Odd Man Out

Martyn Harris

Edited by
Caroline Heler Harris
and Paul Fisher

The Daily Telegraph

First published in 1996
by Telegraph Books
1 Canada Square
Canary Wharf
London E14 5DT

ISBN 0 86367 999 4

Acknowledgments:
The publishers and editors thank the *New Statesman* and
The Spectator for giving permission to reprint articles by
Martyn Harris from their respective publications.
The publishers and editors also thank Jillian Edelstein
for permission to use the photographs of Martyn Harris
on the cover.

Cover design by John Morris
Designed and produced by Well House Publishing
Printed for Telegraph Books by Selwood Printing Ltd

Foreword

When a writer dies at the age of 43, there is bound to be a sense of keen regret for the work which can never now be produced. We all feel this strongly with Martyn Harris. He had written for *The Daily Telegraph* for ten years when he died, and in that period he achieved his maturity as a journalist. If he had lived, he would have gone from strength to even greater strength.

But there is a sense in which Martyn Harris's best work was not cut short by his death, but was inspired by the prospect of it. When Martyn discovered that he had cancer, he confronted the illness not only in his life but in his writing. All the qualities already visible in his work – courage, honesty, wit, a dislike of sentimentality – came to the fore and showed themselves to their best advantage. He made what the prayer calls "a good death", and I believe that the act of composition helped him to do this. It helped him to understand what it was that he faced.

Certainly his writing helps the reader understand. All Martyn's pieces related to his illness are contained in this book; they cover the full range, the angry, the clinical, the accepting, the sceptical, the religious, the comic and the sad. The huge response of readers to these writings has already proved their power. Gathered together, they make a unique testament. I do not want to give the impression, though, that this is a black edged memorial volume. It is a selection from the work of a journalist in the thick of life and under the pressure of a deadline, and of a novelist who hoped to develop further in the genre. Martyn was an interviewer, a columnist, a critic, a controversialist and a reporter, and is represented here in all these guises. As an editor, I print material every day which I think is good. But journalism, by its nature, tends to be impermanent. Martyn Harris was extremely unusual in being a true journalist and yet a writer whose work will last. That is why this book works. On behalf of *The Daily Telegraph*, I am proud to be associated with it.

Charles Moore, *Editor, The Daily Telegraph*

Odd Man Out

Home   109 - 208

Introduction

After 11 years as an editor, I'm cynical enough to have noticed that some of the journalists who are most polite to me in the corridor are those most nervous of being sacked – frankly, the less talented ones.

Conversely, brilliant reporters are often the most awkward to handle, partly because they know they can afford to be difficult because they can always go somewhere else, and partly because almost all gifted performers are tormented by self-doubt, and tend to take this out on everybody else.

Martyn Harris once declared: "Few writers really believe they can write, and fewer still know how they learnt. They think they are pulling off a lucky trick every time they do it." He seemed bemused that I had volunteered for some of my own experiences as a war correspondent, because several times he told me how convinced he was of his own cowardice, and of his inability to cope as a writer with violent conflict.

I said perfectly truthfully, however, that it is far easier for a journalist to write about a great drama unfolding before him – a battle, an earthquake, a riot – than it is to conjure a brilliant literary souffle out of the commonplace ingredients of everyday life, an art in which Martyn displayed his exceptional skill, week in and week out, year in and year out through the best part of a decade in which I was lucky enough to be his editor at *The Daily Telegraph,* and then for Charles Moore after me.

"What's someone like you doing writing for *The Daily Telegraph*?" Tony Blair demanded of Harris four years ago, when Martyn interviewed him.

What indeed? Soon after I became editor in 1986, our Features supremos Don Berry and Veronica Wadley urged me to see this very unusual man from *New Society.* I must confess that if my relationship with Martyn had depended upon that first personal encounter, it might never have got off the ground. Each of us, in our very different ways, might reasonably be described as awkward coves, and not merely physically. Who could ever forget Martyn's raw features and lop-sided gaze from behind the granny spectacles, that slow grin and the strangled vowels? God knows what he thought of me, though I can guess.

Yet I was hooked even before I met him, because I read a piece he had written for *New Society* on the wildly unlikely subject of the difference between electric and wet shaving. Personally, I've never used an electric razor since I read Martyn's explanation of the awful things it does to your skin. That piece, together with another on London prostitutes, convinced me that Martyn Harris could do great things for *The Daily Telegraph* that I wanted to create. In the ensuing ten years, all of us gave thanks many times that we had somehow led into semi-domestication at the paper this extraordinary man who could do brilliant and original things with words.

Successful journalists are those who see the world from an unexpected angle, who take up a seat in the balcony unoccupied by other privileged spectators of the divine comedy. Harris thoroughly understood what some star reporters sooner or later lost sight of, first that they are indeed only spectators and second, that the play is always a comedy. The essence of good journalism is surprise. Good journalists like to make trouble. They instinctively mistrust those who possess wealth, authority or power. It is our job to inform, to entertain, and perhaps most of all, to serve as the grit in the oyster. Over the last years of its old ownership, *The Daily Telegraph* had become a sadly predictable bastion of ageing Tories, a home for readers who wanted a newspaper which would merely nod through the turnstiles the prejudices of Cheltenham man. When we started to rebuild the paper in 1986, I brought in a group of senior editors who I hoped could help to change that. Next, we had to find writers who thought and behaved and wrote in a new way, which a new generation of readers could respond to. Although Martyn could be perverse, graceless, bloody-minded, maddening, from the day he came to the paper we prized his originality, courage, charm, wit, brilliance.

There was never a danger that he would fail to provide the grit in the oyster. The joy was to behold the profusion of pearls which he showered upon us as well. His versatility was astonishing. He could dress up as Santa Claus, sketch the life of a cruise liner, interview a politician or describe a street party with equal facility. He could write a feature about anything or – more important in our trade – about nothing. As a descriptive writer, he could sketch the socks of any rival. His laconic prose possessed a willingness to jar, a power to make the reader think, which is rare even among good journalists.

Martyn scorned the traditional boundaries of taste. He frequently assaulted headlong interest groups which had hitherto been thought inviolate, the Disabled Lobby not least among them. With rare lapses, his judgement was very shrewd. Three or four years ago now, his career took a new turn, when we persuaded him to become *The Daily Telegraph's* star interviewer. Within a few months, he made himself recognised as the ablest practitioner of that craft in Fleet Street.

I sometimes found myself defending him against allegations of brutality towards his subjects. It was not in Martyn's startlingly direct nature to avoid what seemed to him plain truths. His piece on Lauren Bacall 18 months ago, for instance, was savage, but it seemed me justifiable. As a star, she believed that while she had offered herself for interview, she enjoyed the right to set the agenda. Martyn took a different view. He scorned the ritual of allowing a star plugging a book to set the rules of the game. "Bacall is no great actress or intelligence", he wrote, "though she tries to conceal the shallowness behind a battery of hard-boiled mannerisms. It is what she leaves out of her self-account that tells you the most." And these, or course, were the bits Martyn coolly, ruthlessly, perceptively sought to put in. He wrote that piece in the week that he began treatment for his tumour.

Plaster was still falling off the ceiling about his demolition of Bacall months afterwards, and of course the star herself was outraged. I trembled a bit about the row, but at the paper we were chiefly amazed that Martyn could have penned one of his sharpest pieces at a moment in his own fortunes when any of the rest of us, finding ourselves in similar personal circumstances, would have been collapsed in a heap in the corner at home.

He possessed in generous measure the most important gift of any journalist – curiosity about the human condition, matched by fluency, a Rolls-Royce "read me" quality, which co-existed oddly with Martyn's personal awkwardness of body and sometimes of voice also, a condition I know plenty about myself. Martyn wrote wonderfully wittily about that, too: "Most writers are rotten at radio, television – or any kind of live performance. I sometimes think it is precisely because they are so bad at expressing themselves verbally that writers take to pen and paper in the first place. One of the strongest motives for writing is revenge. To get your own back on people. To deliver the clever riposte you thought of on the way down the stairs. I'd love to be able to broadcast, but I can't. An oily film blurs my vision and a roaring fills my ears. I adopt a throttled Liverpudlian accent and the stilted Latinisms of a Bernard Levin think-piece, full of "promulgations" and *loci classici.*

"While writing this I have been listening to myself on *A Good Read.* My accent, which is a fairly classless university drone, resembled a Liverpudlian sailor on a drunken shore leave. I stammered, hesitated, repeated myself. I called the other guest Chris, when her name was Nick. It is being broadcast again on Sunday, and though my mum will be listening, I strongly recommend anyone else not to bother."

For all his spasms of harshness and asperity, Martyn's greatest gift as a writer was that he could generate extraordinary and unexpected emotion in his audience, above all when he wrote about his own illness. He analysed himself dispassionately, yet thoughtfully and with a complete absence of self-pity or sentimentality. While Martyn showed his ability to go the distance as a novelist, it is by his writing for newspapers that he will make his greatest impact upon most of his readers. It was over a course of 1,000 or 2,000 words, writing with irresistible truthfulness about people and things which he saw with his own eyes, that Martyn was supreme. He could waltz words across the page of a newspaper with the assurance of a great ice skater. He represented all the things I wanted *The Daily Telegraph* to be.

Twenty-three years ago, I mourned the loss of a close friend, one of the greatest journalists of his generation, Nicholas Tomalin, who was killed reporting the Yom Kippur War, in which I was also a correspondent. Martyn, by contrast, was a colleague, rather than a close friend of mine. I leave others to pay tribute to his private qualities. But every journalist I know felt this loss to our profession as bitterly as we did that of Nick Tomalin all those years ago, when he died at the same age.

Martyn's funeral in Swansea in October 1996 was a deeply moving occasion for the handful of outsiders like myself, who sat among the gathering of his friends and family in the Wesleyan chapel. Here, we were at the heart of the celtic roots which produced this remarkable talent. Swansea seemed a longish day's walk, or for that matter read, from the work Martyn eventually produced, and from the journalists among whom he lived.

A number of people at the funeral said to me, good-naturedly, that they had always been puzzled about why Martyn wrote for *The Daily Telegraph* rather than for some paper more in sympathy with his personal views, such as *The Guardian* or *The Observer*. I replied that I guessed that Martyn, like many great journalists, felt he performed best against the grain, working in an environment at odds with his own instincts. I don't know whether I am right, but I do know that the decade-long encounter between Martyn Harris and *The Daily Telegraph* produced some extraordinary, indeed unforgettable results.

Harris, like Nicholas Tomalin, was a glittering and wonderfully brave talent whom I am very grateful to have known in print and in person. The tributes of a host of readers on his death testify to the love that he commanded for what he wrote, as much as for what he was.

Max Hastings, *November, 1996*

Editors' note

Less than a week after Martyn's death *The Daily Telegraph's* editor Charles Moore invited us to put together a collection of his journalism. At a time of great sadness and personal loss for us as Martyn's wife and boyhood friend, we both recognised that this project could be a way of focussing our grief. In fact, by reading Martyn, he came alive; he made us laugh again, he astonished us afresh with the range of his subjects, the almost painful acuteness of his perceptions – so this task became a personal quest and a labour of love. His death is a loss to many, including his readers who can through this book recapture, we hope, the pleasure of reading Martyn for the first time.

Martyn wanted to be a writer from the age of eight – an unusual ambition in Fifties Swansea. Nevertheless his early CV reads like a parody of post-war normality; Bishop Gore Grammar School in Swansea; University of Kent where he received a BA in Literature; Keele University where he gained an MA in American Literature by writing a thesis on Norman Mailer. Like many arts graduates in the Seventies, uncertain as to how he could enter his chosen profession, he trained as a teacher. This turned out to be an unexpectedly good decision. A few months teaching computer language for ICL was qualification enough to write for a computer magazine – and he was off. His first mainstream journalism was a *New Statesman* piece covering the Peckham by-election in 1982 and he hit a tone which never faltered. He reckoned the most revealing question to ask an ambitious candidate, particularly one who represented a scruffy London constituency, was where he lived. The young John Redwood claimed his house was ten minutes up the road. "This," Martyn wrote, "turns out to be Lower Thames Street in the heart of the City, which might be ten minutes away by Harrier jump-jet but is more like 15 in a Porsche Turbo."

His Peckham article brought him to the attention of Paul Barker, editor of *New Society* – which he joined in 1982 as a feature writer. *New Society's* unique mixture of politics and social observation proved to be the ideal medium for developing Martyn's talents. Four years later one of his more quirky pieces was spotted by Max Hastings, then editor of *The Daily Telegraph* – the newspaper for which he wrote for the rest of his life.

This selection traces the development and growth of his thinking and writing. *Interviews* is a self explanatory category. *Home* and *Away* contain Martyn's best reportage, features and columns, arranged chronologically written for *The New Statesman, New Society, The Spectator* and *The Daily Telegraph*. We have also included extracts from his two novels in which the writing is at its funniest, sharpest and paradoxically most melancholic. *Do It Again* (published 1989) has Alex Smith, a millionaire socialist, returning to his old university town in a comic but doomed attempt to relive his lost youth. *The Mother-in-Law Joke* (1992) explores London's alternative comedy scene through the eyes of Phil First, an aspiring Welsh comedian struggling to make the big time. Fiction freed Martyn from journalism's lawyerly constraints and allowed him to satirise fashionable North London angst on his own terms.

The final section – *On the Sick* – contains everything he wrote about having cancer. Martyn's wit and power of concentration weren't blunted by extreme illness. Take this from one of his last columns written from his hospital bed: "Army officers must 'toss ideas about' with their sergeants, but the consultant is still an outpost of autocracy. In his power to spend money and terrorise his underlings, he has no secular rival save perhaps the newspaper editor – which is perhaps why I feel so at home." Even less predictably, during Martyn's last six months a growing capacity for spiritual exploration added an extra dimension to his life and his work. The new clarity and richness which he brought to his writing under such testing circumstances is his final gift to his readers, and to us.

We should like to thank all those who supported and helped us produce this book so quickly, especially Joceline Bury, Joy Melville, Vicky Unwin, Sally Townsend, Caroline St John Brooks and Mark Corliss.

Caroline Heler Harris and Paul Fisher,
November 1996

Interviews

Edward Heath

The last time I saw Sir Edward Heath was on Hampstead Heath a year ago, conducting his own 79th birthday concert on the open-air stage at Kenwood Pond. With his vast white tuxedo and picket-fence grin, he looked like a polar bear in a dickie bow, who had surfaced, surreally, from the floating duckweed.

His reception by the youngish, liberalish audience was ecstatic, which seemed odd. The *bête-noir* of my Left-wing youth had become the *bête-blanc* of theirs, which is worse French than Sir Edward's but no matter. My companion explained: "They think he is probably the last socialist Prime Minister we'll ever have."

Our only meeting was in a pub at Bexley, during the 1987 General Election; I had expected to dislike him, but as it turned out, we got on rather well. The Easter Island expression, and stony silences that punctuate his conversation conceal a mordant wit. One story concerned the funeral of the Australian Prime Minister Harold Holt in Melbourne, which Heath had attended. Lyndon Johnson turned up, with about 50 security men, one of them carrying the famous "football" of nuclear codes, "in case he needed to blow up the world while we were in church ..."

Another story, which he does not tell himself, is about the day Margaret Thatcher was ousted from power by her own Cabinet. Sir Edward got the news early and telephoned his old friend Madron Seligman with the simple message, "Rejoice! Rejoice!"

Today's meeting is at Sir Edward's house in Salisbury, which faces the cathedral close and backs on to the river and water meadows which Constable painted. With its Queen Anne facade and 13th-century foundation, it has been described as one of the most beautiful small houses in England. Lord Jenkins, an old friend and rival, once complimented Sir Edward on having, "One of the 10 finest views in the world."

"Oh really?" said Heath, "And what are the other nine?"

Plastic cones prohibit parking within a hundred yards of the iron gates; men with body armour, machine guns and serious moustaches patrol the shrubbery; local legend insists the peaceful

Avon at the foot of the lawn has been mined by "security". I suppose if Lady Thatcher had really hated Sir Edward that much she would have had him make do with a village bobby.

Along the hallway are pictures by Walter Sickert, John Piper, Gwen and Augustus John. He has another house in Belgravia, and has owned five Morning Cloud racing yachts, each of which would cost half a million at today's prices.

Where has all Sir Edward's money come from? As with his sexuality, nobody has quite fathomed it. He netted around £300,000 for his books on sailing and music. He has done lecture tours and musical recordings, and served on the board of Arthur Andersen, the accountancy firm. He is, says his biographer John Campbell: "Distinctly good at getting other people to pay for his major expenses." There are pop stars and grocery millionaires who would envy living on this scale.

Sir Edward turns up in slacks and boat shoes, wattled and mottled, with a swagbag of belly, but plenty of bounce. "So what do you want to talk about?" he demands. I suggest Europe for starters, and off he goes, while I covertly study his CD collection. All the usual classics but also *All Time Party Favourites* and *The Best of Nat King Cole*. "All this nonsense about sovereignty and nation state," Sir Edward is saying. "After the Second World War, we heard nothing about the nation state. We saw where it had led us. My generation, who had fought through the war, wanted a community where this would be impossible."

When you took us into the Common Market in 1972, did you think we would have a common currency in your own lifetime?

"Oh *sooner.* The Heads of Government communique of October 1972 made it clear that by 1980, the Community would be complete."

But did the public understand that?

"The people who follow these things understood it."

It is a wonderfully autocratic phrase – "the people who follow these things" – reminiscent of the Trotskyite formula of the "committed cadres". It is the people who go to all the meetings and read all the documents who matter. All are equal but some are more equal than others.

It is the same when I suggest the only way to confound Euro-sceptic charges of bureaucracy and centralisation is to extend the democratic base of the EU. No no, says Sir Edward. We need more regular meetings of the heads of government. "We need to get that *top pinnacle* in place."

In fact, Sir Edward went to great lengths to minimise the loss of sovereignty in his campaign to carry the Conservatives in 1972. I doubt if a fraction of the people who voted "for Europe" in the referendum of 1974 had a clue they were voting to abolish the pound six years later. I certainly didn't, though I wouldn't have cared much either way. I thought I was voting for a vague ideal of international co-operation which would make wars less likely and myself less liable to be conscripted and killed.

"Do you see why some people have this deep attachment to the sovereignty of Parliament? You are Father of the House, after all."

"Well, it's in their own interests. They want to be self-important, don't they?"

"Aren't Conservatives supposed to be attached to the continuity of institutions?"

"We also commit ourselves to the development of institutions. Look at what Disraeli did to institutions. The Conservatives of 1924-29 gave the women the vote. That's development."

"But this is revolution. You must share *some* of the fears of moderate Euro-sceptics about trying to integrate all these languages, cultures, institutions. It's never been done."

"Oh, it has. It was done in Charlemagne's time. If he hadn't split the empire between his sons, we would not have had half the messes of the last 1,000 years.

Edward Heath was a rotten Prime Minister. His Industrial Relations Act, local government reorganisation, restructuring of the Health Service, internment in Northern Ireland – all were disasters. He won the 1970 election on the "Selsdon Man" platform of tax cutting and low public spending – which he never believed in – and then stoked an unsustainable economic boom and sowed the seeds of hyper-inflation.

His administration was buffeted by the 1973 oil crisis, but the botched confrontation with the miners of 1974 which led to his fall was all his own misjudgment. No leader reduced to asking his country "Who governs?" can expect a vote of confidence.

His only real achievements were the Sunningdale "power-sharing" agreement in Northern Ireland – sold down the river by Harold Wilson and only now being tentatively resurrected – and Europe. Here at least Sir Edward has been consistent throughout his career. At the "Munich by-election" at Oxford in 1938, he opposed

Chamberlain's isolationism and campaigned against the Conservative candidate, Quintin Hogg. (He described Chamberlain's government as "Conservatives with nothing to conserve and Liberals who do not believe in liberty" – a phrase that demands recycling.)

His maiden Commons speech in 1950 attacked Labour's refusal to join the Coal and Steel Community. In 1961, he was the Foreign Office's "Mr Europe", leading the negotiating team in Britain's first attempt to join the Common Market – vetoed by de Gaulle – and in 1972, he was the prime minister who frogmarched a grudgingly acquiescent party and apathetic nation into final membership.

Sir Edward is fond of Brahms and Bach and all that, but he is not a good linguist. Nor is he well read in European literature. The most interesting question about this emotionally wooden and ideologically vacillating man is why he should be so passionate about the single issue of Europe, and the answer, as so often, seems to lie in childhood.

He was born in July 1916, during a German Zeppelin raid on Ramsgate. His father was a carpenter – later a small builder; his mother had been lady's maid to a rich London family and brought up her two sons on tales of their travels on "the Continong". The Heath family house in Broadstairs overlooked the Channel: "So it was natural I should wonder what it was like on the other side."

At 13, he went on a school trip to Paris and at 14, on an exchange visit to Dusseldorf – both unusual for a boy of his age and class. He still talks dreamily of wandering down the Champs-Elysées collecting car brochures from the glossy showrooms, or drinking his first Weissbier at a café in Dusseldorf.

While at Balliol, he visited republican Spain, where he met the prime minister and had the exciting experience of being machine-gunned by a fascist aeroplane on the road to Tarragona. In 1938, he witnessed a Nazi rally at Nuremburg: "Astonishing spectacle and organisation. I could see they meant business." The next year, he hitchiked to Danzig and Berlin "where my German friends were already too frightened to speak to me except in the parks".

He returned to Ramsgate, already filling up with Jewish refugees, two days before Hitler invaded Poland. By the following year, he was a gunner in the Royal Artillery, where he rose to the rank of lieutenant colonel and was mentioned in despatches. He was awarded the MBE in 1946.

There are virtually no women in his life apart from Kay Raven, the daughter of a local dentist with whom he had a long, but apparently platonic relationship until she married a farmer. A well-known Tory lady used to dine out on the story of how she once manoeuvred Teddy into putting his arm around her, "but then he started thinking about VAT or something." Tabloid papers have dug for dirt on him for years and found, or at least published, nothing.

He describes his family as very close, but there were differences between the parents. Thomas was a soccer player, a beer drinker, a bit of a flirt, one of the lads. Edith was pious, puritanical, socially ambitious. Thomas once said sadly in an interview that, "by the end, we didn't have much to talk about". Sir Edward was devoted to his mother and deeply upset when she died of cancer at the age of 63, when he was 31. It does not seem too fanciful to suppose that the only time Heath fell in love, it was with Europe, and that after his mother died, it was his only love.

Lord Jenkins says the best historical parallel to Heath is Sir Robert Peel, another cold fish in public and a charmer in private, who frogmarched his party into Free Trade; who was reviled for it in his own lifetime and later revered. Although Sir Edward is 80 next month, he is standing at the next general election. He has seen off Lady Thatcher, he has decided to see off the Euro-sceptics. He may be around for a long time.

The Daily Telegraph, 17 June 1996

John Redwood

Ystafellnaf says the sign on the door of the Welsh Office waiting room: a dingy place done out in greyish gloss, with paintings of urban blight on the wall by the pupils of Mountain Ash Comprehensive. John Redwood would not be able to pronounce the phrase, nor be bothered by the fact, for the Welsh Office is his waiting room as well: the lowest rung on the Cabinet ladder for a man seen by himself, at least, as leader of the Tory Right, if not a future leader of the party.

So much is apparent from his recent interventions in national policy: his support in the November Budget for cuts in government spending rather than tax increases; his criticism of bureaucracy and waste in the NHS; and most notoriously, his attack last summer on single mothers, which lit the fire beneath the still-bubbling debate on private and public morality.

The Welsh Office is traditionally a backwater where potential troublemakers such as Peter Walker can be sidelined. Redwood sees it as a launch pad.

He is said to be the cleverest man in the Cabinet – he is certainly its only PhD. A Prize fellow of All Souls and formerly an investment adviser with N.M. Rothschild, he was head of the Downing Street Policy Unit from 1983-85. We are meeting to talk about his new book, *The Global Marketplace* (Harper-Collins), a triumphalist account of the advances of privatisation and popular capitalism in Britain and Eastern Europe. He has written eight books in 14 years, a standing reproach to those who see a Fellowship of All Souls as the coffin nail to ambition and achievement.

He is a good-looking man: tall, slim, saturnine, but with an other-worldly air which has led to such descriptions as "half human, half Vulcan", "brother of Spock", and (fancifully) "a Narcissus in a frozen lake". Introductions are minimal: a handshake, a wave to take a seat and a brisk, "Right then?" Does he agree, I ask him, with Professor David Marquand's argument that unbridled free enterprise is a subversive force which undermines public morality and erodes traditional institutions? "You mean is it *popular?*" says Redwood. "Ha, ha." A political adviser, standing guard, throws back his head and also laughs. The minister has made a joke.

"No I don't agree," says Redwood. "Free markets mean that people can express their interests rather than have Mr Marquand telling them what is good for them. It is the ultimate democracy. We all have the right every five years to vote on whom we wish to govern us, but every day we can spend money in the way we see fit, and that is a very real democratic power." His delivery is quiet and confident, and so rapid that it takes three beats to notice he has not answered the question.

"Isn't selfishness the engine of free enterprise?"

"There's nothing wrong with trying to do the best for yourself and your family," says Redwood. "But even if someone wanted to run a wickedly repressive old-fashioned capitalism which went only for profit and wasn't interested in workers and consumers, it would not be possible. To run a successful modern business you need high quality people, and you have to look after them or they go off to someone else. It is better to look after your customers because then you get a reputation for quality and success. So the public interest is taken care of by the private interest of wanting to make money."

As an Oxford undergraduate Redwood studied Marx, and he devotes many pages of his book to forceful anti-Marxist polemic – as if the corpse required any more kicking. But he also betrays affinities with the Marxist mindset: the fondness for totalising theories and prefabricated phrases; an impatience with sentiment; the unshakeable conviction of privileged insight.

His view, in summary, is basically the Gordon Gecko line that greed is good insofar as it fuels competition which provides the best goods at the lowest prices. Furthermore, this same competition will ultimately ensure the well-being of workers, customers and even the environment as the educated consumer demands higher standards of health, safety, ecological soundness and even political rectitude. The state may need to police the frontiers but essentially that is all it has to do. Here is a mirror image of Marxism: once a truly free market is established, a moral order will emerge as a kind of free gift at the bottom of the packet.

Our present difficulty of course is that this new moral order is a long time emerging and seems to have gone into reverse. Wasn't there a national anxiety about the recent spate of political scandals, for instance?

"I do not believe this political generation is worse than previous ones," he says. "People are more accountable because we have a very vigilant press and a very vigilant Parliament. We have never set out to suggest this is an administration of saints, and there will be occasional mistakes and lapses."

He is not always so tolerant, as in his statement after visiting the St Mellons estate in Cardiff, when he criticised "the trend for young women to have babies with no apparent intention of even trying a marriage or stable relationship". He added: "It must be right before granting state aid to pursue the father," which was taken to mean that some mothers and children should be refused benefit, though he has denied this.

All he says now is: "We try to make sure that where public policy impinges on individuals and their conduct it points them in the right direction" – which still leaves the implication that while politicians are the same as they have ever been, ordinary mortals need a shove from the state in the direction of decency.

Redwood himself is happily married with two children, and

remains untouched by the Westminster rumour factory. The fact that he lists "water sports" among his recreations seems a guarantee of his sexual probity, and is certainly the only wet thing about him.

Like Peter Sellers's Dr Strangelove, Redwood cannot always get his limbs to obey his frontal lobes. He begins our interview with knees neatly crossed, but as time passes and impatience rises, the knee climbs higher, exposing several inches of slate-grey shin. He clamps both hands around it but the leg climbs to the level of his chin, as if desperate to lash out a polished black lace-up at his idiot interrogator.

When I observe him later, during Welsh Questions in the House of Commons – seldom a great parliamentary occasion – his head keeps sliding sideways to his shoulder and his eyes roll heavenwards, as if desperately seeking escape from health appointments in Clwyd and redundancies at BP Baglan Bay, until with an effort he snaps himself vertical again.

"As welcome as a rat sandwich" was how Plaid Cymru described his appointment to the Welsh Office, though he is reckoned even by opponents to have made a decent fist of the job.

He was the third successive Welsh Secretary who neither came from Wales nor represented a Welsh constituency. In his first five months in the job, according to the *Western Mail*, he spent only one night in Wales, generally choosing to return to his Wokingham constituency after a day in Cardiff. He responded to the criticism at a Press Gallery lunch by remarking that he must surely be the first government minister to be attacked for preferring to sleep with his wife.

Sensitive to remarks about his extra-terrestrial demeanour, and with his long-term political future in mind, he has taken steps to cultivate "warmth".

At a meeting in Cardiff before Christmas he told an audience of slightly baffled middle-aged businessmen that he would like to be as popular as Mr Blobby. Occasionally he says things like, "Well, I'm off to my flying saucer now".

As he prepared for a transmission from a Westminster television studio, BBC engineers noticed that he was making strange grimaces in the monitor. Was he ill? Had he noticed something disgusting on the floor? After some anxious minutes they realised that the Secretary of State was practising how to smile.

This was told to me as a sinister story, though I found it rather appealing for its vulnerability. Redwood, born in 1951, is the son of an accounts clerk and a shop manageress from Dover: a lower middle-class boy who had to turn himself into an exam machine to get where others have risen more effortlessly.

The vanity, intellectual arrogance and dogmatism which everyone remarks on are, his friends say, merely armour: it can slip to reveal a warm and decent man with a dry sense of humour.

The real obstacle to his advancement is his adherence to an ideology which holds at its core that morality is a matter of economic expediency, which can infect all strata of society. Why not fiddle the dole when the middle class fiddle their taxes? Why not jump the council waiting list when MPs are buying up council houses to sell at a profit, and councils are trading them for votes? Why feel guilty about fathering illegitimate children when the Government have fathered enough to populate Yeovil?

Mr Major's Back to Basics campaign was an obvious if unstated recognition of this growing sense of moral vacuum: a vague but popular appeal for a return to standards of behaviour standing above and apart from getting and spending. So even if the Prime Minister's remarks about "crucifying" and "bastards" are fabrications, it would be easy to understand his fury over the hijacking of his initiative by the ministers most closely associated with the Thatcherite revolution which helped to create the vacuum in the first place.

Like Peter Lilley and Michael Portillo, John Redwood has taken pains in recent weeks to confirm that he is singing from the same hymn sheet as his leader, but even if he hangs on to his waiting room at the Welsh Office after the spring reshuffle, his wait there is likely to be a long one.

The Daily Telegraph, 19 January 1994

John Prescott

The blotter of John Prescott's desk is covered in tiny pieces of steel, like the fragments of some dolls-house hand grenade. I lean across for a better look and see they are the shards of paper clips, systematically dismembered.

Labour's Shadow Employment Secretary, hero of last year's conference and author of this orderly destruction, has gone to the lavatory. I am alone in his office. It has a vaguely nautical feel, with oval portholes looking over Parliament Square, and a model ship's wheel in one corner, which has a carved wooden fist striking through it. Crates of beer are stacked against a wall, with slithering dunes of pamphlets and reports. The one on my lap is called *Financing Infrastructure Development – A Consultative Document.*

Prescott comes barrelling in, heading for the haven of his desk. It is only 11 am, but he starts work at seven, and the tie-knot is well down his chest, the shirt comprehensively creased. "Sorry, I didn't know about the photograph ..." P.J. O'Rourke once asked, rhetorically, why people in politics work so hard (they do), and his answer was because there are no ultimate targets in public life. Streets can never be too clean; taxes can never be too low; Labour can never be too ready for the next election. John Prescott is often here at two in the morning.

News of the day is Bryan Gould's resignation. I just saw Gould downstairs with his wife in the Members' canteen, looking dapper and demob-happy: the opposite of this driven and crumpled man across the desk. What does Prescott think of the resignation?

"Everyone knew Bryan would move on once he had made his play for the leadership."

"He said it was Labour's lack of radical economic policy."

"He is just hacked off with his own career. I came into politics as a seaman, wanting to change laws that affected shipping. People like Bryan come in a different way. They have a career in the Foreign Office, a career in the university, dabble a bit in politics, find they haven't become prime minister, and decide to go somewhere else."

This seems harsh. Prescott and Gould, after all, were both on the Left of the party, pro-full employment, anti-Maastricht ... Weren't they allies?

Prescott snorts. "Nobody had alliances with Bryan. We had shared ideas, but we both got defeated. My movement has taught me that, if you get beat democratically, you carry on doing the job. I am now concerned to find ways to get three million people back to work. I don't take my ball home and run away."

Gould has published several articles, setting out his differences with the Labour leadership with an eloquence and clarity which makes one pine for the chimera of unwhipped MPs and open debate. His gist is that Labour, with its commitment to ERM and Maastricht, has abandoned its traditional policy of economic management for full employment in favour of Conservative monetarism. It is, he says, "a historic reversal". Does Prescott still think full employment is a realistic target?

"Targets are difficult ... We want to provide an opportunity for people to make a contribution and be rewarded for it."

"That's very vague. Labour used to say things like, 'we will create three million new jobs'."

"Does that sound impossible?" says Prescott.

"I'm asking *you*."

"The Tories said you couldn't, but they created 1.3 million jobs in services after the 1987 election."

"But would *you* like Labour to say that?"

"If we say we will do things like release money for house building; restore regulation to transport to encourage bus manufacture – which is what we do say – then you can calculate that in terms of jobs. But it would be stupid to commit ourselves."

As a good soldier – the phrase "practical politician" comes up a lot – he works within the new dispensation, chipping away at vulnerable areas which might yield new jobs, such as the strait jacket of the Public Sector Borrowing Requirement.

As Shadow Transport spokesman, he argued that British Rail should be allowed to lease trains rather than set the whole cost against PSBR in a single year – which the Government has now conceded. A range of badly needed capital investment, in transport, schools, hospitals and housing, is hamstrung he says, by similar "accountancy rules" which are not observed by our European partners.

As an example, he picks the old Labour favourite of receipts from council house sales: "There are six thousand billion pounds held by councils from those sales. Money in the bank. But the Government won't allow it to be spent on new houses, because it's there to reduce the PSBR."

Now, I am no economist, but I think Prescott may be out by a few noughts on his six thousand billion and my economic adviser tells me that this "money in the bank" image is something of a colourful fiction. "It's all figures on balance sheets. If they spend that money then the debit side goes up, and there's no way around it." The idea that PSBR is just a lot of arbitrary accountancy rules seems a little flakey too. It is important, my adviser advises, "as a way of telling lenders the Government will not go bonkers on borrowing, then wipe out its debts with a burst of inflation". Lenders are not fooled because you call their loans by another name.

Prescott is often described as the last old-style working class union leader on Labour's front bench, even a successor to Ernest Bevin, but this is not quite right. He never had a senior position in the Seamen's Union – where, as a young activist, he clashed badly with its leader Bill Hogarth. His grandfather was a north Wales miner, but his father was a white-collar railwayman, a local councillor and a JP. His two brothers and two sisters went to grammar school, but Prescott failed his Eleven Plus and left school at 15.

"I was going out with a girl at the time. She got through and I didn't. I remember sending her a letter expressing my desire – love if you like, a young kid's feelings – and she sent it back with the spelling mistakes corrected ... it leaves you with a bit of an inferiority complex and aggression comes partly from reacting against that."

At 17 he went to work for Cunard – a period he refers to as "my seafaring days", though, as a waiter on a luxury liner, it was not exactly Ten Years Before The Mast. On the Atlantic crossings, he could make £400 a week in tips – a fortune in the 1950s. "They used to call us the Hollywood waiters. These jazzy evening suits with wing collars, white waistcoats – I loved it, and to be honest the women found us attractive."

It may come as a surprise to smoother men, but the bull-necked, bullet-headed, bag-eyed Prescott is seen as a sexy item by several women of my acquaintance. Something to do with the soft brown eyes and boyish vulnerability, apparently. Pauline, whom he married in 1961, and by whom he has two grown sons, is one of the most glamorous of Westminster wives.

As a waiter, he liked to argue with the many famous passengers he met: judges, senators and politicians. He also clashed with officers over petty regulations and was twice charged with mutiny. "I did manage to get one regulation changed. If you are caught with a woman passenger, you are no longer charged with broaching ship's cargo." Tory MPs in the House of Commons still like to shout. "Mine's a gin and tonic, Giovanni,." when Prescott rises to speak.

At 25, sponsored not by the Seamen's Union, but by the Conservative Cheshire County Council, he went to Ruskin College, Oxford. "My mind was opened to the pleasures of learning ... It taught me I had no need to feel inferior to anybody." In 1966, he heard himself denounced by Harold Wilson in the House of Commons as one of the "small group of politically motivated men" behind the national seamen's strike. "Politically motivated" was code for Communist, but the Prime Minister could hardly denounce someone who was by then Labour parliamentary candidate for Southport.

Entering the Commons in 1970 as MP for Hull, he made his mark as an effective Transport spokesman in the late 1980s, over issues such as the Clapham rail crash and the Lockerbie bomb, wearing down Transport Minister Paul Channon with persistent questioning and mastery of detail. He never got on with Neil Kinnock, and what he called "the beautiful people" of the New Model Labour Party. Kinnockites, in turn, attacked Prescott as a "loose cannon" for his challenge to Roy Hattersley as deputy leader in 1987, his outbursts of temper, and his "old-fashioned" pro-union attitudes.

He has been happier with John Smith: "You know where you stand with him. Integrity is important to him."

"Are you saying Kinnock lacked integrity?"

"Nobody could have given more to Labour than Neil Kinnock. But, at the end of his leadership, the feeling developed that all he had to do was smile and government would fall into his lap. Well, I think you have to earn that respect."

"So you'd agree with those who can't see what Labour stands for now?"

"Labour stands for a publicly owned railway – that's a clear difference. Labour will build more houses; restore the health service. These are real differences."

"But the fundamental difference was that Labour stood for state direction of the economy – and that is *not* clearly stated."

"I am more *concerned* with *how* you get a thing to *work*," says Prescott, with a sudden blaze of vagueness, "and *how* to relate that to our *policies.*"

Prescott's speech at the party conference in October, which secured one-member one-vote for selection of MPs, inspired newspaper talk of him as a future Labour leader, though, as one senior Labour source says wearily, "There is a lot of patronising Tory-inspired crap talked about Prescott. Sheer propaganda to boost someone who is, in many people's view, not the greatest asset to the Labour Party."

He would be hurt by this. He is hurt by remarks about his family, his lapses into nervous incoherence, by the gin-and-tonic taunts. He could not bear to watch his conference triumph on video for two weeks, because of a *Guardian* leader making fun of his syntax. "Can you imagine Prescott facing the Prime Minister at Question Time?" another Labour source asks. His attractiveness and candour are the other side of a man still finding out about himself, but leaders of political parties, Tory or Labour, are not allowed to be in the business of discovering their personalities – if indeed they are allowed to have personalities at all.

The Daily Telegraph, 16 February 1994

Lord Hailsham

Lord Hailsham has written his autobiography, *A Sparrow's Flight*, largely from memory, and there are several small errors. Edward Heath is referred to as Chief Whip during the Conservative leadership struggle of 1963, which he was not. Mr Peter Hain becomes Haines, Mr Anthony Howard is promoted to editor of *The Observer*, and so on.

I was looking forward to irritating Lord Hailsham with these trivial matters but sadly he pointed them out first, together with the fact that he appears as "Quentin" and sometimes "Quinton" Hogg.

Did he know that Wynford Vaughan Thomas had once composed a limerick on his name? He did not, so I recited it:

> *The girls of Blaenau Ffestiniog*
> *Can be had for a penny (Welsh: ceiniog)*
> *This I know for a fact.*
> *I was caught in the act.*
> *By Lord Hailsham, formerly Quintiniog.*

As Lord Hailsham is sometimes a sanctimonious old poop, I had hoped this might irritate him too, but he laughed long and wheezily and offered me a rhyme in return composed by Oliver Goldsmith for a lady called Mrs Hunbeigh (my spelling is guesswork):

> *You make a mistake*
> *If you think I can't make*
> *A rhyme on your name, Mrs Hunbeigh.*
> *Your face is so fair*
> *Though exposed to the air.*
> *How transcendently fine must your bum be.*

The former Lord Chancellor has a fondness for things lavatorial. His book contains a gruesome description of the toad-infested latrine at prep school, and an epigram from the Eton lavatory wall to the goddess Cloacina. Its first page describes how he was circumcised, at the age of seven and without anaesthetic, held down across the knee of his family doctor while his mother looked on.

"What would Dr Freud have made of this?" I ask him.

"My mother may have thought it would make me less lustful. She had peculiar ideas of her own – a strong minded lady, like Mrs Thatcher, which perhaps has helped me get along with Margaret."

We are talking in the garden of his Roehampton home, where he is stoking one of the four compost bins which seem to absorb him a good deal. When he runs short of grass clippings he sets out on expeditions to the nearby common, where he gathers nettles and weeds. Ranging outside the back door are hundreds of large plastic pop bottles filled with a murky fluid. This is Lord Hailsham's bathwater, which he is storing against the next hosepipe ban.

His sitting room is shabby-genteel, with threadbare rugs covered in dog hair, scuffed Rexine sofas and dust-laden beams of sunshine. The day is warm but Lord Hailsham wears the black jacket and waistcoat, striped trousers and high-laced boots of the pre-war Cabinet Minister. He swings along rapidly between two sticks, and when he wants to sit he topples backwards with a crash like a felled tree, his floury jowls atremble.

His grandfather was founder of Regent Street Polytechnic. His father was Attorney-General, Lord Chancellor and President of the MCC. Hogg was educated at Eton where he won a Newcastle scholarship, and at Christ Church, where he took a double first in Mods and Greats (six mentions in three pages). I begin, uncontentiously, by remarking that he had a privileged background.

"I disregard and spit out the word privilege," he says. "There is no privilege in being well-off. A privilege is a thing which gives you rights which other people don't have. I had advantages. It is a totally different conception."

I learn, as we proceed, that Lord Hailsham is fond of such donnish discriminations. When I refer to the Cabinet, for instance, he takes great pleasure in telling me there is no such thing as the Cabinet, only an *ad hoc* committee of the Privy Council. Elsewhere he remarks, "There is no such thing as sport ... only a heterogeneous list of pastimes with different governing bodies." He delivers these platitudes with an air of immense significance.

All this is part of the logic-chopping skill of the professional debater, which has given him a reputation for great cleverness, and which served him well as a barrister and Lord Chancellor. It was less helpful in practical politics, where he often found himself fighting hopeless, even shameful positions, with great intellectual tenacity but little profit.

He entered politics as Conservative candidate at the famous Oxford by-election of 1938 where he defended the Government's Munich sell-out against a popular front candidate supported by practically everybody, from the young Denis Healey to the young Edward Heath.

He says emphatically now: "I have never doubted that I took the right line ... or that, at an absolutely critical moment in our nation's history, and totally unprepared and inexperienced as I was, my victory at Oxford played a not unimportant part in our nation's ultimate salvation."

Others such as Denis Healey point out that, moral issues aside, Munich meant sacrificing 30 Czech divisions to the Nazis, and that it was Hitler who used the breathing space to build up his forces rather than Chamberlain. It is an argument that will go on for ever, of course, but in the short term Munich clouded Hogg's career in the new Churchillian Tory party.

At Suez he again backed the wrong horse, by supporting Eden's crackpot intervention to the hilt, though this did not prevent Macmillan promoting him to Minister of Education and then chairman of the party. Here he was effective if eccentric: ringing his famous handbell at the Tory Conference, and taking dips in the October sea, with snorkel, flippers and half the Fleet Street press corps in attendance.

Hogg's showbiz flamboyance may have cost him the Conservative leadership when he stood in 1963: his Moulton bicycle; his baby-brandishing; and the flat cap he affected on his visits to the north-east. It might, as he argues now, have been necessary to restore the spirits of the shattered Tory Party after Suez. He may even, as he claims, have been largely responsible for Macmillan's victory in 1959. But in the austere councils of the Carlton Club that man Hogg had become irredeemably a little unsound.

As a Lord Chancellor he was popular with lawyers but not innovative, leaving reforms to his successor, Lord Mackay. He is opposed to Select Committees, one of the few democratic innovations of the last 50 years, and he disapproves of public inquiries in general as pandering to public prurience and curiosity. Although he applied to Attlee for permission to renounce his title, he did not fight for the right, as did Tony Benn, from whose struggle he benefited, but whom he scorns in his book for "flouting the law".

His real talent is for defending a brief at a moment's notice, and his political convictions do not appear to run deep. In his early career he was a big spender, promoting investment in the Foulness Airport, Channel Tunnel and Concorde, while under Mrs Thatcher he has paid lip service to sound money. When Labour was in power he talked about elective dictatorship and the need for constitutional reform. When the Left picks up the idea and the Tories are in office, he grows quiet.

In person he is charming and hospitable. In print I find him snobbish, arrogant and self-justifying, but always readable and interesting. I did not know before I read his book that the Woolsack is stuffed with horsehair, nor that he was responsible for coining the expressions "unflappable" and "lunatic fringe".

At 83 he has suffered great personal tragedy and written about it movingly. His mother died when he was 17; his half-brother Edward committed suicide with Hogg's own gun. He caught his first wife *in flagrante* with another man, and his second died in a riding accident after 34 years of happy marriage.

But he has also been a lucky man, chiefly inasmuch as he has benefited from two of the great illusions of English public life. One is that anyone with a good Classics degree must necessarily be a genius. The other is that any politician who has passed the age of 70 and can still eat a soft-boiled egg is necessarily a great statesman.

The Sunday Telegraph, 1 July 1990

Lord Longford

I n October 1955 Lord Longford and his wife Elizabeth were staying with Evelyn Waugh. "Frank made a splendid entrance to Sunday breakfast," writes Waugh in his diary, "his face, neck and shirt covered in blood, brandishing the Vulgate, crying: 'Who will explain to me second Corinthians, five?' Of every name mentioned at table Frank asked: 'What chance of their coming in (to the Church)?'"

Waugh gets almost every aspect of Longford in this paragraph: the clumsiness, enthusiasm, erudition, piety and innocent snobbishness (collecting society scalps for Jesus). Frank Pakenham, seventh Earl of Longford, aka "Lord Porn", "the potty peer" and champion of "Moors Monster Myra", has never been afraid to be a silly ass. He is too busy, passionate, and sincere to cultivate the detachment of those, like Waugh, who value poise over principle.

His recent book, *Avowed Intent*, is, I think, his fifth work of autobiography but still contains stories that are fresh and funny. In the Thirties, as a very green Conservative Party researcher, he is staying at the same country house as Stanley Baldwin. The Prime Minister invites him for a walk, which passes in silence until Longford nervously inquires: "Who would you say has most influenced your political ideas, Prime Minister?"

"Sir Henry Maine," says the great man, eventually.

"And what did he say?"

"That whereas Rousseau argued all human progress was from contract to status, the real movement was from status to contract."

Baldwin hesitates, his face furrowed with horror. "Or was it the other way around?"

In other stories one is not sure how self-conscious the comedy actually is, as when he describes his very limited acquaintance with the notoriously chilly Edward Heath. "One day it was announced in the newspapers that he [Heath] had lost a stone in weight by careful dieting. I found myself standing next to him in a function at the Savoy. 'Hello Ted,' I said, 'How's the weight?'

"'All right,' he said coldly. 'How's yours?'"

The Pooterish imperviousness, a rich stratum of amiable idiocy, runs through Longford's career, though whether he doesn't know, or just doesn't care, what people think of him is hard to say.

We talk in the sitting room of his small Chelsea flat: a gloomy place of sticky brown varnish, withered pot plants and a view of a smoke-blackened brick wall. The dominant feature is a large drawing of Queen Victoria – "that gigantic dwarf", as John Fowles unimprovably described her. She died only two years before Longford was born, and her shadow, as he admits, overhangs his life: the energy, piety, prudishness and productivity, from books (26), to careers (at least five), to children (eight) and grandchildren (26).

He will be 90 this year and still jogs four miles every Sunday along the lanes near his country house in Sussex ("though I am so slow I really must stop boasting about it"). His famous hair, the caricaturist's crutch, is a dandelion clock whose time is almost up, and he shuffles carefully to the drinks cabinet to fill our sherry glasses (a good quarter pint apiece) but he is as sharp as a tack.

He has lived such a long time that he has known everybody: Waugh, Betjeman, John Buchan, Keynes (who turned him down for a job as a stockbroker), Beveridge (whom he worked for on the Beveridge Report), Attlee (served in his first government), Gaitskell (they shared rooms at Oxford) – it goes on and on. He is frequently related to them as well, through his own family or Elizabeth, who is a member of the Chamberlain clan. Anthony Powell is his brother-in-law. Auberon Waugh is his godson. Harriet Harman is his niece, Harold Pinter his son-in-law.

He is the second son of an Irish earl, and was educated at Eton (Captain of House) and Oxford (a First in PPE). "What have been the main circumstances of my formation?" he asks. "Privilege, obviously must be mentioned early …" He joined the Labour Party in 1936, influenced by his wife, and his experience as a Workers' Education Authority lecturer in the Potteries. He has sat as a Labour peer all his life, serving as First Lord of the Admiralty in Attlee's government, and Leader of the House of Lords in Harold Wilson's.

"One of the things which struck me most about your book," I say to him, "is the way that in spite of your socialist conversion you managed to maintain your friendships with people like Waugh and Birkenhead …"

"F.E. Smith? He would be very Right-wing in today's terms. But one of the most amusing men I ever met. You don't have to agree with people's ideas to get along with them."

"Do you lack a gut feeling for socialism?"

"I don't think politics are the deepest things in a man's character. That's a very *crude* idea."

"But there must have been people whose ideas were so repellent you could not stay friends?"

"The only one with actually *repellent* ideas would be Diana Mosley, who still has a few kind words to say about Hitler. But I knew her before she was a fascist, and we are still friends."

Longford belongs to the same Labour tradition as Attlee, Gaitskell – or Tony Blair, for that matter. He is a high-minded public schoolboy ignorant of, or indifferent to, both theoretical socialism and class antagonism, who has seen in the Labour movement a vehicle for his own do-goodery.

There is nothing wrong with that, but it means that he sees nothing amiss, for instance, in the fact he is a believer in social equality and a Knight of the Garter, "unless you are a republican and you aren't *that*, are you?" He sees no contradiction between the fact that he served in the Labour Cabinet which established the comprehensive system and that he sent his sons to Ampleforth – the leading Catholic public school. "I think one's first duty is towards one's children's education …"

"Lord Bath sent his children to a comprehensive and they both went to university."

"I won't take guidance from a man who has had 62 mistresses."

"But isn't private education the chief way in which the privilege you oppose is maintained?"

"You must think of the children."

"Why shouldn't they do perfectly well at a comp?"

"It would be unnatural for them."

Longford resigned from the Wilson Cabinet in 1967, over the decision not to raise the school leaving age, and has devoted himself since to a variety of good causes: as chairman of Mencap and as a prison reformer and visitor – most notably of Moors murderer Myra Hindley.

"What are your arguments for releasing Hindley?" I ask.

"Very simple. Myra has been in prison for 30 years. She is a good, religious woman."

"What about the families of the victims?"

"I treat that argument with contempt. You cannot keep someone in jail to please the victims' families. People can be exploited by the tabloids year after year. Wheeled out on television, their hatred kept alive. Can you bring yourself to believe she is a good woman?"

"I don't know."

"All the evidence is that way," he says.

"I don't think it's relevant whether Hindley is good or evil. Even evil people should be released if they are not dangerous and have served their sentences."

"I see what you mean," says Longford, "but it is relevant in this way: because the tabloids call her Evil Myra it is necessary to refute that. She was a good woman before she met Ian Brady and she shook off that influence very soon afterwards. Rationally it should not matter but it is essential in this debate."

I am not sure if it is, and I wonder if by blathering on about good and evil Longford has not muddied the waters and made the issue subjective and theological, when it should be a straightforward matter of justice and decency. Hindley has served more time than many comparable offenders. She is not dangerous.

The feelings of victims' families are irrelevant. Indeed the whole point of having a legal system is to remove punishment from the realm of rage, grief, vendetta and local powers. The courts exist to depersonalise justice, not to be influenced by weeping relatives, screeching tabloids or theological argument. Ergo Hindley should be set free.

"Have you helped her?"

"Very difficult to say – well, I think so. In the years when no one else backed her."

"Wasn't there a point when she didn't want you visiting any longer?"

"Yes, but as a matter of fact I have just seen her again."

In many respects Longford's career has been one of failure: he has no great social or political reform to his credit like Lord Jenkins or Sir David Steele. He has never run a great department of state. Dick Crossman described his Cabinet career as "farcical", and Wilson was reputed to have said he had "the mind of a 12-year-old", though Longford says, indignantly, that it was "the *judgment* of a 12-year-old".

His ill-informed crusade against pornography became a comic opera for the press, and his campaign on behalf of Hindley, however generously intended, has succeeded only in projecting her image so strongly on the public mind that no Home Secretary dares to set her free.

He is quite candid about most of this, awarding himself only a "second class honours" or "borderline two-one" in most areas of his life. He was chairman of a clearing bank, but not a major one; chairman of a publishing house but not a great one; an Oxford don but never a professor; a social worker, but not in the league of Leonard Cheshire; a successful author but never a literary star. The only exception to this parade of nicely calculated modesty is his marriage of 62 years, to which he awards a First.

"All this time," he says before I go, "you have been scolding me for my aristocratic friends and for sending my children to public school. Yet here you are, a republican and a socialist, writing for the *Telegraph*."

"Well, I'm only playing the interviewer you know."

"And I suppose I am only playing the interviewee," says Lord Longford. "Isn't life complicated?"

The Daily Telegraph, 23 January 1995

Ros Hepplewhite

There are no mothers and fathers at the Child Support Agency, only Absent Parents and Parents With Care: APs and PWCs. The AP, of course, is nearly always a pa: "We have to face the fact that nine tenths of Absent Parents *are* male," says Ros Hepplewhite, the CSA head, but she prefers the non-judgmental initials. Enraged and impoverished fathers have already laid siege to the Tory Conference, created the biggest MPs' postbag since the poll tax, and helped boost the CSA's incoming phone calls to a fantastic 800,000 a month. And the focus of their loathing is the mumsy lady in the armchair opposite, in the yellow blazer and print frock, with a mouth full of Civil Service pabulum. "There has been a *very* well-organised campaign by *certain* groups of Absent Parents," Mrs Hepplewhite says.

I'm an Absent Parent myself by definition, even though the children of my first marriage spend a third of their time with me; though I pay their mother maintenance; and though she received a house in our settlement. I don't cite these facts in bitterness (we get on quite well) but as confession of bias and to illustrate that many APs don't feel like APs, and resent the classification. They feel like fathers who are already discriminated against by the courts (which award care and control of children to the mother semi-automatically), and who are then treated by the CSA as cash-cows, or rather bullion-bulls.

But indignation is running ahead of information. We are on the 24th storey of Millbank Tower with a dim view, through summer smog and filthy windows, of the new MI6 headquarters across the Thames. The room looks like the suite they use to dose drug-runners with castor oil at Heathrow, but this is Mrs Hepplewhite's personal office. There are no photographs, no pictures, no books, and the desk is bare. A press officer called Karen pointedly switches on a tape recorder at the same instant as mine – always a sign of PR naïvety. There is little time wasted on pleasantries.

"I was surprised you agreed to do this interview, since you turned me down nine months ago. Have you decided you need some good publicity?"

"I try very hard to make sure I am accessible and give an account of the agency," Mrs Hepplewhite says. "Clearly, there are occasions when too many people are asking me at once, or when the Minister is a more appropriate person."

What she said at the time was that she would answer no questions about personal matters, or policy, or matters concerning the running of the agency which had been extensively covered elsewhere – which didn't leave very much. Over the past year Mrs Hepplewhite has regularly taken refuge in the mandarin's mantra that "policy questions are for politicians", though in reality the Chinese Wall between policy and administration is not very solid –

especially in semi-detached, "first step" agencies such as the CSA.

The largest single grievance of fathers is that the CSA takes no account of "clean break" settlements where money and property have been given to the mother instead of maintenance. Mrs Hepplewhite has defended this on the grounds that the gift of a house does not directly benefit the children – which is clearly nonsensical. She defends it now, on the grounds that "in many cases it wasn't just the property that was transferred, it was also the mortgage debt – which meant the cost of housing benefit to pay that debt was also falling on the taxpayer".

"But we are not necessarily talking about people who are claiming benefit at all."

"Well, if you are not on benefit there is no need to come to the CSA," she says. "But anyone can come to the CSA for an assessment of maintenance, can't they? So housing benefit has nothing to do with clean breaks."

At this point Karen the PR steps in: "I'm sorry to interrupt, but this is going a long way down the road of policy issues."

"But, look, for years the courts and lawyers have been recommending to fathers that the most humane way of settling the question of money in divorce is the clean break."

"No, you are going right down the policy road, which only a politician can answer."

"I am just trying to find out if she believes there is a serious flaw in the legislation."

"That clearly is not an issue that I can express an opinion on," Mrs Hepplewhite says.

"But you just *were* expressing an opinion by defending it. And presumably you took the job on believing it *was* a correct position, so how can you say you have no opinion?" But there is no point continuing, for the Chinese Wall has descended.

Mrs Hepplewhite, as even the people who loathe the CSA admit, is a perfectly nice woman. She was a successful Health Service administrator in Sussex and a popular head of MIND, the mental health charity. Nobody seems to know her well, though, and there is something curiously opaque about her. Her odd-sized eyes wander all the time, as if seeking escape; her voice is a soothing, counsellor's monotone; her language is full of Majorish phrases such as "inappropriate to speculate" and "a not unrealistic assessment". Perhaps the oddest thing is the way she talks about her background, which she is ready enough to do at first but then becomes hopelessly stranded.

She was born in Stoke-on-Trent in 1952, but was brought up in Portsmouth by her mother, a school teacher. Her father left home in 1956 but remained sporadically in touch throughout her childhood, taking out her and her brother Roger once or twice a year. He remained on good terms with his wife, whom he never divorced but never supported financially. This in itself sounds rather odd, but it becomes odder still.

"What did your father do for a living?" I ask.

"He did a variety of things."

"A businessman?"

"No … a variety of things is a very realistic assessment."

"Give me a couple of examples."

"Well, he was in the Army when I was born."

"An officer?"

"I'm not sure … he thought so."

"Well, what did he do after the Army?"

"Well, as I say, he had a variety of jobs."

"If you know he had a variety of jobs you must know what some of them were?"

"You could say he was a casual worker."

"Manual or professional?"

"He tried his hand at anything."

"Did he have some kind of a problem? Drink?"

"In that respect you probably know as much about him as I do."

The PR, the photographer and myself are shifting in our seats, and rolling our eyes, but Mrs Hepplewhite is quite implacable.

"Why do you think he left your mother?"

"I really have very little information on this. I don't think it's appropriate to speculate." So I decide to change the subject: "Were you very poor as a family` with your father gone?" I ask, but Hepplewhite is evidently stuck in a groove, and produces an answer which is quite crackpot.

"I really could not speculate on that." An embarrassed silence falls.

"Am I wasting my time?"

"I am not trying to say nothing. You keep asking questions I don't have the answer to."

Of course it is absurd, as some newspapers have tried, to link Mrs Hepplewhite's errant father and her own pursuit of today's APs. She is a civil servant executing a policy entrusted to her by our elected masters, but all the same there is a kind of marmoreal stubbornness about her, and in the way she has done her job which suggests what the shrinks call "unresolved conflicts". In a recent case for instance, the CSA demanded £98 a week maintenance from a grandfather who had adopted his granddaughter 13 years previously to prevent her going into care. The child's natural parents were alive, and the uncle and aunt she lived with both worked, but the CSA was immovable. A CSA spokesman I asked about the case said: "We only administer the law. What else could we do?"

I said they could have lost the file, like any sensible bureaucracy, and she looked at me dumbfounded. Mrs Hepplewhite's CSA evidently has no truck with such pragmatism, and accordingly has spent its first year staggering from one public relations disaster to the next: maintenance demands to dead people; to "fathers" who had never met the mothers, and for sums which were larger than some fathers' gross incomes.

Worst of all, perhaps, was a leak of agency documents which revealed it had been dealing as a priority with 250,000 cases where absent fathers were already paying maintenance. One management memorandum told staff: "The name of the game is maximising the yield – don't waste time on the non-profitable stuff." Mrs Hepplewhite herself was revealed to receive a performance bonus on her £48,000 salary if the agency hit its goal of £530 million benefit savings, though as it turned out there was to be little danger of this.

At the end of its first year the agency had fallen £112 million short of target and Mrs Hepplewhite made an abject apology for failing to meet acceptable standards.

Labour's Social Security spokesman, Donald Dewar, said the CSA had undermined the public confidence needed for its survival: "Laws rely on consent and we are near the point where consent is being withdrawn." Labour MP Frank Field remarked that it was "disappointing" that the agency was recovering little more money that its predecessor, in spite of having cost the taxpayer £230 million in start-up costs.

Divorce is a messy business, which may be amenable only to the pragmatic procedures of the courts rather than the narrow formulas of a bureaucracy. Everyone welcomed the Child Support Act when it was passed, but hindsight argues that perhaps all that was needed was a little reform of the existing system. The CSA has been reformed once and will be reformed again when the Social Security Select Committee reports in the autumn, but the odds on

Mrs Hepplewhite surviving as head must be slim.

Before I left I returned hesitantly to personal questions: to her children aged 16 and 17 who are both at boarding school; to Julian her husband of 23 years, who is company secretary of the Alliance and Leicester. "You were married very young weren't you? Before you even went to university. You must have been about 18?"

"I just met the right person at the right time," Mrs Hepplewhite says. "It's very hard to speculate why you do these things. I suppose I have been very purposeful in my personal life as well as my career – in getting things sorted out."

The Daily Telegraph, 20 July 1994

Norman Mailer

Norman Mailer spins a small coin on to the glass table top. Its serrated edges yatter crossly in a brief, downward helix, towards silence.

"That is the irritation of the god you can hear," he says. His sharp blue eyes dare me to smile. He is talking about *Ancient Evenings*, his monumental, and well-nigh unreadable novel on the Egypt of the Pharaohs. "Try to imagine a world where people believed intimately in gods. Where they hear a god in the strike of coin on glass." I try, obediently, as he flips the coin again. The susurration of traffic seeps in from Piccadilly, the big jets groan in their holding pattern over Hyde Park, the reels of the tape recorder click and the overstuffed sofas and chintzy drapes of Brown's Hotel scoff mutely at the pretension. But Mailer's Magus intensity holds back the encroachment of smug common sense for a moment, and yes, there is the hint of an angry snicker in the coin's last echo.

Probably the most interviewed novelist of all time, Mailer is inevitably a portmanteau of small tricks and parlour enchantments; a walking library of conundrum and anecdote, he has all but vanished up his own dust jacket. Harvard at the age of 16, graduating *summa cum laude* in aeronautical engineering; an infantryman in the Pacific war; internationally famous at the age of 25 with the publication of

The Naked and the Dead; successively a marxist, existentialist and self-appointed court jester to the Kennedys; five children and six wives, the second of whom he was imprisoned for stabbing; drug taker and drunken beast of the TV chat show; a leader of the anti-Vietnam war movement; candidate for Mayor of New York; 25 books and two Pulitzer prizes.

We are supposed to be here to talk about Mailer's latest novel, *Tough Guys Don't Dance* – a potboiling murder thriller – but Mailer knows a fan when he meets one, and we are into the Mailer Big Country now of God, totalitarianism, sodomy and madness.

"Would you like a throat lozenge?" Mailer asks. "No? They *do* taste awful." And he pads away to the bathroom for water. He will be 62 next birthday, on 31 January. Aquarius. That was the name he chose for himself as narrator of his book on the first moon landing, *Of a Fire on the Moon* in 1970. Narrators don't have names like that any more.

He used to talk proudly in those days too, about all the punishment his body had taken: the bourbon, seconal, benzedrine, marijuana, LSD, fist fights – and that actor who hit him on the head with a hammer while he was directing his film, *Maidstone.*

I don't suppose he would boast about it now, because it shows. He is smartly dressed in soft black loafers, grey flannels, navy v-neck sweater and regimental tie at half-mast, but his face is grey and crumpled with tiredness and his whole body sags. He has a bad cough and is beginning to walk with the carefulness of old age. The dust jacket photo on *Tough Guys* must be five years out of date at least.

His old rival and contemporary Truman Capote died just a few months ago, and I ask him his feelings about death. "The idea we go through all the things we go through, good and bad, and have it all end up with oneself as a piece of sod, has never made much sense to me. It's more interesting to think there's some continuation."

More interesting. Like the great, hypostatic sentences of his novels, crammed with conditionals, he qualifies his statements reflexively. So is his belief in an afterlife, and in a Manichean universe run by God and the Devil just a literary notion, a bit of scaffolding for the novels? He considers. "Thirty years ago I used to ask, 'What if God were an embattled general fighting for his vision of the universe? What if we were his troops? – all that kind of stuff, as a literary conceit. Then after ten years or so I decided to take the next step and say he *was.*"

In *Tough Guys Don't Dance*, God abandons his military role to appear as a kind of celestial bookmaker. The story, in brief, concerns a failed writer, Tim Madden, living in Provincetown, Cape Cod, who wakes up one morning after a blind drunk to find a tattoo on his arm that was not there before, and the seat of his car soaked in blood. Later he discovers two severed female heads in the cave where he keeps his marijuana, and begins to get worried. The rest of the book is a lengthening trail of corpses and suspects who include Madden himself, Madden's wife, a psychopathic police chief, a homosexual millionaire, a black stud ex-boxer and so forth.

In one scene, Madden's father, Dougy, argues that betting on the points "spread" in a football game, God would win 80 per cent of the time, compared to 75 per cent for a corporeal bookie. "Why not 100 per cent?" his son asks him. "Because footballs," says Dougy, "take funny bounces."

So God is up there, doing his best, but he can't keep an eye on everything. Man has to save himself, through familiar Mailerian rituals – confrontation with violence, personal courage, the self-assertion of the existential hero. At the start of the novel, Dougy is dying of cancer – caused, he believes, by the fact that as a younger man, after being shot four times, he prudently admitted himself to hospital instead of trying to kill the guy that shot him. At the end of the book he has cured his cancer by cutting up six dead bodies – the fruits of the intervening mayhem – and dumping them in the ocean.

Teased out of a brilliant and restrained narrative like *The Executioner's Song*, such ideas can command interest, but nailed on, as so much metaphysical baggage, to the ramshackle structure of a sub-Chandler plot, they are just preposterous. But Mailer is pleased with *Tough Guys*. It is one of the novels, he says, along with *The Deer Park* and *Why are We in Vietnam?* that he is most fond of. "I wrote it in two months, and the price you usually pay for speed is a sloppy, leached-out surface. But I think the sentences come out well."

In fact the surface of the book is awful. "Two steel bolts drilled in a rock," is Mailer's description of the police chief's eyes. "What is the first maxim of the street?" the narrator, Madden, asks himself. "If you want to die with a slug in your back, fool around with a cop's wife." Surely that would be the seventh or eighth maxim of the street?

Of course, it is a first-person narrative, which as any first-year

English student knows, means you can blame all the stylistic infelicities on the ham-fistedness of your narrator and call it ironic distancing. But that doesn't explain the unevenness of the badness. Sometimes characters talk as if they have hangovers from *Ancient Evenings*. "Our seed has got to be too hideous to continue," Dougy (a docker) tells his son when he begins to suspect him of being the murderer. When the dog shits itself, "The treasures of its belly befouled the linoleum." And the whole text is studded with playful archaisms ("wont to do," "of other ilk") and fancy Teutonic inversions ("Madeleine was living in an apartment totally drab"). But of that for now, enough.

A more serious charge is that Mailer is plagiarising not only his own metaphysics but his favourite phrases. "Any lady who chooses to become blonde is truly blonde," he writes of the "porny" star, Jennifer Welles, which is just what he wrote about Marilyn Monroe twelve years ago. Of a modern housing estate, he writes: "The shape of our twisting roads came from the draftsman laying it out on drawing paper with French curves," which is not a bad perception, were it not lifted from *Of a Fire on the Moon*.

Not that it matters a great deal. Mailer can write very well, (*The Naked and the Dead, Armies of the Night, Why are We in Vietnam?, Executioner's Song*). But if his appeal rested on good writing alone, the mob would have strung him up when the atrocious, ideology-stuffed, *Barbary Shore*, came out in 1951.

Nor is it his intellectual rigour. Mailer is responsible for some of the maddest, most sophomoric formulations in modern literature. The huge popularity of Darth Vader and Luke Skywalker, he told me at one point, "could be due to some unconscious agreement by the hordes of the populace on what the structure of the cosmos might be. Who knows?" Women's Lib, on the other hand, came along just when the computers "needed" to abolish the difference between men and women in order to double their storage capacity.

No, the reason even hostile critics continue to pay attention to Mailer is that he is a genuine original, working against the grain of most of his contemporaries in American literature. "Passive, timid, other-directed," is his contemptuous description of the fictional heroes of Bellow, Malamud, Roth and the like. "Up to their nostrils in anguish, the world is stronger than they are, suicide calls."

Against this literature of the victim, Mailer has erected a fictional world of vigorous possibility and personal responsibility. On the one hand the Devil, totalitarianism, corporation, conformism, computers, deodorants, contraceptives, smog and plastic. On the other hand, God, magic, smells, telepathy, dialectic, animals, cruelty and love.

God as general, or God as bookmaker, whether he is metaphorical or actual, entails a universe in which everything people do *matters*. Every act of love, bravery, cowardice, destruction adds to or subtracts from the forces of Vader or Skywalker. Everything has a meaning, down to the chink of a coin on a glass table.

"If that was all it took to be a Catholic," Mailer says, "then I would become a Catholic. I've always been impressed by the Catholic notion that at every moment a man is a little bit more or less good than the moment before."

It is an austere and forbidding theology; a demand for perpetual vigilance, constant struggle. It has led Mailer into uncomfortable and unpopular social positions. Contraception is bad because it corrupts the dialectic of sex, as does sodomy and masturbation. Murder and violence, on the other hand, may have their redemptive qualities insofar as they may reveal a person's true nature to himself.

It can easily become an advocacy of moral Puritanism and social barbarism, but it is hard to imagine anything more civilised and less barbarous than the pudgy Jewish boy from Brooklyn who gets up to shake hands before I go. "If there is a purpose to my writing now," he says, "it is to keep alive some notion of the varieties of human experience." The sofas yawn, the big jets groan and the traffic snores, but Norman Mailer sends me away whistling.

New Society, 18 October 1984

Roald Dahl

R oald Dahl is ill when we meet, but he is being ill in great style: propped up in bed with his dog Chopper, a giant jar of jellybabies and a pack of Cartier cigarettes. He even has the rather stylish ailment of gout.

"Excess of uric acid. Swells up your joints, see?" The ring finger of his shovel-sized hand is swollen to the dimensions of a parsnip. "But the doctors can cure it with pills these days."

I arrive forearmed with tales of Dahl's legendary grouchiness, but he is all charm today: a Big Friendly Giant in striped flannel pyjamas. "So glad you smoke. I try not to inhale. It scares me to death when you see people – women especially – sucking in great gobs, and then nothing comes out. But I couldn't write without one."

"You write every day?"

"When I'm well. Two hours in the morning and two in the afternoon. Never do more than that, it buggers up your family life. I got masses of teaching from old Ernest Hemingway who said when you're writing well you should stop. Never write yourself out."

He works in a garden shed where he also keeps his two arthritic hip-bones and a vertebral disc, floating in a jar. There is a matching pair of bottle-green BMWs in the garage and a scattering of F-reg hatchbacks in the drive. The house, near Great Missenden, is low, white, rambling and beautiful with a kitchen full of pretty blondes who might be his daughters, step-daughters, housekeepers or cooks: all are present at one time or other. I register oil paintings by Matthew Smith and Francis Bacon and a wall of Henry Moore etchings.

Dahl is the most successful children's writer in the world. His last book, *Matilda,* sold 160,000 copies in hardback in the UK, and when *Charlie and the Chocolate Factory* was published in China it had a first print-run of two million, which is thought to be the biggest printing of any book, anywhere, ever. I bought a copy of his latest book, *Esio Trot* – a tale of love and 140 tortoises – for my daughter this week. It was very slim, it cost £6.50 in hardback, and to my great chagrin, she read it under the bedclothes in one hour flat.

"Why do you still do interviews?" I ask him.

"Well, I don't want to sound sententious, but you should give something back. And I love reading about the chaps I like reading."

The chaps he likes reading are the American crime writer, Elmore Leonard, and the novelists of his youth: Faulkner, Waugh, Steinbeck, Greene. "I read the reviews of people like Martin Amis, but when I buy the book I'm disappointed 95 per cent of the time. I don't think the novel is what it used to be."

"You created a row at a literary prize-giving last year by saying the only purpose of the novel was entertainment."

"I meant that. It's why I disagree with people like Rushdie. This creed of his that the writer is a privileged person – the creator of the future – it's absolute balls."

"Do you know many other writers?"

"Hemingway always used to say writers that hang out together are no bloody good."

The independence, pugnacity and cynicism have their roots in a wretched childhood. Dahl was brought up in Wales by prosperous Norwegian parents, but his sister died when he was three, followed a few weeks later by his father. At Repton he was beaten savagely and regularly by the headmaster, Geoffrey Fisher, who later became Archbishop of Canterbury – an irony which Dahl says put him off Christianity for life. He escaped to an overseas job with Shell, and then joined the RAF where he flew Hurricanes in bloody campaigns over Greece and Syria.

And then a charmed, magical quality seems to come into his life. He is wounded, and posted to a plum job as Assistant Air Attaché in Washington. The novelist C.S. Forester asks him to make some notes of his flying experiences for the *Saturday Evening Post*, which Forester will write up. Ten days later Dahl gets a letter saying "Did you know you were a writer? I didn't change a word." And enclosed is a cheque for $900.

Then Dahl makes up a story called *Gremlins* (he coined the word) about the demons which inhabit fighter aircraft. It is snapped up by Walt Disney who flies him to Hollywood and introduces him to Jimmy Cagney. The story is read by Eleanor Roosevelt who invites him to dinner at the White House, where he meets Martha Gellhorn, Hemingway's wife. He becomes a friend of Hemingway and a protegé of Franklin Roosevelt, who takes him on country weekends from which Dahl feeds titbits to the British Secret Service.

These are real events and real surrogate fathers. And they make the events of his stories – the orphan girl who is taken up by the Big Friendly Giant, or the poor boy who is adopted by Willie Wonka the chocolate millionaire – seem almost mundane.

He emerges into the 1950s with an established career as a short-story writer, and a beautiful Hollywood wife, Patricia Neal. But then the spell is lifted as mysteriously as it was cast. His eldest daughter dies of measles; his infant son is brain-damaged in a traffic accident; his wife suffers three major strokes.

He nurses her back to health, but falls in love with her best friend Felicity and they divorce. Patricia writes a painfully revealing autobiography, and his daughter Tessa a thinly fictionalised novel with Dahl as villain. A month before we met, his step-daughter died suddenly of a brain tumour. There are more magical transformations and tragic reversals here than would be reasonable in any work of fiction.

He made his first reputation of course, as a master of the short story with the cruel twist. Is he pleased to find himself largely known as a children's writer?

"I love it. It's very worthwhile, encouraging children to read."

"But if novels are only entertainments, what's the point of getting children to read even more?"

"The value of reading for them is not the reading itself, but to get somewhere in life: doctor or lawyer or vet or whatever," – which seems a curious ambition for the anarchic Dahl, but there you are.

"What do you think makes a good children's writer?"

"It's a mysterious thing. Almost every writer I've known has tried to write a children's book and they can't do it. Hemingway wrote a story about a lion once which flies to Rome – great start, but then the lion goes down to Hemingway's favourite bar and orders a Negroni – buggers it up completely."

"Perhaps you have to like children to write well for them?"

"I love them, but I don't think you have to, Beatrix Potter hated children and had none of her own. When she saw one coming down the street in the Lake District she used to throw stones at it."

So it is a puzzle, and an irritating one for the liberal parents who would prefer their children to be reading more conventionally safe writers than Dahl, with his vulgarity and anarchism, and disrespect for the adult world. But all the great children's writers, like Potter, and Lewis Carroll and Lear and Kipling – alongside whom Dahl surely deserves to be ranked – are unusual, thwarted personalities.

They are all partly marooned in childhood themselves by the intensity, and often misery, of their own childhood experiences, and it is this which gives great children's stories their special, unfakeable energy.

The most important question though, and the one which my daughter wants answered most urgently, is when will Mr Dahl write another one?

"There are various mumbly little things going on. An idea in my notebook about an old gipsy woman with a dog which can understand language. It might work." I hope it does, I hope it will be soon, and I hope it will be long.

The Sunday Telegraph, 13 May 1990

A.L. Rowse

It is a cold, monochrome day in Cornwall: grey sea, grey laurels and grey lawns running up from the shore to A.L. Rowse's square grey house. There is some problem with the hot water system. "He hasn't had a bath for a month," says Phyllis, the elderly housekeeper, in a helpful *sotto voce*. Alfred Leslie Rowse, 90 next month, is rather deaf.

"Are you married?" is his first question. I say I am. "He won't like *that*," says Phyllis.

"Pity," says Rowse. "And you have children?"

"Three, I'm afraid."

"He won't like that *at all*."

But Rowse likes the fact that I am a fellow Celt, from Swansea, and falls to talking about Dylan Thomas. "Quite a good poet, though he wasted it on drink and his awful wife. You know A.J.P. Taylor's wife was potty about him. She got me to take Dylan and Caitlin to lunch once in Oxford. It was wartime so I offered them beer or cider. 'Oh no', says Caitlin, 'We'll have a bottle of white wine'," Rowse prods me in the arm, shrill with the indignation of this 50-year-old slight. "That's the kind of *bitch* she was."

Conversation is a steady snowfall of great names. "You know Montgomery sat in that chair? ... He told me that Clem Attlee was a far better chairman of Cabinet than Winston ... Attlee was a *great* man and so was Ernest Bevin ... but Winston was a *genius*. I met him when I wrote my history of the Churchills ... Winston and Lloyd George were the only first-rate men of genius to lead the country this century ... You know, I met Lloyd George? He was a *naughty* boy but naughty with the girls, not the other way. He had such a *lot* you see and had to have somewhere to put it ..."

We sit side by side in his great study with its bay window looking out towards the sea: he clutching my upper arm, and I scribbling. The great Elizabethan historian, Shakespeare scholar and sometime poet, was born just down the road, son of a china clay worker. With his brown tweeds and blunt, rosy face, he could be a labourer in Sunday-best, though dialect has disappeared under the arch accents of the Oxford High Table. But his sentences still climb Celtic escalators of emphasis to the final syllable, a triumphant parakeet screech.

Nominally I am here to discuss his latest book, *All Souls In My Time*, a rambling and wretchedly proof-read memoir of Rowse's 50 years as a fellow of that college. But his attention is taken up by the two great grudges of his life: the pre-war policy of appeasement and his discovery of Shakespeare's "Dark Lady" of the Sonnets. We, or rather he, return to them relentlessly, and there are connections as we shall see. His early life, vividly recounted in *A Cornish Childhood*, was the epic struggle of the grammar school boy to make his way in the world. "Of course, I didn't really like living in a working-class household with no books, no music, no lovely rugs or beautiful pictures. I was by nature an aesthete you see, and I didn't fit into that kind of life."

At 17 he won the only university scholarship in the whole of Cornwall, through prodigies of effort that almost destroyed his health. At 23 he was elected a Fellow of All Souls – "the blue riband of an Oxford career" – though he never became a professor, and has yet to collect a knighthood.

"Of course, as a young man I was very much on the Left, but not a communist. I was looked down on by the fashionable Cambridge spies lot like Blunt because I was a straight follower of Ernest Bevin and Clem Attlee. A good middle of the road Labour man, which was working class and I'd had an awful raw deal when I was young. But what kept me on the Left was the absolutely shocking policy of Baldwin and Chamberlain going in for appeasement with Hitler. But they never knew Germany or German history as I did. I was right and they were *wrong*. They were *ignorant*, and would not be *told*."

The Dark Lady was Rowse's great discovery of the Sixties – an elusive figure in Shakespeare's sonnets whom he identified as Emilia Bassano. She was of Italian and possibly Jewish extraction; the mistress of the Lord Chamberlain who patronised Shakespeare's company; she was around at the right time, and knew the right people. "I'd *got* her," says Rowse, and there was certainly a fanfare of publicity, followed by equally noisy rebuttals from a chorus of what Rowse dismisses as "journalist clowns", "journalist professors" and "third raters".

This journalist clown is not qualified to made a judgment but there is an obvious echo between the two crises, of appeasement and Dark Lady, where Rowse twice appears as lone iconoclast, chip heavy on working-class shoulder, to challenge established and Establishment opinion. English history for Rowse is a process of steady, and heroic ascent – parallel to his own laborious self improvement. It was deeply galling for the young romantic to arrive at the top of the heap at the very moment, in the Thirties, when the silly toffs were turning it into a second-class heap. "They well nigh ruined this country and reduced it to a second-rate place in the world."

He has published more than 50 books and was a staple of my own A-level course 23 years ago, but I have no idea of his academic standing these days. Patrick Collinson, Regius Professor of History at Cambridge, and a leading authority on Tudor England, says: "Some of his early work, like *Tudor Cornwall* and *The England of Elizabeth*, were very rich books but there has been a progressive degeneracy. Decades of increasing scorn for professional standards; a quirky anti-professional streak in which all the experts are bound to be wrong. He has not been taken seriously by professional historians for a very long time."

Jonathan Bates, who is Professor of Literature at Liverpool University and an editor of *The Arden Shakespeare*, argues that Rowse's problem is "he does not understand that Elizabethan writing is not concealed autobiography. That is a much later, Romantic idea". Stanley Wells, Professor of Shakespeare Studies at Birmingham University, director of the Shakespeare Institute at Stratford and general editor of *The Oxford Shakespeare*, says "his Dark Lady theory is not accepted by the world of scholarship in general. But he's a character isn't he? An opinionated person who thrives on controversy."

Against this one should probably add that the academic trade union is rotten with professional jealousy, particularly for those such as Rowse whose works have sold millions, who tramples traditional demarcations and who has never been polite about "second rate" colleagues. But even so …

There is always a tension between scholarship and style, and Rowse's curse perhaps is that he is such a gifted writer – *A Cornish Childhood* is marvellous – that the power of polemic erodes the scruple of scholarship. The Dark Lady theory is an interesting patterning of circumstantial evidence but not a proof.

Among modern historians, who tend to be sceptical about "great men" and to question the neat labelling of historical periods – the

Elizabethan "age", the "English Reformation" etc – Rowse's attitudes have become quaint, and his confident generalisations about personality and race, anachronistic. In *The Spirit of English History* he writes: "There was a strong contrast between the Britons and the Saxons. Where the former were imaginative and extreme, moody and discordant ... the Saxons were earthy, laborious, stolid. They were a virile, masculine stock."

Of the Germans he says: "In the ascendant arrogant and brutal, in defeat base and grovelling." Of his great heroine, Elizabeth: "Hers was a subtle and brilliant Renaissance personality ... she was young but she was wise and something of a sceptic." It is not quite *1066 and All That*, but sometimes not far off.

The key to Rowse is in his poetry, which is sometimes fine, sometimes plonking and derivative, but where he appears again and again as a solitary figure in the crowd. In *Farnham, Surrey* fruitful autumn is the "Season of mists and mellow insignificance/Of domestic dogs and perambulators pushed/I watch with no affiliation the human zoo."

Rowse is as camp as a Boy Scouts' outing; his horny old hand is seldom absent from my knee or upper arm. He says that "My sympathies are *entirely* homo", but he is also of a pre-outing generation skilled at evading direct inquiry, as when I ask when his "sympathies" were first apparent? "Oh, the gay lib people are such fools. My line is just that homosexuality is a variety of ordinary sex experience. A fact of everyday life, so what is all the fuss? It is just childish and silly."

He is a delightful old man and a wise one, who has given entertainment and enlightenment to millions. I liked him and never more so when I asked if he minded the prospect of dying. "No. I think that is what's so boring about Philip Larkin. An awfully good poet but every bloody poem ends up with *death*. The thing is to get on with your *work*. People should fulfill their abilities as deeply and as fully as they possibly can. That is the way to happiness."

"So what has been your happiest moment?"

A.L. Rowse does not hesitate for a fraction of a second.

"When I was elected a Fellow of All Souls."

The Daily Telegraph, 17 November 1993

Nigel Kennedy

The rumour mill has given Nigel Kennedy a good going over in the past few years, since he dropped out of the classical music circus. Drying out clinics, drug rehabs, mental breakdown – and there were grounds for the whispers. He was giving interviews while swigging champagne, a bottle in either hand. He did £3,000 damage to his Berlin hotel suite. He had developed a habit of driving backwards in the dark with his eyes closed "to see what happened".

In 1993, Kennedy announced, portentously: "At some point, I'm going to have to consider if it is my responsibility as a musician to get into heavier drugs to find out more about music ..." And then three years of silence.

It looked for a bit as if Nige might be heading down the same route as his rock hero Jimi Hendrix, but we needn't have worried: after all, nobody called Nigel is ever going to make a convincing decadent. Jimi, Janis, Keith and Kurt may all spectacularly self-destruct, but the Nigels of this world always go on to another Grand Prix, chess tournament, or gold disc.

Nigels may be naff, but they are nickel-plated, and Nigel Kennedy is on the comeback trail: as bright-eyed, bushy-tailed and mildly irritating as ever. "Oh cool, man," he says, as I offer him my hand in a Malvern tea-shop, and "Oh, monster, man", when I say how I enjoyed his new album which is called *Kafka* ("cos, like, it's all abaht changes").

With his pudgy face, electric-shock haircut and slackjawed amiability, Kennedy could pass for 14, though in fact he is nearly 40. The teen-genius was invented by EMI to promote sales of *The Four Seasons* in 1989 (fastest selling classical record ever) and perpetuated by Kennedy's stubbornly juvenile tastes in rock (Hendrix, Portishead), clothes (Camden Lock/Oxfam Shop) and language (cats, vibes, man, cool, monster).

If anything, he is a late developer: the quiet, almost withdrawn child of a musical family from Brighton; regarded as technically competent but lacking in flair by his teachers at the Menuhin school.

Monster Nige emerged only in his late twenties, after a spell at the Juilliard Academy in New York and the end of an early marriage. With him came a strange new accent to replace the modest middle-class tones of his youth. "Where did you get that accent, Nigel?" shouted a hack at an early press conference, and Nigel shouted back, "From Tesco, where do you ----ing think?" Nige may be naff, but he is certainly no numbskull.

We sit in the window of the tea-shop, on the western flank of the Malvern Hills, looking across the Marches to the Black Mountains. Outside is Nigel's F-reg Jaguar, which is sprayed with the slogans of Aston Villa FC. He lives in Malvern not because of Elgar, but because it's only half an hour from Villa Park. "Only missed four games this season." He has had a steady girlfriend for the past year; ("not a musician, someone I met locally"). Every morning, he runs up the Beacon, and the drinking is down to a glass of champagne a week. "I've given up for a year now."

"Were you overdoing it?"

"I'd got to this point where me and my mate Steve Duffy – he's a songwriter – would go to the pub at lunch, go back home to do some work and pass out, go back to the pub at night, go home to do some work and pass out, then get up the next day and do the same thing again. I thought I'd better get a grip."

"Have you tried performing on acid, or other things?"

Nigel giggles. "I have tried playing in *various* states of mind which haven't been very beneficial to the people around me. I have found that I work best straight."

According to Nigel, he took the three years out largely because "it bugged the s--- out of me that I had to do these subscription concerts that are booked so far ahead, and frankly are for the benefit of mainly rich, upper-class audiences who aren't that discerning anyway". (Hooray!) He needed time to recover from two operations on his neck, "and I needed to convince EMI that I wasn't going to do a *Four Seasons Two.*"

Instead, he has produced *Kafka*, a collection of his own songs which range from rock anthems to Celtic folk dirges. The second track is called *I Believe in God*, which I take to be a statement of spiritual awakening, but Nigel says is a tribute to Paul McGrath, the Aston Villa defender.

"So you haven't gone spiritual?"

"Only in the music. I do three or four hours of practice a day, and I can find myself approaching some sort of state of spirituality then."

"And are you ever transported when you are performing?"

"Yeah, definitely. Maybe one time in 10, it's as if I'm in the audience looking on and the composer has taken over my body. "That's the best feeling you can have really; when the ego has been cast aside and the music is speaking for itself. One time, I had left my body and it was so graphic I was wondering whether to leave the concert hall, but I was too scared to do it in case I couldn't get back and left this guy sawing away for ever ..."

"And when you are playing your very best, where does it come from?"

"Some emotional or spiritual core, which is in everybody. A pool of common knowledge we all have from birth. Good music comes from a desire to communicate, and the fact that it actually happens shows it is in the person who receives it as much as the person who composed it."

This is an admirably democratic view of high art, and Kennedy has spent much time in sniping matches with more elitist members of the classical music establishment. His career took off in the late Eighties, when the *Nessun Dorma* theme for the World Cup, the explosion of CD sales, and the appearance of unpretentious music magazines such as *Classic CD* seemed to signal a new mass market for classical music (which has rather declined since people completed their CD collections).

EMI marketed "punk prodigy" Kennedy and *The Four Seasons* in a way no performer had been packaged since Paganini, and he has never been forgiven. There were bits of *The Four Seasons* that sounded like Hendrix on Ecstasy, and Nigel declared: "As far as I am concerned, Hendrix composed classical music. He is also a much more influential composer than, say, Vivaldi, in the effect he has on his contemporaries."

The music writer Michael Kennedy said in this newspaper: "Nigel has been conned, under the specious guise of anti-elitism into the belief that the concertos he plays are on no higher level than rock or pop or jazz. But they are, and he demeans his own immense gifts by pretending otherwise."

Well *does* Nigel think pop can stand comparison with classical music? "I think there are probably rock musicians turning out better realisations of what they want to express than some of the classical composers of today. But if you compare *any* modern day artist with past centuries, it is hard for them to survive."

So Nigel is a closet conservative really, who doesn't much like the plinkety-plonk sounds of modern minimalism, "or only if I am totally out of my head". He disapproves of over-edited studio recordings and of the modern emphasis on perfect technique over emotional power. He doesn't think music progresses either, "just swings between simplicity and complication: Bach complicated; Mozart simple again; Beethoven complicated; then back to Stravinsky."

And what about the conservative idea that classical music stops in about 1920?

"I've got half a foot in that camp. The central German composers like Bach, Beethoven and Brahms probably do encapsulate the greatest classical music ever written."

"You said once that the English snobbery about classical music was because we didn't have many composers of our own."

"That's right. If you count the composers who have busts made of them, you'd be lucky to find Elgar and Handel in the line-up – and Handel wasn't really English."

"Why is that?"

"Dunno. In the 1500s, we apparently produced some of the most beautiful music around. Perhaps it was like our cookery. Oliver Cromwell put a stop to that, didn't he?"

I am pretty cloth-eared about classical music, so I turn to the critics for guidance on how good Kennedy really is. Richard Morrison calls him, "The finest violinist Britain has produced since 1945"; Hugh Canning says he has "a style and technique which 20 years ago would have placed him firmly in the second rank". Sir John Drummond, former head of Radio 3, calls him "A Liberace for the Nineties"; John Peel of Radio One calls him "a w-----".

It helps confirm what I already know for a fact about literature, which is that all criticism, above the level of basic competence, is a matter of personal taste and bold assertion supported by a meaningless welter of undefined terms. Reticence and commitment, sweetness and abrasion, depth and threadiness, allure and attack – they are all words one comes across in appraisals of Kennedy, and mean as much as "nice" and "nasty".

Personally, and with cloth ears confessed, I quite enjoyed Kennedy's *Four Seasons* and loved his Elgar Violin Concerto, though I found the fiddle playing a bit mannered and intrusive for repeated listening. It is much the same with *Kafka*, which has some nice tunes (and a possible hit single in the football chant, *I Believe In God*,) but too much nagging *virtuosity* for real enjoyment, rather like

Blind Faith and those other "supergroups" of the late Sixties which became showcases for tedious solos on drum and guitar.

Kennedy is very likeable, far more so than some of the snotty characters who criticise him for his showmanship and his accent and the appalling way he sells millions of records to vulgar people who haven't listened to classical music all their lives. If, as a complete outsider, I were ever forced to take sides in the classical music battle, I would definitely be on the side of the Nigels. There will always be more of them about, and they always come back.

The Daily Telegraph, 3 June 1996

Charlie Richardson

Charlie Richardson has written a terrible book, full of rage and hatred and involuntary insights into a disturbing character. As a book – as a literary achievement – it is very far from terrible, being exciting, funny, and much better written than the usual kick-and-tell, criminal autobiography.

Richardson is the South London gangster, the "Torture Gang Boss", whose name is forever linked in the public mind with a sinister black box with a crank handle. It was called the "Megger" generator, and was used, according to the prosecution at Richardson's trial in 1967, to torture victims by means of electrodes taped to their genitals. I have seen it myself, on display at the Black Museum in Scotland Yard, alongside Dennis Nilsen's gas cooker and Crippen's acid bath.

Richardson's name is linked too with the Kray twins, whom he knew as friends and rivals, and whose gang was broken up in the same year. But in terms of wealth and influence, if not showbiz flash, Richardson was a far bigger fish than Reg and Ronnie – who were really rather hopeless hoodlums.

By the time Charlie appeared at the Old Bailey he was operating a business empire which ran from South London scrapyards and West End drinking clubs to Welsh slag heaps and South African mines, and he had powerful contacts at the heart of both the British

Conservative party and the South African Broederbond.

Six years after his release from prison, he is a wealthy man again, to judge by the tan and manicure and the foppish beard of the Euro-businessman. His origins are apparent only in the knotted cartilage of his nose, and breathy "Sarf London" accent, which lends a bleating stress to the ends of sentences: "I didn't want to meet you at all really. I been losing sleep over it, and it's not as if I need the money. But the publishers, they give you such a build-up." He is very fidgety to begin with; it is the first promotional interview he has done and he doesn't know the ropes. He turns up at the Savoy with armfuls of letters and documents as if we were going to try his case all over again. His wife Veronica sits across the tea table: a handsome, likeable, capable woman, some 20 years his junior, dressed in a smart suit. She intervenes only occasionally: "That's off the record Martyn." "I don't think you should go into that subject Charlie." Richardson's book is dedicated: "To my wife Veronica, who is a brilliant brain on beautiful legs" – but this is one of the few tender sentences in it.

In the opening chapter on his trial for instance, the spectators in the public gallery are: "Sad little grey people with sad little grey lives ..." The journalists are dismissed as "dandruff, pot bellies and spotty fat arses". Later on, the police are described as "the most lucrative, powerful and extensive protection racket in existence". Prison officers "escaped ordinary life one step ahead of an overwhelming sense of their own inadequacy". Teachers are "tired and underpaid social failures who took their solace in the dubious pleasures of discipline and control". There is a strong strain of physical disgust in the book, from his regular descriptions of body odour, to his adolescent distaste for sex: "My thrills were not from slipping a sweaty hand up fat sausage thighs to sticky knickers. I got my pleasure in a clever deal where I sold scrap for a good price."

It would not be too strong, on this evidence, to describe Richardson as a psychopath, in the strict sense of being a sane person who is indifferent to formal social relations. He has no belief in justice: "There never has been justice for anybody, ever. It's only another myth really, created by the Establishment. Veronica's mum, and my mum, they believe in this sort of myth."

His trial, according to Richardson, was a total fit-up. The chief witnesses against him, his former associates Lucien Harris and James Taggart, had been pressured by police to perjure themselves. The torture generator was a fabrication. The tale of nailing Lucien Harris's foot to the floor with a knife was a colourful lie, as was the account of screwing scampi into his eye sockets, as was the description of Taggart being forced to swab his own blood from the floor of Richardson's office with his underpants. Richardson's own account of himself is "a slightly bent businessman" and "not such a bad bloke really. So I have smashed a few people in the mouth because they owed me a few quid, but I've given a fortune to charity. I love my mum and I've got five kids. All I ever wanted was to have a good life." He says he knows I cannot retry his case for him in the space of an article, but he wants me to get those things down, and so there they are.

He was born in 1937 and brought up in Camberwell, the son of a merchant seaman and a Lyons Corner House waitress. Richardson makes a good deal of his childhood poverty as reason for his criminal career, but in fact the family do not seem to have been particularly badly off.

His grandparents owned a couple of shops: "They were very strict and proper people, but easy to manipulate." An uncle was a Baptist minister, while his mother was an honest woman in steady work. They were no poorer than the family of Lord King or Lord Delfont for instance; a good deal better off than someone like Derek Jameson, and Richardson himself seems to have been a cherished little boy. The decisive influence seems to have been his father, who was seldom at home, but had been something of a war hero, and whom Richardson describes approvingly as "a lifelong villain and local Casanova".

His mother was the respectable matriarch-cum-martyr of working-class tradition, whose heart her husband and sons spent a lifetime in breaking. When Charlie was evacuated during the war he ran away from his foster home, was recaptured and held in hospital. Magically, his father arrived from nowhere and with a wink at the nurses, slung his son over his shoulder and walked out. Later, when he was 14, he made a break from reform school, and found his father, waiting for him outside with a change of clothes.

He spent his teens stripping lead off church roofs and stealing cars, and was in and out of reform school. He had his own scrapyard by the time he was 17, but at 19 was called up for military service. He decided to work his passage by feigning madness, and was sent to the army glasshouse at Shepton Mallet, where he first met the Krays, for whom he has affection but no great regard as intellectuals: "Ronnie Kray was terrified that people might think he was soft, and there were several ways he could deal with the problem. He could establish himself as a dynamic force with the use of his highly developed intellect, or reduce people to jelly with his disarming wit. Alternatively he could blow their heads off with a shotgun, or stab them with a big knife." And yes, I'm afraid that Richardson makes me laugh more than once during our interview.

Out of the army, he set about building up the scrap metal business, with a profitable sideline in "long firm" fraud – setting up a phoney company, buying a lot of goods, selling them cheap and then not paying the debts. "Like Robin Hood really," Richardson says. "The rich got robbed, the poor got bargains, and we got rich," By the age of 30 he was very rich indeed, and moving into legitimate mining deals in South Africa, when the roof fell in. A close associate in South Africa was charged with murdering Richardson's partner, and suspicion fell on Richardson himself. His brother Eddie was arrested after a shoot-out in a Catford nightclub, and Charlie was charged with trying to nobble the jury, and separately for a series of assaults.

The real extent of Richardson's villainy is only possible to guess at, and my guess is that he was guilty of more than he admits to here, but probably less than the police accused him of. The original Megger generator, if it ever existed, was never produced at the trial, and I am persuaded by Richardson's own account of the psychology behind the allegation. "When you bring out a black box with a handle and wires and you connect it up to someone's testicles there's a ritual involved and the British love ritual. The inventor of this story had a thorough grasp of British psychology." The Megger was just too complicated and too theatrical when the same results could be obtained with a lump of wood.

Similarly the other most serious allegation – the nailing of Harris's foot to the floor – made for a colourful headline but was only flimsily supported by medical evidence. The final sentence, of 25 years for five counts of grievous bodily harm, was exceptionally harsh when Richardson had only one minor adult conviction, for receiving stolen goods (six sides of bacon).

My own guess would be that the Richardson gang was less of a gang, and less violent than the police made out, but was nevertheless a serious threat. The young Charlie Richardson was a very bright, very ambitious businessman who had no compunctions about oiling the wheels of his business with intimidation, arson and violence, and none of his cheery old lag's language about "mischief" and "high spirits" should obscure the fact.

The police normally keep this kind of racket in check by locking up some of the key participants every few years when it is "their turn", but Charlie was breaking the rules, and raising the stakes, by fixing juries and fixing witnesses on a large scale, and even beginning to fix a few politicians. He was fixing so well in fact, that he looked as if he might even become invulnerable, so when his turn came up the police may have decided it should be a long one. But as I say, it is only my guess.

The Sunday Telegraph, 24 February 1991

Damien Hirst

S hall I show you my cigarette trick?" says Damien Hirst. He pinches a Marlboro between his thumb and forefinger. He cups his hands around it. He opens them and the cigarette is gone.

"That's good. Do it again."

He does it again.

"So how do you do it?"

"Ah … a magician should never explain his tricks."

We are in Berlin, sitting in the sunny garden of the Café Einstein, a fancy place on the Kurfürstendamm, on the ground floor of the Daad gallery where Hirst is preparing his new show.

It is a series of sealed rooms filled with plants and butterflies, with a glass corridor winding through for the visitor. The corridor is made of heavy angle iron, ugly with bolts and bright ground welds, and the glass is 16mm shatterproof plate.

There will be 500 butterflies and 1,500 larvae flown in from Malaysia. The gallery manager says it has cost 40,000 Deutschemarks – about £17,000: "The most expensive thing we have done."

The show is called *A Good Environment For Coloured Monochrome Paintings*, and Hirst has a companion piece running in Pittsburgh, featuring bluebottle flies, and titled *Bad Environment for White Monochrome Paintings*. Next week he is "curating" a show at the Serpentine Gallery in London featuring 15 other artists.

This is big-time stuff for a 28-year-old, and Hirst is already seen by some critics, such as our own Richard Dorment, as the most important artist of his generation, though there are others who would view him as its biggest charlatan.

He is best known for sawing pigs in half, displaying cows' heads covered in maggots, and for his 1992 work, a shark in a tank of formaldehyde. They are "Sterile exercises in Dada taxidermy" according to one critic, and "Commonplace ideas disguised by the overwhelming theatricality of presentation" to another. For *Isolated Elements Swimming in the Same Direction* (40 fish suspended in separate tanks), the *Daily Star* sent a photographer equipped with chips and vinegar.

When I arrive at the gallery there are men on stepladders with paintpots, and Hirst is busy masking a tiny hole in a door lintel. "Because there's a *hole* in it, that's why." His style is the up-all-night-getting-wasted-look of the Eighties arts school: cropped hair, shapeless dark clothes and a pale, doughy face which lends itself to a deadpan drollery.

He drinks a lot: "A bottle of wine last night, five schnapps and three Long Island Teas. That's a mix of tequila, gin, vodka, rum, sekt, Coke and lime juice. It's too much, but I like drinking."

We watch Roland from the Berlin butterfly house releasing the hibernating insects from the little paper envelopes they have travelled in, breathing gently on them until the wings inflate and they flutter stiffly away. In minutes the room is full of butterflies the size of saucers, dipping around the fluorescent lights and clinging to the glass.

"Do you know what they are called?" I ask Hirst.

"Oh yeah. That one there is Helmut, and this one is Nigel, and that is Fritz …"

The larvae and pupae have arrived in a box, tucked snugly between layers of cotton wool. Little bullets of silver and gold and turquoise, some stirring with life. "I'm going to glue these on the canvases when he's finished with the adults."

"*Glue* them on?"

"Yeah. Stop them dropping on the floor."

"What do you glue them with?"

"I find Copydex usually does the trick."

In the hall a box of red plastic roses has arrived, which will be sprayed with synthetic nectar to feed the butterflies. "But I'm going to change them. I thought I'd use those red things you have for washing up."

"Pan scourers?"

"Yeah. I can't stand artificial flowers."

What, I am thinking by now – what most readers are thinking, I expect – is how can this be art? Imported butterflies? Copydex? Pan scourers? Anyone could do that. It's the cry of the bewildered gallery-goer down the post-war decades, but Damien Hirst is ahead of the game.

"I've got this show of spin-art: cards rotating on an electric drill. You draw on them with pencils as they spin, so everyone can create their artwork. I have some of my own on the wall, but I sign other people's as well. I like the idea that everyone can do it."

But we can't really: the dead animals; the tanks of carcinogenic chemicals; the rubber protective suits; the breathing apparatus; the chainsaws; the dissecting tools; the welding gear – not to speak of the logistics and planning and manic attention to detail, right down to the masking tape on the nail hole.

As Richard Dorment says: "It is actually very difficult to render a so-called 'ready-made'. People talk about the lack of craft skills, but it's a million times easier to paint a picture than to do what Hirst does, which is disgusting and dangerous and very hard work. You don't *just* order up a tank and pop a shark in it."

And then there is the idea, for as Hirst says: "It's all very well to look at something, and say, 'I could do that'. The point is that you didn't and I did."

But is the idea worth it in the first place, and what is it anyway? Clearly Hirst's work is dominated by death and decay, but is it precocious profundity or an adolescent morbidity?

"I think of decay as intensely active," he says. "There is more going on in your body then than before you die."

"Are you frightened of dying?" I ask.

"I don't think I *am* going to die."

"Literally?"

"No. I mean that it's impossible to believe. It's why I called my shark piece *The Impossibility of Death in The Mind of Someone Living*. I did get very frightened about death when I was six or seven and asked my granny about it. She was one of these people who was always saying, 'Now be careful across the road or you'll be run over', and 'Wrap up warm or you'll catch your death'.

"And I said to her, 'Granny if I am really, *really* careful, will I live for ever?' And she said no, I would die of natural causes. *Natural causes*. I mean, look at this." He slaps his firm young arm which is resting on the table between us. "I'm not going to die. It's impossible." Then he grins and points an imaginary pistol at my head. "Bang!"

He was brought up a Catholic: "Everyone says 'Oh you're a *Catholic*. That explains it.' But all I remember was being bored. Sitting in church every Sunday wanting it to be over. Looking through the illustrated Bible for the gory pictures of the Crucifixion."

He liked to read pathology books as a child. "Or not read them, just look at the illustrations of dissections." His bedside reading at the moment includes Brian Masters's book on Jeffrey Dahmer, an American mass murderer; something else called *How We Die;* and *Criminal Profiling* by Robert Kessler, the FBI man who invented the term "serial killer".

"That all sounds a bit ..."

"Morbid", says Hirst. "But I'm also reading Les Dawson's autobiography."

He is fascinated by Dahmer: a monster who tried to make animated zombies from the bodies of his victims by injecting their brains with acid.

"You see, there are two kinds of necrophiles. One kind is like Dennis Nilson, who is lonely and wants the murdered body as a friend, and the second kind is like Dahmer, who has a kind of terrible curiosity to find out how living things work, by taking them to pieces."

Hirst was brought up in Leeds, the eldest son of a car salesman who divorced his mother when he was 12, and whom he has now lost touch with. "He used to take me to the cinema every weekend when I was a kid, and I used to try to talk to him, but I never really got through. He was not very free with his emotions, so I got very frustrated."

Hirst became a bit of a delinquent in his teens: "I did the minimum in school, and I was naughty outside, doing a bit of shoplifting and burglary, for which I ended up in court." He scraped through A-level Art with an E, and was turned down for Central School of Art. "But I went to London anyway and spent two years on building sites, earning £30 a day and drinking £30 a night."

Even at Goldsmith's, where he eventually studied, he got only a "so-so" degree, though he shone as an art impresario.

Did his parents' divorce have a long-term effect, I wonder.

"I think it can be good for you to find that something as solid as your parents' marriage isn't really. It helps you to be careful about relationships, and it can be good for you as an artist."

"In what way?"

"In that you take nothing for granted. You look at things from every angle. Turn them upside down."

"Take things to pieces?"

"Yes."

One of his projected works, which he admits he will probably never be able to make, would consist of the bodies of a man and woman coupling, but sawn vertically through the middle, "so you could walk between the halves".

Its title is *The Secret Of Creation Explained*, which seems to encapsulate the spirit of his work: on the one hand, the ruthless intensity of a child dismembering a butterfly; on the other, the recognition that in trying to understand the flux of life we kill it.

Before we say goodbye I am determined to get from him the secret of the cigarette trick. "You know these new wave conjurors, they always tell you how their tricks are done. It's post-modern. And my kids would love it …"

So he relents, like the nice chap he is. "You just wet the fag, so it sticks to your thumbnail." He flips his hand open and the cigarette is gone again, neatly concealed behind the thumb.

"You see? There's nothing to it really."

The Daily Telegraph, 27 April 1994

The Marquess of Bath

There are no lions to be seen at Longleat when I arrive, and none of Lord Bath's wifelets either, which is a greater disappointment. My taxi driver, supplied by Central Casting for his reactionary views and Mummerset accent, has sworn there will be dozens of willing women roaming the estate. "That dirty old booger might let you 'ave one if you're in luck."

"They don't approve of Lord Bath around here?"

"Nah." We round a bend and a sunlit valley opens up: woods, lakes, churches, hamlets, grazing sheep – and at the centre the lovely pile of Longleat, all honeyed stone and glowing domes.

It's a lot, though not so much as 10 days ago, when thieves broke into the State Drawing Room and made off with a £5 million Titian. It was the jewel of the Longleat collection and a key attraction for the 150,000 people who visit the house each year, but Lord Bath is disappointed rather than distraught. "Just one of the penalties of living in a glass house. The sad thing is we may have to consider limiting access to the house." This *is* sad, because Longleat is the most open of stately homes, with visitors trooping through not only the state apartments, but bedrooms, nurseries and Lord Bath's private office.

It is where we are at the moment: a comfortable, shabby room. The eye takes in at random: a guitar, a box of Black Magic chocolates, an overstuffed Safeway carrier bag, an office shredder, a book on Rouault, a copy of the *Daily Mail* and a giant bottle of Lilt.

The walls are decorated with Lord Bath's own murals, in oil paint and sawdust, and depicting the various ages of man, pre-nativity, innocence, adolescence, etc, in a graphic style reminiscent of Chagall. The colours are dark and the paint is crusted so thickly that the room reeks of oil. The ceiling is painted in similar fashion but is protected by a sheet of perspex. His lordship explains that some chemical reaction makes it spit gobs of wet paint on the visitors below. "I think my mistake was using quite so much black pigment ..."

His lordship's estranged brother Christopher once called the murals "pornographic pizza". I would describe the overall effect as more like sitting inside a huge and filthy old cooker.

Alexander Thynn is the 7th Marquess of Bath, but the first to spell his name without the final "e", which he dispensed with in 1976. "There was a slide in the pronunciation which I wanted to arrest: it should rhyme with 'sin' rather than 'swine'. And it was really an Anglo-Saxon name, though The Builder wanted to pretend it wasn't."

"The Builder" is John Thynne, Comptroller of the Kitchen to Henry VIII, who rose to become the second most powerful man in England. He was a hard-nosed Tudor bureaucrat who followed the Tudor route to respectability by picking up cheap land after the Dissolution and building a very pretentious house. ("But not before he was nearly executed for embezzlement" – Alexander.)

The two men look very alike. Alexander has the jut jaw and fierce nose that you see in all the family portraits: but his blue eyes are hazy-soft, and underneath his leopard-print poncho is a belly the size of a flour bag. The family has a long tradition of enmity between fathers and sons, and of mild eccentricity, but it has come to full flower in the 7th Marquess.

Alexander Thynn is married to Anna Gael, a Hungarian model whom he picked up outside a Paris cinema when she was 15, but he has also enjoyed the company of 62 "wifelets" (their oil and sawdust portraits are displayed on a spiral staircase known as Bluebeard's Collection). He has decorated a whole wing with his murals, including the erotic Karma Sutra room which he likes to show visitors around himself. He has stood as European parliamentary candidate for the Wessex Regionalist Party, which believes in a world government based in the Sinai peninsula. He is writing a 25-volume autobiography which has currently taken him to the age of 26 and 1.5 million words. He sent his children to the local comprehensive. His favourite dish is grey squirrel in mushroom sauce. Where does one begin?"

"I suppose you *are* best known for the wifelets."

"I am a polygamist – though most of *them* are polyandrists as well. They have their hublets."

"Do you go in for group sex and orgies and so on?"

"Ah, you'll have to wait for my autobiography."

"How would you justify your harem to respectable readers of *The Daily Telegraph*?"

"I would say that previous generations paid lip service to marriage then had affairs on the side, which to me seems hypocritical."

"Aren't you using your wealth and privilege to please yourself?"

"Not at all. I think we are moving from a monogamous to a polymorphous society where mothers will choose the family form that suits them: single motherhood, marriage or polyandry."

"Who's going to pay for all these fatherless families?"

"A resuscitated welfare state. An increased general taxation."

"Why did you send your children to a comprehensive school?"

"Because the worst thing about British society is its class divisions. It is up to people like me to break the pattern."

"How did the children cope?"

"Lenka, my daughter, got 10 grade As at O-level and two As and a C at A-level I think it was. She went to a good Oxford college, took a 2:1 and is now making her way in television."

"And what about your son?"

"Not *quite* so straightforward. Caelwyn did his O-levels, but then he sent himself off to Bedales for his As. They sent him down after six months, which made me feel rather vindicated. He's at London University now and doing well. I think they are both glad they went to state schools. They have a lot of friends in the area, which I never had."

Alexander was educated at Eton, where he was a member of Pop and Keeper of Boxing. He went on to do National Service in the Life Guards and then PPE at Oxford, where he ran with the monied set and was president of the Bullingdon. Contemporaries at Eton recall him as "tall, handsome, athletic ... something of a school hero ... totally straight up and down." His rebellion began only in the Sixties, when he was nearly 30, though he traces it back to a "traumatic incident" with his father when he was 16, though he will not say more. "My early life was trying to be the man my father wanted me to be, and there were various steps of disillusionment until I decided to work out my own morality, my own politics, my own religion."

"In reaction to your father?"

"In reaction to the absurd attitudes he had."

"Which were what?"

"Fascism in politics, for instance."

"Literally?"

"Oh yes. He was passionately pro-Hitler. In 1962 there was that headline, 'Hitler a Helluva Guy'. But normally he toned down in public what he would say at the dinner table."

We get up for a wander – through industrial passageways with gloss painted walls, meaty pipework and racks of fuse-boxes. A pair of overalled girls, rinsing clothes in a stone sink, give an almost curtsy and a giggly "Afternoon, your Lordship." Isn't it rather hypocritical, I ask, for someone who is opposed to the class system to be called his Lordship? For someone who believes in equality to be sitting on top of an enormous pile?

"It's more equality of opportunity I am interested in."

"But at some point the children will inherit all this, which is hardly equal opportunity for all the other kids in the comp is it?"

"But in a way it's just a business like any other, and the title is a useful marketing tool."

We enter the maze of private appartments, every surface clotted with Thynn's immense murals. I don't know enough to say if they are good, bad or mad. All I can say is they are not the work of a dilettante, but the hard labour of 30 years. This leads to another thought, which is how typically aristocratic is this compulsion to anthologise and commemorate oneself.

Thynn is portrayed by the press as a lovable buffoon – the Hippy Peer, the Loins of Longleat – but the picture misses out all the toughness of the man: the Army Officers welterweight boxing championship, for instance; the way he sacked his brother Christopher from running Longleat within a week of inheriting the title; the unsentimental decision to bring a CenterParcs holiday village to Longleat. This is not to say that Thynn is insincere, but eccentricity has long been the essential camouflage of the aristocracy.

On my way back to the station from Longleat my cabbie points out an extensive timberyard beside the road. "See that? He sells the tops for Christmas trees, the branches for fencing, the trunks for timber, the bark chippings to garden centres, and the sawdust to the local butcher at so much a bag. Tight as that." He pinches a finger and thumb.

"It doesn't seem to go with the wifelets and all that."

"Nah," says my cabbie, whose great-great-great-great-great-great grandfather might have driven The Builder up this hill in his trap to view the estate of Longleat for the first time. "They know how to hang on to it."

The Daily Telegraph, 16 January 1995

Ian Botham

It is a chilly autumn morning in Somerset, but Ian Botham wants to sit out on the terrace, breathing in the flowering mallow and cut grass of the little country hotel. He has always suffered from claustrophobia – "which may be why I never like net practice. If people saw me there it would be, 'What? Beefy in the nets? He must be ill'."

In truth, nobody would ever think Beefy Botham was ill. At 38 he is in his prime: clear-eyed and ruddy, over six feet tall and 16 stone. The dining room floor trembles as he walks. His haircut is awful; his waistcoat could have been hacked from the hotel carpet; his big, cricketer's bum is crammed into jeans that are far too tight. But the man is formidable.

"Did you like the book?" he says, straight off, and for once I can say honestly that I did. Botham's *My Autobiography* is ghostwritten, of course – he left his secondary modern at 15 without an O-level. But among the hired hackery and the plonking "setting the record straight" there is plenty of indiscretion, malice and comedy.

He makes no bones about having smoked dope since he was 18 (once with a vicar in a church porch). He is very open about family rows: the time he threw pizza at his wife; the time his son, then eight, had to put him to bed, dead drunk.

Subtitled *Don't Tell Kath*, it is, in large measure, an act of reparation to his long-suffering wife. "I have been a selfish bastard. At times I have been aggressive, tyrannical, chauvinistic and hot tempered ... Over the years she has suffered more aggravation and heartache than anyone deserves. I honestly don't know how she has put up with it ... I had been a bloody idiot ..."

Candid though he is, Botham treats Kath more as a presentational problem than an actual person. It wasn't the drug and bimbo tales so much as his failure to be by her side and explain things properly; not so much what he did as what the tabloids said he did.

Clearly he has promised to be a better boy. And clearly Kath didn't just stand there and take it, as when his marijuana habit found its way into the papers: "She came into the sitting room where I was stretched out on the sofa and hurled a glass-topped table at me. Luckily her aim was somewhat affected by her state of mind, but the message was clear."

He is wonderfully rude about stuffed shirts like Ted Dexter ("amateurish", "unreliable", "a complete and utter fool"), while Geoffrey Boycott is "selfish" and "egotistical".

Ian Botham is the greatest all-round cricketer England has produced this century, and still well within plausible playing age. When he declared his retirement from the first class game last year, many suspected he would soon fall prey to the comeback bug, but after the bridge-burning in this book that will surely be impossible.

One of the fiercest chapters is an attack on former Pakistan captain Imran Khan and ball tampering, which Khan admits he has done (one time using a bottle top), and which he claims has been practised by almost every seam bowler. Botham says that outside the Pakistan team it is nothing like as widespread or accepted as Khan alleges; that it is "cheating" and that "with hand on heart I can categorically state that never once have I done anything illegal with a cricket ball".

Of the recent Atherton affair, he says: "I never believed for a moment he was cheating over that dirt in the pocket business. Not in the showpiece match of the decade with millions watching on TV."

"Aren't you making one rule for England and one for Pakistan?"

"No. It's a completely different thing. You are talking about bowlers who peel one side of the ball like an orange, which will give it the most incredible swing. The Atherton business was a molehill out of a mountain – or maybe the other way around."

As he confesses in the book, Botham has never liked to admit a mistake. The excuses he devised for losing his wicket were legendary, from the man in the crowd who opened a newspaper at the crucial moment, to the wink of sunlight on the window of a passing bus. "Yes, it's a weakness. A sign of immaturity. But it's also part of being competitive, and any sportsman who makes it to the top has to be ultra competitive."

"So a top sportsman must be immature?"

"Yes. There are no shades of grey. It's all black and white. Which can be very hard for the people around me like my wife."

Clearly Botham thinks those days are behind him, but there is still a strong streak of self-justification in the book: as in his highly partisan account of the Australians' opening match of their 1993 tour against the Duchess of Norfolk's XI, for instance. His performance was mediocre, but Botham is convinced it was Dexter's prejudice that kept him out of the subsequent England side.

Botham makes much fun of the fitness fetishism and psycho-bashing which goes on in the current England team. He has often been criticised for being overweight, for smoking (which he has now given up), and for his prodigious thirst. He has never been an alcoholic, but is proud of being able to sink three pints in a minute, while every emotional crisis in the book seems to be answered with two bottles of brandy. Does he think his career might have lasted longer had he been fitter?

"Nah. There are different kinds of fitness. Cricket is a six-hour fitness, while something like football is more a ballistic fitness. If you trained cricketers like footballers they could never maintain the concentration needed for a Test match."

"But you have said your bad back started in the early 1980s because you hadn't warmed up properly."

"I've had 21 years in the game. You can't ask for more than that."

Botham was born in Cheshire and lived for a while in Northern Ireland, where his father was serving with the Fleet Air Arm, but was raised mostly in Somerset.

Both parents were sporty, but Ian was a prodigy from the age of seven when he was playing football for his primary school, a year under age, and practising his autograph for when he became famous: "All through my life I have possessed an extraordinary self-belief. There were no doubts about what I would be when I grew up. I was going to be a professional sportsman."

The only thing he didn't know was what kind, because at 15 he had offers from Crystal Palace and five other League clubs. It was pretty much a toss-up that he went to Lord's as a trainee cricketer (and was taken up by John Arlott who educated him both in cricket lore and vintage wine). "If I'd had an offer from Chelsea, which I supported then, I might never have lifted a bat again."

The facts of his cricketing career, with Somerset, Worcester, Durham and England, are too well documented to repeat any but the most remarkable. He is one of only six men to have played in more than 100 Test matches; one of only nine to have taken more than 300 Test wickets; one of only 11 Englishmen to have scored more than 5,000 Test runs, and holder of more Test catches than all but four other men.

The high point of his career was in the summer of 1981 when he scored centuries against Australia at Headingley and Old Trafford and bowled a spell of five for one at Edgbaston. England won the Headingley Test after following on – only the second time this has ever happened. Botham followed his six for 95 in Australia's first innings with 149 not out, off only 87 balls. More than one newspaper called it the greatest Test innings of all time. Botham insists it was "a bit of a fluke".

He is not a cultivated man, nor a tactful one. He offended the Pakistanis by remarking that it was somewhere he would not send his mother-in-law, and upset the Australians by saying how much he liked to beat them at Melbourne "in front of an audience of 100,000 convicts". His idea of a great joke is to stuff a few prawns in a friend's batting glove or set fire to a newspaper, but he is not a lout, and is certainly not stupid. And he has a nice line in self-deprecation: "When I was captain my idea of man management was to make sure everyone stood a round at the bar".

At times he likes to play the yokel, but as the *Telegraph's* Christopher Martin-Jenkins has said, he has a better tactical cricketing intelligence than he is sometimes credited with. He speaks confidently, fluently and amusingly about what he knows about, which is cricket, and stumblingly about politics, books, art, religion, or ideas of any kind.

"Weren't you a big Thatcher fan at one time?" I ask.

"Only the early Thatcher."

"I bet John Arlott didn't approve."

"I don't think we ever talked about politics. It's not a subject I give any thought."

A great athlete is always a simple character. Introspection is fatal to sporting achievement. His intelligence is distributed through his body, giving him clever hands, smart legs and brilliant eyes. His body takes intelligent action without that cumbersome chain of command between brain and muscles – which may be why the English, with their horror of cogitation, revere the sportsman so highly, though they are not so happy when they become too successful.

As Botham himself points out, when we produce a world-class sporting hero such as Steve Davis, Nick Faldo or Nigel Mansell, the instinct is to hunt for the flaws rather than to lionise. So we have Steve "Interesting" Davis; the taciturn Mansell and the robotic Faldo. Botham enters no plea for himself, but it is absurd how his career has been dominated by petty stories of carousing and soft drug smoking. In America, when a football star is charged with double murder, the nation plunges into an orgy of denial. When Ian Botham is fined £100 for possessing a few grains of cannabis, we turn to each other and say, "Well, what do you expect?"

The fact is that Botham is almost certainly the best athlete we have produced in the last quarter century (copyright Christopher Martin-Jenkins). Above and beyond that, though, he is a genuine hero, in the Arthurian mould, possessing as he does the authentic heroic quality of vulnerability. There is a mythic feel to Botham's career, reminiscent of Bernard Malamud's great baseball novel, *The Natural*, which was itself based on the Arthurian legend.

He comes from nowhere; he is adopted as a youth by a cricketing magus (John Arlott); his talents arrive and depart him mysteriously; like the Fisher King he is pursued by afflictions, demons and predatory females. There is even a Morgan Le Fay character in the shape of a former Miss Barbados to denounce him to the tabloids, but our hero preserves his energies through renewed commitment to purity (Kath, his wife) and the sword (his bat).

It is hard to imagine him doing nothing now. He talks about *A Question Of Sport*, his road show with Allan Lamb and his business interests, but it doesn't seem to add up to much. Botham says: "I enjoy being on my own. There's nothing I like more than tramping across a grouse moor alone. That's one of the reasons I enjoy my charity walks for leukaemia. It gives me a lot of time to think and chew things over. And besides, it's a good battle. Me against me."

The Daily Telegraph, 12 September 1994

Martina Navratilova

As I arrive at Martina Navratilova's hotel suite, a tray of breakfast is leaving. It is just fruit, fried eggs and toast, but she has done something to the eggs I have not seen before, which is eaten all the whites and left the yolks whole and staring on the plate. Just the latest bit of West Coast, live-forever lunacy I suppose, but it reminds me of a piece of convoluted Central European wisdom Martina once delivered, on the subject of commitment. "You have to think of a plate of ham and eggs," she said. "The hen is involved but the pig is committed."

Martina's career, the implication ran, was all about this kind of pig-solid commitment, about serving herself up, year after year, on the skillet of a thousand show courts; about maximum training, optimum fitness, total aggression – and never eat the egg yolks. She is the only woman in history to win nine Wimbledon singles titles, the winner of more singles matches than any player ever, the winner of more titles (an amazing 167) and of more prize money – over $13 million. And now it is all over, to be replaced by the exhibition matches, the celebrity appearances, the commentary box at Wimbledon, the where-are-they-now? articles. Margaret Court, Christine Truman, Virginia Wade ... where *are* you now?

We are here to talk about *The Total Zone*, "her" "new" "novel". It is about a teenage tennis star who disappears and is tracked down "across the international world of pro-tennis, uncovering a startling story of abuse, suicide and murder". Martina is doing the press in the hired beige-out of a suite at the Hilton, where the only clues to personality are a bottle of mineral water (room temperature) and a copy of *The Day of the Triffids*. She is wearing a red velour sweater, man's watch and black stretch pants, and has arranged herself horizontally over several hotel chairs. With her big, capable hands and tawny horse face you might cast her as the gym mistress of an expensive girls' school.

"Why did you want to write a novel?" is the first question, and Martina is baffled, as if asked why she endorsed a tennis racket or gave her name to a shower gel. To write a novel is something a sports celeb *does* at a certain point in her career.

"Wall it came up a couple years ago. My achent asked was I inarresded in doing some fiction with another rider to pud it together." The accent is almost American but she still has a European way with soft consonants like the "g" in "agent".

"So you did it for the money?"

Martina laughs. "I could earn that much money a whole lot faster doing something else." And this is true, even if the book sells out its 20,000 hardback run, for she can still make $50,000 for an exhibition game.

"Then you must have done it as an ego trip."

"Are you kidding? They had to pull my arm even to get me to publicise the thing." And this is true too, because the publishers have been apologising that she was not around for the launch some months ago. It cannot have been the pleasure of literary composition either, because *The Total Zone* is ghostwritten by someone called Liz Nickles, whose name appears prominently on the cover, which is accepted publisher's code for "the author never wrote a word". According to Martina: "We met several times. We talked on the phone a buncha times. She would send me what she wrote and I would correct it."

"But you didn't put any words on paper?"

"My job was to provide the tennis background."

It is hard to convey how bad this book is within the confines of an interview, but I must quote one passage where the heroine, who is a kind of cross between Martina and V.I. Warshawski, is describing her house: "There is no leather of course, and I've tried to use natural materials and colours. One of the reasons I bought the house was because the builder was ecologically sensitive. For instance, there are watersaver shower heads in the bathroom and built-in recycling bins in the kitchen. I use rechargeable batteries and recycled toilet paper, and there is no styrofoam in my cupboards. I went into the kitchen and squeezed myself a couple of oranges and made a bowl of custom-mixed granola and soy milk"

Dontcha just *love* it? The vacuity of this globe-trotting tennis star, preening herself on her rechargeable batteries? The exquisite snobbery of the "custom-mixed" granola, mingling with the self-congratulation of the soy milk? A new literary form seems to be shyly emerging here, bastard child of food-porn and eco-fascism – let us call it the art of conspicuous abstention.

"But look," I say to Martina eventually, since she doesn't seem to get my point. "How would you feel if I went out on Centre Court with a hired tennis pro to hit all the hard balls, and then called myself Wimbledon champion?"

"Hey," says Martina. "Would you rather I hadn't written the book?" – to which the honest answer would be "yes", though it would also signal the end of the interview. I console myself with the thought that this kind of rubbish does have one function, which is to siphon off moron-money into the pockets of the publishers, so they can afford to pay decent advances on real books.

The other Martina clone in *The Total Zone* is an older player called (ahem) Mariska, "who had won more Grand Slam titles than any woman in history, one of those people who has achieved a pinnacle so rarefied that her last name is an unnecessary appendage ..." She already sounds appalling, but the description goes on: "She's known for being an aggressive, tough even brutal player ... In interviews, she can come across like a sharp stick in the eye ..."

It is a great relief, then, that the real Martina is a delight to interview: friendly, relaxed and candid, even with the more prurient probings.

Part of the reason she is in London is to visit her girlfriend, Danda Jaroljmek, a former fashion PR who is now a student at Chelsea College of Art. Last summer, it was reported that the pair were planning to have a child, with the help of Italian test-tube baby doctor Severino Antinori. Was this true?

"When Chrissie Evert left the tour to have a baby, I said I might do it one day, but I don't know if I will. Out of that, came these reports I was trying to have a baby."

"Some people are shocked by the idea of a single lesbian woman having a baby."

"There can be more love and stability from a single mom, whatever her sexuality, than in many marriages."

"Why have a baby yourself rather than adopt?"

"If I did have kids, I think I would like to adopt some and have one of my own – but still don't know if I want to change my life so drastically."

Martina has always been admirably frank about her sexuality – right from the moment she applied for US citizenship, as a timid, 17-year-old Czech defector – "this chirpy, chunky, Czech chick", as Frank Keating called her. "Since I was under oath, I did not want to perjure myself, and so I just gulped and said I was bisexual." Her coach/stepfather was so outraged he refused to join her in America: "I would rather you slept with a different man every night than slept with a woman." In fact, she had already slept with a man, an architect four years her senior. "But when we got down to it, there were no bells, no stars, no flashing lights – not a lot of affection or skill either."

"Do you think sexuality is an absolute thing?" I ask her now. "People like Tom Robinson have been gay and straight."

"People change, and your sexuality can change with you. But you cannot *make* yourself gay or *make* yourself straight."

"You sound as if you were always sure what you were."

"Not really, I think the important thing is not just that you want to have sex with a person, but you want to *be* with them all the time. I am attracted to men, but I don't want to *live* with them."

Her relationship with Danda is monogamous – "all my relationships have been monogamous" – but there has been quite a string of them over the years: tennis players, golfers, basket ball stars, pop singers – some very colourful. Rita Mae Brown, for instance, was a feminist novelist from Virginia, who was so outraged when Martina left her that she threw a pistol at her departing car. The gun went off, shattering the rear window of the car and narrowly missing Martina (I'm just repeating this story as it was printed). Judy Nelson was the Texan doctor's wife and mother of two whom Martina seduced while staying at her husband's home, and who eventually sued Martina for several million dollars in "galimony". Bizarrely, Judy Nelson was last reported to be living with Rita Mae Brown.

Martina doesn't think her "orientation" as we bashfully refer to it, had anything to do with her family background. Her father left when she was a baby, but her step father had moved in by the time she was three, and her memories are of a happy, tomboyish, not especially driven childhood.

Martina grew up in a little town called Revnice, 15 miles from Prague. The family had been solid citizens who lost it all to war and communism. The key image is of Martina, aged three, living with her mother in a single room of the big house that once belonged to her grandparents. Outside the window is the overgrown tennis court where her grandmother Agnes Semanska used to practise, becoming good enough to rank as Czech number five, and to defeat Vera Sukova, the only Czech woman to reach a Wimbledon final. Granny's racket becomes Martina's. She remembers the feel of it 40 years later: "An old wooden racket with a wooden handle. No leather grips. I just hit two-handed backhands against the wall all day." Nobody had to tell her; the message in the racket was "Win it all back for us, kid".

The grown-up Martina was never a great technician, with her swinging left-hand serve and limited repertoire of groundstrokes. She did not even have a great temperament for a player, especially in her early years. Ted Tinling once described her style as "arrogance or panic, with nothing in between". Navratilova was the self-created player *par excellence* who developed a ferocious serve and volley game that terrorised the more sedate stylists of the women's game, and who built a body which rivalled the men for athleticism. All the same, it is hard to see exactly what it was that made her the greatest tennis player of the century, and so I ask her the question I always ask in interviews: "Where do *you* think you get all this commitment from? Why are *you* such an achiever?"

"I am always more surprised that everyone else is *not*," Martina says.

The Daily Telegraph, 6 February 1995

Bob Monkhouse

Bob Monkhouse is the great technician of British comedy. He knows more, and has thought harder about the subject than any comic alive. He knows why Eric Sykes's walk is funny, and Max Miller's shrug, and Arthur Askey's little skip. He performs them for me here in his living room, these tiny tics of other personalities, and they are weirdly flawless, like hearing your wife's voice from a stranger's face. "It's all details, details. There's a gag I do about my wife watching TV over my shoulder while I'm making love to her. It gets a laugh, so I top it by saying, 'And she's channel-hopping.' And it gets another laugh, so I top it again by saying, 'And we haven't got a remote control ...'"

Monkhouse frowns to himself. "The peculiar thing is, if you just say, 'and we haven't got a remote', like they do in America, the joke doesn't work. You have to trail off with the whole phrase, 'remote control ...' And then they laugh, and I don't know why." But you feel he is working on it.

Twenty years ago, in an interview with David Nathan, for his book *The Laughtermakers*, Monkhouse said a strange and terrible thing. He said: "By that time [the age of 28] it was clear to me that I had no talent. What I had was a certain facility, that was all. The people around me with exciting personalities and originality were Norman Wisdom and Tommy Cooper. I had no more than the perky mind of the average compere presenting cabaret in a northern club."

No talent! There are myopic TV critics who savage "smarmy Bob" and viewer polls which find him the most loathed entertainer on TV after Jeremy Beadle. But nobody has been more ruthless about Monkhouse than Monkhouse himself; no one has commented more freely on his own oily, Uvasun veneer, his studied smoothness, and his magical warmth. "Unctuous", "oleaginous", "three-faced" – these are all words he uses in our interview about himself, or rather his stage self, for the real Bob Monkhouse is rather apart, and rather surprising.

He lives in Bedfordshire – the house is Tudor, red brick and beautiful, but a big farmhouse rather than the mansion of tabloid profiles. There are a lot of good books and pictures – the names which stick from a fast scan are D.H. Lawrence, H.G. Wells, Maxim Gorky, Russell Flint, Arthur Koestler. One wall of the sitting room is a black cliff of electronics, with five remote control units on the coffee table. "Four actually control things and the fifth is supposed to learn what all the others do, but I haven't taught it yet." He watches every game show that comes out of America: "About 200 in two years, but they're all rubbish, and never new." His new series for Central TV, *Bob's Your Uncle*, sounds like a hybrid of *Blind Date* and *The Golden Shot*, kept afloat with massive injections of Monkhouse mordacity.

He dresses well, his hair is real, and his smooth brown throat unlined by his 63 years. "A critic once said I looked like a cross between Clarke Gable and Archie Andrews, and of course my ego instantly erased the Archie Andrews." His mid-Atlantic accent is entirely inexplicable, for he was born in Beckenham and educated at Dulwich College, alma mater of P.G. Wodehouse and Raymond Chandler. He says he doesn't notice it himself.

His father was chairman of the family custard-powder firm of Monk and Glass: "I was brought up in an atmosphere of 'Some day son, all this custard will be yours'. But I didn't like the feeling of so much security and the prospect of so much cornflour." At Dulwich, during the war, he started writing and drawing for magazines like the *Beano* and *Dandy*, and soon was producing his own. "I liked the formality of the humour. The fact that if you were rich you always lit a cigar with a £5 note, and if you were even richer you went to the Hotel de Posh and had a completely spherical plum pudding with custard on top like snow and a piece of holly. It seemed to me a world where I could operate quite successfully."

He opened his own office in Penge and started commissioning adult artists and writers, using a deep voice on the phone and paying them in postal orders. He had made himself a small fortune – some £20,000 – before he was called up for National Service at 18. "I assembled the stuff, sent it to printers and then distributors in London. I was such a hustler. Looking back on it now I am simply agape. I don't know how I could have had such a hunger ..."

He had already started performing, having joined four different political parties under four different names so he could do turns at their social evenings. He was Gabby Gibson to the Youth For Labour Group in Penge, Chris Webb to the Beckenham Young Conservatives, John Frederick for the Bromley Young Liberals, and

Colney Hatch, after the London lunatic asylum, for the Young Communists. By the late 1940s, he was gag-writing for radio and appearing in revue with Benny Hill, but his parents disapproved. They wanted him to follow a career in commercial art, and they disapproved still more when, at 21, he announced his decision to marry ("They were quite right"). His mother resolved to send him to Coventry and, fantastically it seems to me, she did not speak to her son again for 20 years.

In that period, his wife lost four premature babies before giving birth to Garry, who is a spastic and lives in a residential home near the Monkhouses. They also had Simon, now a 36-year-old teacher, and adopted Abigail, 31, who is a social worker. Bob's marriage broke up, and he married Jackie, his former secretary (who was not involved in the divorce). And in all that time he didn't see his parents?

"I think my father came to one of my shows. I looked out of the Cambridge Theatre once and I thought I saw him in the queue, but I couldn't be sure." When his father had a heart attack, Bob visited him. But his mother sent him away, and the next morning his father was dead. "I only saw my mother again when she was ill, and that was because Jackie insisted I should lay the ghost."

"Did you hate your mother for all that?"

"I suppose I do blame my feelings of insecurity on that tremendous coolness she had. A tremendous strength. She had this stoicism in the face of pain or worry. She and my father seemed to have reached an agreement that they would demonstrate very little to each other, but would get on extremely well. My brother is the same. But here was I, in the middle of this, with a very emotional nature ..."

"But did you forgive your mother?"

"I get sloppier as I get older. I remember how she used to paint faces on the hard-boiled eggs she gave me for school lunch. And she would always tell me the story of King Kong before I went to sleep."

"So you never got angry?"

"I only get angry when people get between me and an audience."

He drinks a lot: a bottle of wine and half a bottle of malt a day, but he looks fine and is apparently invulnerable to hangovers. And he works ferociously, filling a 2in thick ledger with gags every few months, all of them written out under subject headings like

"Chiropody" and "Firemen", and in different coloured inks. Black is for bluish jokes, red is for gags written with somebody else, blue is for his special favourites and green is for thinnish jokes. There is quite a lot of green.

I get a good feeling from spending time with Bob Monkhouse. Of an intelligent man who has been through a lot and dealt with it as best he can, and preserved his balance and good humour, and carried on doing what he is good at. It may even have made him better, for there is a saying among comics that "comedy is honesty", which means that you never get really funny until you get to know yourself. The ordinary stand-up, the patter merchant, whatever you call him, is what Monkhouse calls "a joke announcer". The greatest comics, like Tommy Cooper, Ken Dodd and Frankie Howerd, are the ones who have the least to do with telling jokes, and the most to do with exposing the gothic structures of their own personalities.

Certainly something changed in Monkhouse's humour with the end of his marriage and the death of his parents. You have to look at the cabaret act rather than the TV appearances, but there is a shift, from the bumptious, invulnerable, intolerable Bob, to a self-conscious version of the same thing. He is still glossily veneered and relentlessly fluent, but the carapace itself is the subject; the Monkhouse persona the joke. "I look around an audience and wonder how many men there are making love to a woman who doesn't want them to? And since I have experienced something of the same pain myself, what do I say about it? 'I was thinking of getting a vasectomy because it seems wrong to use live ammunition on a dead target.'"

And I laugh at this, and wince, and say that it is awful and tasteless. But it also works – because it slides out through that remorselessly sunny delivery, and implacable Archie Andrews face of his. And yes, Bob Monkhouse has become dangerous now, in the same way that Frankie Howerd and Les Dawson are dangerous – because underneath being funny, they are not funny at all – which is reason to laugh all the harder.

The Sunday Telegraph, 31 March 1991

Jasper Carrott

O ne of Jasper Carrotts's regular lines is that he is not a "natural" comic like, say, Billy Connolly, whom he closely resembles in other ways. Similar age, similar provincial backgrounds, same early career in Sixties folk clubs, and the same prickly integrity which instinctively rejects the "opportunities" of panto and quiz panel.

But Carrott doesn't think he is funny: "I'm as boring as old wallpaper paste. It's just that one in five people in Britain watch me on TV – which frightens me into being funny."

He hasn't performed live on stage for the past year ("but it's not a problem, really") and in the couple of hours we spend talking, he doesn't make me laugh once – or try to. This is in a dark red lozenge of a room at the Mountbatten Hotel in Covent Garden. Royal portraits scowl down from the walls. Enormous chinoiserie vases are wedged into the corners like funerary urns. Carrott is sitting on the sofa, his face tight as a light bulb, his teeth small and receding.

He is dressed in jeans and navy sports shirt. He has been working at the coffee table: pages of a script with scribbled alterations; a pair of steel rimmed spectacles. The white stripe on the collar of his shirt is a bit naff (there is always something slightly naff about Carrott; he keeps open his lines to the anorak brigade).

But the general impression is professorial: the comic technician at work, tightening the final nuts. In fact, he has spent the afternoon fitting the laughter track on a new series of *The Detectives*, which begins on February 15 (BBC1).

"I thought we didn't do canned laughter on British television?"

"Oh, it's *real* laughter. We play the tapes to a live audience. You might dub it when you're expecting a laugh, and it doesn't come. But it is not *mechanical* laughter, like in the States." This is evidently an important distinction.

At the age of 50, Carrott is the most consistently successful comic in Britain, with a television career going back almost 20 years. *Canned Carrott* has pulled audiences of 13.5 million, second only to soaps 'n' Cilla, while *The Detectives* is now on its fourth series since 1992 and still attracting audiences of 11 million-plus.

Uniquely, Carrott appeals to both twenty- and fiftysomethings, reflecting his interesting position in the history of comedy, lodged between the fag end of the old music hall tradition (Jimmy Tarbuck, Les Dawson) and the "alternative" comics who began to emerge during the first Thatcher government.

The traditional British comic was a fat man in a frilly shirt who machine-gunned his audience with one-liners based on stereotypes of sex, class and race: the wife's mother, the Irish labourer, the upper-class idiot. The comedian never called them jokes, but gags; a gag being something that makes you laugh, but also ties you up.

The limited nature of the dialogue was expressed in the careers of the genuinely talented comics of that generation (Frankie Howerd, Tommy Cooper, Morecambe and Wise) who all tended to drift away from gags to a comedy of character, where the persona of the comedian himself became the focus of humour.

Carrott himself was a gag merchant in his early days, pinching one-liners from Bob Monkhouse to pad the introductions to his songs – an assortment of folk standards and Tom Lehrer ditties, like *Poisoning Pigeons In The Park* – which he had memorised in his early teens.

"Then, in about 1973, I did a very enlightening week at a cabaret club called the Cresta, in Birmingham. By the end, I had it down to 40 minutes of one-liners. Your absolutely *basic* comedy, just designed to get *through* to the audience. To *spray* them with gags. Anything to do with orifices, you know – and by then, I knew that my integrity was not to go out there and get a laugh at any expense."

And so he turned to something more personal and anecdotal. "I decided to do about four minutes of Lehrer-style material based on my experiences working at Butlins. 'Knock, knock. Have you got a girl in that chalet? No? Well, we'll soon find you one.' Etcetera. It was four minutes without the safety net of a punch line, and I remember turning green with the fear of it, but also being incredibly elated."

The character he evolved was one of goofy amiability: a baffled Midlands everyman, perplexed by the surrealism of life, who wanders about the stage asking the audience, "Have you ever noticed ...?" or "Haven't you ever worried about ...?" "Betamax Man" is one label Carrott coined for the persona. Its success relied heavily on trust and honesty. He could talk about collecting sex instruction videos, for instance: "Of course, they're just hard porn, really, but because it's sex instruction, you can have it next to Nick Faldo ..."

And because of the vulnerability of the character, he would also get away with being pretty cruel: "Old people. You can wear what you like, can't you? Tea cosies, loft insulation, tartan zip-up bootie slippers. Old people. You've got your own shop – Littlewoods. You can shove into queues, 'Get out of my way. I'm old'. And when you forget everything and start to dribble into your Wincarnis, they make you into a judge."

As Carrott got older, domestic detail began to appear: Biffer the Labrador who has "the intelligence of a daffodil" and likes to chase parked cars; the hopeless attempts at DIY: "Someone gave me a Black and Decker Workmate for Christmas – like giving a kaleidoscope to Stevie Wonder."

It is a style built on a habit of *noticing* things which other people don't. "Tree surgeons," he will remark, *à propos* nothing. "What a pompous title. They're just bloody gardeners, aren't they?" It can be very funny, but can also ossify into mannerism, which sophisticated audiences rapidly tire of.

In his book *Comedians Talking*, William Cook sketches the personality of the typical alternative comic: youngest child in family; distant father; state school; adolescent appetite for horseplay (but not class clown); mediocre exam results; string of dead-end jobs; insatiable appetite for ironic introspection – Carrott fits on every count. His real name is Bob Davies, he was born in Acocks Green, a working-class suburb of Birmingham, and grew up in a terrace house with no bathroom and an outside lavatory.

He was educated at Moseley Grammar ("God, I went to a rough school. Had its own coroner") which he left at 16 with two O-levels (art and maths) to work, successively, as a sales rep, factory clerk, barrow boy, tote operator at a dog track and kitchen porter at Butlins.

His father was a self-employed electrician, Communist Party member and would-be entrepreneur: "I remember coming home once to find 10,000 streetlamp covers stacked in the back garden. He'd bought them from the local council, with no idea what to do with them. A strange man."

"And you've got a brother eight years older. What does he do?"

"A clerk."

"And your mum?"

"A cleaner."

"Which parent was most important to you?"

"I don't think that's a fair question. My father's dead and my mother is 83 now."

"All right. Which has had most influence?"

"My father, in that I was determined not to do what he did. I think he messed his life up ... um, but probably I don't really want to talk about my mum and dad, is that all right?"

He is proud of having kept in touch with his roots, "probably more than anyone else in showbusiness". Married for 26 years to Hazel, a former journalist, and with four children, he still lives only a few miles from where he was born. "Depending on whom I want to impress, it's either 12 miles south of Birmingham or seven miles north of Warwick. Basically, it is Solihull."

His best friend is Bev Bevan, drummer with The Move and Electric Light Orchestra, whom he has known since they were 11, while his accountant is Phil Ackrill, one-time guitarist with Denny Laine and the Diplomats. Other friends include a panel-beater, a hairdresser, a man who makes pie fillings.

Every February, 30-odd mates take over a hotel in the Lake District, and every summer they head for villas in Minorca: "Counting kids, there were 65 of us having dinner in one restaurant last year." I say that I'm jealous, and Carrott says, yes, he's lucky.

His father died at 67, of diabetes, and eight years ago Carrott was diagnosed with the same disease. Instead of accepting insulin treatment, he set off on a round of alternative therapists, and now successfully controls his blood sugar with a diet that excludes bread, cakes, pastries, potatoes, beer, caffeine, sugar, sweets and chocolate.

Along the way, he became interested in a whole range of New Age ideas – homeopathy, acupuncture, and "hands-on-healing" for which he believes he has some talent. "Though anyone can do it to some extent. You've only got to look at the way a mother touches a baby."

All the same, it is a problem for the professional sceptic, which every comedian has to be. On stage, he is taking the mick out of astrology nutters: "You know these people who come and say 'What sign are you?' 'Hump-back bridge,' I tell them. Or 'Slippery when wet'."

In private life, he is visiting an acupuncturist every month and selecting services from *Yellow Pages* with a dowsing pendulum:

"The things that are important to me now are a bit esoteric, and that's not good for comedy, because you are trying to relate to people on common ground."

And so he isn't performing any more, though there are other reasons. "Every subject I can think of I have done three times. Comedy has to be dangerous, and once it gets comfortable, it loses its appeal."

To raise his adrenalin, he booked a theatre in Amsterdam last year and went down well with a mainly Dutch audience: "You wouldn't believe how hard it was to find out the name for Polyfilla in Amsterdam – but it was the best night of my career."

The Detectives, one suspects, is largely just a meal-ticket for Carrott – a feeble burlesque whose high ratings are chiefly the product of generous scheduling and the oatmeal texture of "family" entertainment, graded to that precise level between irritation and ignorability which prevents you from quite summoning the energy to turn the damn thing off.

In the meantime, he is looking around for something new: he is interested in the anti-environmentalist rap of the US comedian, George Carlin, in the anti-PC attitudes of P.J. O'Rourke, and in the wild excesses of Right-wing shock comics like *The Dice Man*.

It is hard to imagine the amiable character of Jasper Carrott in such a role but, as he says, he has never been your standard "Left-wing bedwetter" and he is sure there is *something* there. An alternative to the alternative – and as the man who virtually founded alternative comedy, who better to finish it off?

The Daily Telegraph, 5 February 1996

Lauren Bacall

Outside San Lorenzo's a snapper is hunched, with his collar up against the drizzle. "Lauren Bacall will be along in a minute," I tell him, and he cheers up and starts fiddling with his lenses. What a ridiculous restaurant this is, no different from a dozen Knightsbridge pasta joints, but always a Princess Diana or a Jack Nicholson to pull the paparazzi. The big deal is this chunky old lady called Mara in a navy cardie, who comes and gives you a big welcome, mwah, mwah, and asks after your dog and your prostate and your new wife. She is doing it now to a noisy bunch on the corner table.

"Anthony!"

"Mara. *Cara. Bellisima!*"

"So you *know* my Mara?"

"Mara and me, we are old, *old* friends ..."

Yucky stuff, though good luck to old Mara if it pulls in the punters. Amazing, though, how stupid rich people can be, or perhaps it's just how lonely.

Bacall arrives late, looking like an advert for mobile phones: taupe silk; blonde streaks; good bones. She gets the full Mara treatment: Mwah, Mwah! *Cara! Bellisima!* There is much fussing after olives and bread and water and crudités and calories. Bacall is a big woman with big feet and a big mouth. Her triangular eyes are faded like sea glass. Her manner is don't mess with me, buster, though it overlays a certain anxiety. In her new volume of autobiography, *Now*, she says how, even 40 years after the death of her husband Humphrey Bogart, she still dreads entering a public place alone.

But I am nervous too – this is a teenage lust object we are meeting – which is why I now say the stupidest thing that comes into my head.

"I saw you in *Prêt A Porter* yesterday."

"Oh yeah? What did you think?"

"I thought the film was ... ah ... untidy ... but you were great." Actually the film was awful and so was Bacall, playing an old-fashioned editrice. Her scenes have been so heavily cut it is hard to see why she is in the picture by the end. "You know when Altman told me about the film, I thought it was going to be all about me. He is such a great salesman." She shrugs. "But it was four months in Paris, which is not so terrible."

I first saw her in *To Have and Have Not* (1945) playing Slim, the dirty girl from nowhere who tells Bogart if he wants her, all he has to do is whistle: "You know how to whistle don't you, Steve? You just put your lips together ... and blow." Slim was a girl who smoked, drank, picked up sailors in bars, had an 18in waist and a smart answer for everything. She was 19 and Bogart was 44, but they fell in love, married and made three more movies: *The Big Sleep, Dark Passage* and *Key Largo*.

Bacall became the essential complement to the Bogart cult, though this did not really begin until after his death in 1957 and reached its height only in the late Sixties. He was the prototype of the Cold War loner whose pose and irony and refusal to choose sides came to symbolise wider cultural discontents. She, with her shamelessness, intelligence and independence was his female counterpart in the war of the sexes that was also gathering pace. Bogart and Bacall, Bacall and Bogart ...

"But you don't want to talk about all that," she says now. "You want to talk about my book ..."

And this is difficult because *Now* is about the past 20 years when, frankly, not a lot has happened. Blenheim, her dog, died (a chapter); she remodelled her kitchen (a chapter); her three children got married, divorced, had their own children (umpteen chapters).

She has always worked, in films such as *How to Marry a Millionaire* (1953), *Murder on the Orient Express* (1974) and *The Shootist* (1976) and she had great success on Broadway with *Cactus Flower* (1965) and *Applause!* (1970), but she has never reached the early heights. She has known a lot of extraordinary people: Ira Gershwin, Noel Coward, Hoagy Carmichael, John Huston, Spencer Tracy, Frank Sinatra (whom she almost married), Adlai Stevenson (a prolonged flirtation) and Jason Robards (who became her second husband). The trouble is she lacks the anecdotal gift even when the interviewer adopts his most fawning chat show manner.

"It must have been amazing for someone of what, 19, to meet George Gershwin ..."

"I was in total awe. Just total *awe*. How could you not be in *awe*?" Then, accusingly. "Wouldn't *you* be in awe?"

"Well yes, I suppose, but what was he *like*?"

"I didn't have a negative feeling about any of those people. It was just fabulous to be in their presence. Would *you* be negative?"

"And then there was Adlai Stevenson. You were *very* close to him, weren't you?"

"A wonderful, wonderful man ..."

"What did you talk about together?"

"He was charming, witty, brilliant ..."

"Yes, but what did he say?"

"Intellectually we were hardly on the same level, but I had *no* problem with him."

And then Mara turns up again at the table for another endless round of Mwah, mwah! *Cara! Bellissima! Cosi fan tutte! Gino*

Ginelli! And I am sitting there sweating, thinking God, we are halfway through this thing and I haven't got a decent quote yet, so perhaps I had better be completely *direct* ...

"Give me a good story about Stevenson."

"I don't *have* a story," she tells me, and turns the sea-glass eyes on full-frost. "Mister, you are looking for trouble. Well you aren't gonna find it here. You came to the wrong party. Back to the book." But there is nothing to ask about the book, which is mostly page after self-absorbed page of vapid musings. I resort finally to the patsiest question you can feed an old luvvie.

"Why did you want to act?"

"I used to dream of being other places, other people. It was an escape for me."

"Was your home life not so great?"

"No, I had this fabulous mother, fabulous uncle, fabulous family ..."

"What makes a good actor?"

"You have to have ... a natural gift."

"What is the essence of the gift?"

"I don't think it is definable. Everything can't be explained."

"What are your gifts?"

"I think you are third degreeing me, mister. I have no idea. I leave that to others." The sea-glass eyes are on full frost again with anger, panic, dislike. "I think you are looking for angles mister. For devious things in me that are not there. It's very straightforward. Acting is a life of rejection." And so finally we have our quote, blurted out, and picked up only later on my tape recording. Acting is a life of rejection.

On screen she was the well bred girl and Bogart the stubbled slob, but in life the roles were reversed. Bogart was the son of a patrician East Coast family, a classically trained actor (and reputedly the first to say "Anyone for tennis?" on Broadway). Bacall on the other hand, was born Betty Joan Perske, daughter of Jewish immigrants from the Bronx. Her father, a salesman, left home when she was six and she was brought up by her mother, a legal secretary, who sent her away to boarding school at eight.

"I grew up believing that women had the upper hand – got things done – were listened to. It's women I admire more for character, honesty, daring, courage ..."

She took acting lessons from infancy but was first spotted as a photographic model in *Harper's Bazaar*, by Slim Hawks, wife of film director Howard. He saw her immediately as someone he could mould into a fantasy figure. "I'm going to create a girl as arrogant as you are," he told Bogart, but Bacall was panic stricken. "How could I play a woman when I was a girl? How could I have the upper hand in an exchange with a man, when I knew so little about them, was still a virgin? How could I be insolent and independent when I was terrified?"

The answer was by Bogart carrying her. "He handed her the movie," Slim Hawks said, and he won her heart. He was a drinker on his third marriage and 25 years Bacall's senior. "But I fell in love with and wanted to marry Bogart as badly as I wanted to breathe ... I wanted to give Bogie so much that he hadn't had. All the love that had been stored inside me all my life for an invisible father, for a man ..."

It should have been a disaster, but became one of the great Hollywood love stories, up to and including Bogart's early and agonising death from cancer after 11 years of marriage and two children. Bacall's unsparing account of that death in the first volume of her autobiography is one of the most honest and harrowing things you will ever read about love and bereavement, and perhaps the best, most important thing she has ever done. "Since Bogart? I haven't even met a man I want to go to dinner with ..."

Bacall is no great actress or intelligence, though she tries to conceal the shallowness behind a battery of hard-boiled mannerisms. It is what she leaves out of her self-account that tells you the most, which is of course her father, who is barely mentioned, even though, so far as one can gather, there was fault on both sides of the marriage and it was her mother who terminated it. And if this sounds too neatly Freudian, then consider Bacall's reaction when the subject is raised:

"You are quite hard on your father in the book."

"How would you know?"

"You say yourself you hardly knew him. There are usually two sides ..."

"You know I really don't like your tone, mister. You have a hell of a nerve. You are looking for nasty unpleasant things. I am not gonna deal with that kind of crap ..." The sea-glass is sea-ice now, and the voice only a little below a screech.

"Perhaps I should leave ..."

"I think maybe you better had ..."

And so, rather gracelessly, our meeting is concluded, the first time I have walked out, or been slung out, of an interview, which is a pity because grown-ups should be able to preserve the basic courtesies. So the fault is partly mine, though it is Betty Perske's bottom I would like to boot as I leave San Lorenzo's.

Acting is a life of rejection, she said, and she learnt rejection early, from the father who walked out on his little girl, to the beloved husband who turned away from her to die. Of course people should get this kind of stuff sorted out by the time they are 71-years-old, but perhaps this lack of self-knowledge is the secret of Bacall's still potent charisma: to be still slouched against the doorframe, forever the truculent teenager, inviting, repelling, irritating: "You do know how to whistle, don't you ..."

The Daily Telegraph, 13 March 1995

Arnold Schwarzenegger

Arnold Schwarzenegger plays a pregnant man in his new film, *Junior*. As part of his research, he tells me, he spent a lot of time hanging around doctors' waiting rooms, observing the expectant mothers. "They always had this like *daydreaming* expression, you know?" I do know, and he imitates it very well, that ecstatic, ruminant stare. What I don't see is how a man the size of Woolworths, with the most famous face in the world, can hang around observing expectant mothers, when the only thing expectant mothers would be observing would be Arnold Schwarzenegger.

Twenty years ago, when nobody knew what Arnie looked like (I'm already tired of typing his surname), he was up for a part in the Bob Rafaelson movie, *Stay Hungry*. Rafaelson was fixing him some lessons with an acting coach, Eric Morris, and arranged for them to meet in a parking lot. "But how will I recognise this guy?" said Morris, and Rafaelson said simply: "You will, Eric."

Oddly enough, I don't recognise Arnie when we first meet, perhaps because he is so intensely familiar that you don't notice him, like your own living-room sofa. This is in the Dorchester Hotel, where the Arnia has taken over the whole first floor: producers, directors, co-stars, trainers, agents, doctors, PRs, gofers. Even the gofers have gofers, and one of the lowliest shows me into a room full of anxious journalists, photographers, mendicants, supplicants and petitioners. "This is the holding tank," she says cryptically, and whisks away to a smaller room full of the same kind of people, which might be the header tank or possibly the septic tank. They are running late but we will soon be "filtered through".

In the meantime I talk to a photographer who has been here all morning, and two make-up girls who have been waiting since yesterday. It seems perfectly possible that, like some minor envoy to the court of Elizabeth I, you could take up residence here for years without ever getting to meet the monarch.

Then suddenly he is here, in a cloud of cigar smoke, light bounding off the angles of his face, and the gap-toothed farmboy grin. He has been in the room for ages apparently, talking to members of the Arnia. "Ya, I chost god in from Owstria yesdiday. Chost byoodiful up dere in de moundins." The room seems to have grown smaller and the ceiling lower. A hand the size of a hot-water bottle wraps mine up to the wrist. "Good to meet you Mardyn. Chost follow me." And I follow him through the septic tank to an enormous panelled room – the shark tank? – with me watching the tidal roll of Arnie's shoulders under his candy-striped shirt, and the cannonball bulge of his calves in the washed-out jeans, and the shelf his buttocks make at the bottom of his back, like a firing step.

"No, I don't train any more, sank Cod. Chost half an hour of cardio-vascular and half an hour vid der veights every morning."

"You are quite a bit smaller than when you were bodybuilding?"

"Oh sure. About 215 pounds now, compared with 240-250 before. You don't want to look too overwhelming in the movies. And it's good to get into normal clothes."

"So you are down from about 18 stone to 15 then?"

"You kill me you guys wid your stones."

It is only 10 am but the cigar, a $24 Davidoff, is smoked down to resemble a cold and toxic Toffo. Close up, there is a nicotine sheen to Arnie's skin, a tobacco bubble to his voice, and tiredness in the corners of the eyes. The press calls, parties, interviews, hotel meals and interlocking periods of jet lag can get even the Terminator down.

He is 47-years-old and the biggest box office star of all time, able to command $15 million a picture, though he is more likely these days to go for a percentage, as he has with *Junior*, in which he stars with Emma Thompson and Danny De Vito. This is a likeable screwball comedy in which Arnie plays a research scientist who decides to test his own fertility drug by making himself pregnant. The scenes in the nursing home, which he plays in an appalling wig and immense prosthetic belly, had the case-hardened preview audience choking on their popcorn.

I tell him so, and he says: "Yeah, you know but some journalists wrote that Arnold got soft now he's doing all these movies with kids and families. They had this headline in Austria. 'Terminator to Flabbynator', but as a matter of fact it takes a lot more balls to play this character than to play an action hero."

"Was it embarrassing, getting into the women's clothes?" "No. In fact I used to wear the drag out shopping in the street in San Francisco. I like to shock people a little."

He has three children with Maria Shriver, television presenter and niece of John F. Kennedy. "And I don't think I could have done this role without the kids and the wife who had gone through all this. The way a woman starts to look around her for someplace to hide when she gets morning sickness. The way she gets up from a chair when her belly is big."

"Did it change the way you thought about women?"

"One gets more respect for women. The way they go through these hormonal changes. The way things just *happen* and they have no control over their bodies ..."

"And you are always seen as this very controlled person."

"Absolutely. To make it as a bodybuilder, or as any kind of athlete, you have to be disciplined, you don't let anything overexcite you or disappoint you. But in acting you have to do the opposite of that and let the emotions come out."

Arnie – Schwarzenegger means "black ploughman" – was born in the small Austrian town of Thal, second son of the local police chief. According to Wendy Leigh, his unofficial biographer, Arnold's father, a charismatic man, was also an ex-Nazi, a drunk and a bully who terrorised Arnold and his older brother Meinhard, making them race and box and continually compete. Meinhard was the blonde handsome favourite, Arnold the weedy, bespectacled one with prominent ears and a sunken chest. At the age of six he saw Johnny Weissmuller, the Hollywood Tarzan, opening the new swimming-pool in nearby Graz, and by 13 he was visiting the cinema to watch Hercules starring Steve Reeves, and the body builder Reg Parks. He began training four hours a day, seven days a week, at the Graz

Athletic Union, was on steroids by the age of 14, and by 20 became the youngest Mr Universe in history – a title he would win a record six times.

Freudian psychology maintains that children who are terrified of their parents often cope by seeking to become the parent, and there are echoes of such a strategy in Arnold's career.

"Little boys in gorilla suits," was how Arthur Jones, founder of the Nautilus empire, described his bodybuilders. As a child, Arnie liked to try on his father's uniform, but by his teens he had replaced it with the gorilla suit of his tremendous musculature. By his late teens he had become a bully, whipping girls' legs with nettles, and beating up a milkman with his brother.

As an adult in California, one of his jokes was to order a dish of cream and meringue known as Mile High Pie for his girlfriends – and then to push their faces in it. It might be true. Myths accumulate around this man, like the time a waitress asked how he wanted his steak and Arnie said: "Just wipe its ass, baby, and bring it to the table."

Arnie won't say much about his family – but when his brother died in a drunken car crash in 1971, and his father died a year later, he did not attend either funeral. His reason: "I was in deep training."

At 22 he emigrated to California with nothing but a few words of English and a gym bag. George Butler, who directed him in the pseudo-documentary, *Pumping Iron*, remembers a phenomenally determined young man, whose outlook was "a mixture of Nietzschian philosophy and Stalinist Five-Year Plan. It involved getting to America, becoming the greatest bodybuilder ever, getting an education, investing in real estate, becoming an actor, director and producer, collecting art, marrying a glamorous and intelligent woman, and being invited to the White House before he was 32 – Simple!" And he did it all.

Pumping Iron was followed by *Stay Hungry* – a proper Hollywood feature – and then *Conan the Barbarian*, *The Terminator*, *Commando*, *Predator*, *Total Recall*, *Terminator 2* ... Arnie didn't act much in those early roles: he spoke six lines in *The Terminator*, but combined stony charisma with such finely graded self-mockery that almost every line he spoke became a catch phrase: "Hasta la vista, baby"; "I'll be back"; "Consider this a divorce" (after shooting his wife).

Arnie belongs to a small group of people (Jeffrey Archer and Madonna spring to mind) who have made one of the great discoveries of the 20th century – that you don't need to have talent, intelligence or even anything to say to be a success. Arnie's choice of the non-sport of bodybuilding is significant here, in that all you need for it is determination, but determination of such a high order, and coupled to such nullity of insight and ignobility of purpose (to get big, to get rich, to get famous) that we are talking about a species of derangement, or at least obsession.

The American Dream is essentially to do with the invention, and continual reinvention of self. It sounds like an abstraction, but for the first religious rebels, political fugitives and pioneer farmers, it was practical enough. Over centuries it has become the central myth, the *stuff* of America, just as the Arthurian legend, with its conservative message of cyclical decline and renewal, is the matter of Britain.

Arnie represents the dream in an extreme, late 20th-century form, where it has gone beyond fantasies of wealth and power and freedom, to the boundaries of personality, to reinvent himself as superman, robot, cyborg, man-machine. Even in a comedy, such as *Twins,* he is the product of a genetic experiment, and in *Junior* becomes the subject of his own experiment, turning himself from man to woman; terminator to creator.

People have wondered when Arnie will take the dream to its limit by becoming President of the United States. His instinctive politics: entrepreneurial, anti-communist, anti-government, pro-capital punishment, coupled with his great wealth, would make the governorship of California his for the asking.

Gore Vidal has predicted, with patrician melancholy, that the election of 2004 will be between Arnold Schwarzenegger and Stormin' Norman Schwarzkopf.

The only real obstacle in Arnie's way is that nobody can be President who wasn't born in America, but when some pedant points it out, Arnie will have only to turn that look on them and ask: "Why baby?"

The Daily Telegraph, 12 December 1994

Tom Jones

'Number One approaching Stage Door ... No, yes, yes. Number One *inside* building ..." Backstage at the Glasgow Royal Concert Hall, walkie talkies squawk the news of Tom Jones's progress from hotel to dressing room. I am sitting in Phil the tour manager's room, as roadies and liggers come and go, begging and bullying for free tickets. "Aw c'mon Phil. Just a couple of comps – you can sit them behind the mixer. It's the bass player's sister-in-law from Tannochbrae or somewhere ..." There are 46 people in the Tom Jones entourage and everyone has a sister-in-law in Tannochbrae. "I got three nights sold out solid," says Phil, "I'm the most hated man in Glasgow."

Phil's mobile office goes to every gig: a dense collage of laptop computers, phone chargers, red wine bottles, photocopiers, printers, portable filing cabinets. The labels on the drawers say: hole punches, photo passes, ear plugs, batteries, laser toner, cables, pens, tools, shoe shine, envelopes. The corridor is a cliff of flight cases: scuffed black chests with battered aluminium angles, and a sprinkling of ancient decals: "Roger Daltrey Tour '89", "Eurythmics, Percussion – Eastern Europe ONLY." When Tom Jones was touring the working men's clubs of the Welsh valleys it was him and his dad in the car with the PA in the back. Now it is three 18-wheel wagons; two floors of the Glasgow Hilton, booked 12 months in advance, and 4,000 Scots women queueing up Sauchiehall Street every night with a pair of knickers in the handbag.

"Number One in dressing room," a radio squawks, but there is no need because he is here already, red as a radish and sweating pints in black jumper and tight black corduroys. "Gaw, 'sbloody 'ot in 'ere again. 'Avnay fixed 'at radiator valve yet? Nor that window lock neither. They 'aven got a bloody clew, honesty they 'aven." Emergency calls go out on the walkie talkie for radiator experts, valve engineers, thermostat technicians, window theorists, lock philosophers and temperature counsellors. They arrive. The problem is solved in seconds.

"*Very* sorry about that Mr Jones."

"Aw, s'alright mun," he murmurs. The star's pre-performance tantrum is over, and we are on our own.

After 30 years in Las Vegas and LA he still sounds and looks incredibly Welsh. The body is standard-issue miner's build with broad shoulders, narrow hips and thighs like Christmas turkeys. His face, with its black curls, high cheekbones and rosebud lips would fit behind a pint pot in any public bar from Merthyr to Mumbles.

When I was growing up in Swansea and Tom Woodward from Ponty became Tom Jones on *Top of the Pops* everyone suddenly knew him and had stories to tell. Was there any truth, I ask him now, in the one about him driving his motorbike through a chip shop window in Pontardawe? "Oh no, no. That was totally made up," says Jones. "I was *nutted* through a chip shop window in *Pontypridd.*"

And what about the time he and his son Mark were stuck at an airport between planes? Did they really refuse to wait in the stuffy First Class lounge, and head instead for the public bar where they drank eight pints of warm, flat Welsh bitter beer apiece? "Rubbish," says Jones. "It was a lot more than eight pints."

He is the son of a miner, from a big, warm Welsh family. "Both my parents came from families of six, and all my uncles, aunts, cousins, grandparents – they all stayed in Ponty." He left school at 15, married at 16 and was a father at 17. He worked in a glove factory and a paper mill ("Earning a man's wage there, I was"), and he would probably be there still, but for a magic millimetre or two on the vocal chords, and a lot of time in bed with TB, listening to blues on the radio.

He became a novelty act with a name borrowed from the fashionable Albert Finney film: a greaser from the valleys with tight pants, flounced shirt, and a shelf-life of 18 months at the outside. He didn't really fit into the Sixties scene. The BBC wouldn't play *It's Not Unusual* because it had this vulgar, old-fashioned big brass sound. Jones was the same age as John Lennon, but he looked older ("A bricklayer in a blouse," he says now) and his fans were hard to categorise, as they still are. Grannies and gays liked him for his bodice-ripper looks, and the hip crowd for his camp-chic, and the soul fans for his reverent reworking of Stax and Motown classics – but was he Radio One or Two?

Gordon Mills, his old-school manager, took him off to Las Vegas, where he was a great hit with the pink rinses. Elvis, who had flopped in the casinos in the early Sixties, came to learn from Tom

Jones's act. By the Eighties Jones was making $100,000 a show, with houses in Bel Air and Wales, but he was locked into a contract with Polygram who had decided he was really a country singer, and he hadn't had a hit record for a decade.

The new Tom Jones we see is the result of the end of the Polygram contract, the death of Mills, and the assumption of Jones's management by his son Mark, 37. The makeover began in 1988 when he recorded Prince's song *Kiss* with the conceptualist duo Art of Noise, while in his latest album, *The Lead and How to Swing It*, he collaborates with such impeccably hip producers as Jeff Lynne and Trevor Horn, and singers such as Tori Amos.

This type of opportunistic alliance between old pros in need of a career boost and young guns in search of a gimmick has become quite common. Take That and Lulu; Pet Shop Boys and Dusty Springfield; Bono and Frank Sinatra – but Jones could fairly claim to have pioneered it. The makeover has also included what manager Mark describes as: "Shifting the focus of public attention about three feet higher." At 55, and with two grandchildren, it has been decreed that the great Welsh Undresser should keep his jacket on, his gold medallions off, and not move about so ... well ... so *much*.

"Ah yes, the Underwear Situation ..." Jones says sadly.

In 1968 he was playing the Copacabana Club in New York and perspiring a lot ("When I sing, I sweat"). Women in the audience began passing him napkins to wipe his face, until eventually one removed her knickers, which he used and returned with thanks (he has beautiful manners). Earl White, the showbiz journalist, reported the incident, and a blizzard of underwear began to fall at the Welshman's feet. "And did you check them beforehand for ... um ... hygiene?" I ask him now.

"Oh I have a good look at the knickers, you know. But the British women's ones are always laundered and ironed in their handbags."

Knickers are ignored these days unless a woman holds them right in his face: "It is *difficult* then. You don't want to seem *ungrateful*."

In the Glasgow concert audience (80 per cent women) the knickers have become largely symbolic: waved above the head like football scarves or draped along the upper balconies like lines of washing. Many are not sexy in the least, but parodic Donald McGill bloomers in coral pink with chest high waistbands and elasticated legs – and so we have managed, in our British way, to turn the erotic into the comic. "Do you think he's sexy?" I ask the woman sitting next to me, who is about 30. "Och no. He can't dance and his gut is hanging over his trousers. He does have a good voice mind you."

"So why have you come?"

"Och, my friend here is sister-in-law to one of the band."

The older generation are kinder on the Jones physique; "I think he has a greeeet body," says a lady of 50 or so, in a see-through black mesh top. "I like a man who looooks after hisself. Are you here all alone ...?"

Knickers or no, Jones is still an accomplished manipulator of sexual hysteria: tossing his coat to the wings as he warms up; loosening a collar button as he gets hotter; swiping the sweat down his face with the blade of his hand; hitching the buckle of his trouser belt. Each gesture brings a wave of screams, more intense as the evening wears on and the songs build in tempo: *Delilah; It's Not Unusual; What's New Pussycat.* The eight-piece band and double percussion section create a beat that comes right up through the seat, and after two hours the lady in front – a grey-haired matron of 60 with Dame Edna glasses – is gyrating in a simulated sexual abandonment that would make her grandchildren die of shame.

"Why do women find you sexy?" I ask Jones, back in the dressing room, and he says: "I think it's just the voice. It's a big, Welsh voice, heavily influenced by American black music – with all the passion behind that." According to tabloid legend, Jones is a bit of a superstud, fond of three-in-a-bed sexual marathons, during which he perks up his parts with Listerine mouthwash. "You must have had a fair number of women throwing themselves at you over the years."

"A husband came up to me once and said, 'Hey Tom, you pump up the tyres but it's me gets to ride the bike'."

"But you get real offers?"

"I am not as pure as the driven snow, but it's not as many as the papers say."

"This girl in New York, Katherine Berkery, who said she had your child. You were paying $2,000 a month to her ..."

"That's all over now. It was difficult to disprove at the time and so we paid the maintenance. But that is over."

"And this Nicole Hall, whom the *National Enquirer* said you were seeing."

"She was just a fan and a fitness trainer I went jogging with. I'd hardly go jogging on the Boardwalk with someone I was having an affair with."

And so we leave it because he has said the main thing, which is that he has strayed, but in a 38-year-old marriage. His wife, Linda, spends as much time as she can in Wales, doesn't mix with showbiz people, doesn't talk to reporters and avoids reading the press. It seems evident that an understanding exists.

Toward the end of his Glasgow concert a woman walked boldly to the front of the stage and held a pair of black frillies up to Jones. He took a quick glance to either side; the reptile tongue flicked along the lips; dabbed his forehead with the panties and handed them back. It was a delightfully theatrical piece of furtiveness, which seemed to say, well we are not really allowed, but just this once, and between you and me.

"So for the benefit of your audience when you go south, I can write there is not a total ban on knickers?"

"I wouldn't want to put anyone *off*," says Tom Jones.

The Daily Telegraph, 21 November 1994

Marti Caine

"I'm the Mother Teresa of showbusiness," says Marti Caine. "Heal sick babies and bring back the dead." As they still haven't invented that useful typeface called "Ironic" I'd better say that Marti doesn't mean it. She is not serious. She is making a joke. At her own expense.

After five years of cancer treatment she is weary and a little wary of tabloid hagiolatry. "I can hear them sharpening their knives for me now," she says, and there have already been pinpricks. After her bone marrow transplant last January – her first NHS treatment – a newspaper spitefully noted that Marti Caine had "cost the NHS £40,000".

Mind you, she says, if you're going to get cancer, she can recommend hers, which is malignant lymphoma ("Does that make me a lymphomaniac?" she asked the doctor who told her. He didn't laugh.) It is slow and relatively painless, though the radio and chemotherapy are vile. "I lost my hair and nails for a bit and there was some scarring of various intimate orifices."

Five years ago she was given five years to live, and has already had the three remissions which are usual. But it is 10 months now since the bone marrow transplant, and the scans are clear.

She is appearing in panto this year in Cardiff, but rehearsing in London, where we meet. It is the lounge bar of the Royal Lancaster hotel, with a pianist tinkling *Don't Cry For Me Argentina* and snotty waiters highly trained in avoiding your eye. It is the worst place in the world to do an interview, but Marti has a gift for intimacy.

She was sitting in the cafe at John Lewis recently when a woman came and sat at her table, burst into tears, and told her she had just shoplifted a knitting pattern and what should she do? I believe it, for though she strides in like a star, with her dramatically backswept grey hair, she has a recognisable ordinariness about her. A woman who has been through a lot, who knows not to condemn, and who still cleans her own windows.

She loves interviews, and is amazed when I tell her she is a vanishing species of celebrity: "But it's *fantastic* to talk about yourself for two hours." So many public people are so tediously secretive about their mundane little lives that it's a pleasure to meet someone who will talk about incest, adultery and incontinence.

Marti talks about all of them, in that flat, husky, confidential Yorkshire tone that can make comic the most appalling detail – the same tone of humorous fatalism you overhear in shops and bus queues in the North: "She had to have it all took out ... He were never the same man again ... Found him trapped under the Christmas tree four years later ... Buried three husbands before she were 40 ... A prolapsed womb it was – on the table for three hours."

Female comics are two-a-penny now: French and Saunders, Ruby Wax, Josie Lawrence – but Marti was the first woman stand-up to break into television, via the New Faces show in 1975. She also patented what is now a universal style: slagging off the men and siding with the women, with a string of self-deprecating gags studded with beadily observant domestic detail.

But there was also a strain of daftness descended from older, music hall turns such as George Formby and Norman Wisdom. My favourite Marti joke is not about sex or marriage or domesticity, but two dyslexic skiers on a mountain in Switzerland.

"Let's zag-zig down this slope," says one.

"No, it's zig-zag," says the other.

"No, no. Zag-zig."

"ZIG-ZAG!"

They appeal to a passer-by, but he can't help them because he doesn't know anything about skiing: "I'm just a tobogganist," he explains.

"Oh, all right then," says the first skier. "Could you give me 20 Benson & Hedges?"

She served, the hardest apprenticeship possible, 13 years in the working men's clubs, which gave her a boiler plated comic persona and a whiplash tongue for hecklers. One night she was booked to appear after three strippers when the last failed to turn up. "They'd had bangers and mash for lunch. The mash was all over the flock wallpaper, and the second stripper was performing with what were left of the bangers."

Marti went on stage "with me pipe cleaner legs and flat chest, and this drunk stood up and shouted: 'I want tits'. And I heard this voice, very fast and confident saying, 'You'd look a right c--- with tits'. And it were *me*."

She often talks about Marti Caine as a separate person. The stage Marti even has a different face. "You can see it change. I'm putting on me make-up, there's a knock on the door, and they say 'Five minutes, Miss Caine'. I look in the mirror and I've gone and *she* is there." It is the oldest cliché in showbiz, but Marti really is sick before she goes on stage: "The dresser's there with a bucket because it happens every time. Yellow bile, because you can't eat when you work."

"You go on stage tasting the bile?"

"Oh no. *She* doesn't taste. She doesn't feel. She doesn't hear. But when the spotlight goes off so does she, thank God, because she's not someone I'd like to live with."

Her real name is Lynn Stringer and she was born in Sheffield in 1946, to a Scots mother and Yorkshire father who worked as a steel company draughtsman. Her parents were in love, she was a cherished only child, and it was a glowingly happy childhood until she was seven, when her father died of lung cancer.

"Your mother was knocked out by that?"

"She might as well have died with him. She spent the next 14 years dying slowly. She was an alcoholic and well into drugs – anything to reduce her to a state of semi-awareness."

She moved constantly between Scotland and her mother and grandfather's houses in Sheffield, and attended 15 different schools: "I honestly thought Algebra was the language spoken in Algeria." When she was 11, and living in Scotland, her mother went into hospital and Marti into care: "The woman in charge was soft and squashy with a wrapover pinny that smelled of flour and carbolic – a very comforting smell."

When nobody would tell her what was happening to her mother she ran away. "My granddad sent me half a crown a week and I'd saved seven and six. The day I left, someone pinched it so I took some money from under a milk bottle, bought a platform ticket and hid in a guard's van. I ended up in Carlisle, where the porters all plied me with chocolate to get my name out of me. In the end I told them my granddad was a pattern maker with English Steel in Sheffield, and he turned up to collect me."

She lived with "Pop" off and on for the rest of her childhood. "He was very ambitious for me. Sent me to a dancing school and he tried to get me into sport. Had me swimming up and down the pool after a brush, and leaping over a washing line in the backyard." He was the closest person in her life until she awoke one morning to find his penis in her hand. "He started babbling that I'd had a nightmare. But I wasn't stupid. I found he'd tried it with my friends as well, and that he was well known for it in the family, which upset me, because my mother could have stopped it. In itself it were nothing, but it had the most profound effect on me."

"What was that?"

"A feeling of worthlessness. You blame yourself. And I felt betrayed that he didn't really love me after all. And if I am honest I think I was jealous of the attention he had paid to my friends.

"I was a bitch to him from then on. Demanded locks on my door. If he said black then I said white. I understood he probably couldn't help it, but I never really forgave him."

At 16 she was pregnant and at 17 she was married. "My granddad wanted me to go to me Uncle Frank's in Blackpool. Have it in secret and have it adopted. But I didn't want anyone else to have my baby. I thought me life was over." Her son, now 32, has just presented her with a "beautiful" grandchild.

"Was it the end of your ambitions?"

"I was never ambitious. I only went on stage because I wanted a three-piece suite and a fitted carpet." During her first performance, singing at a working men's club, she wet herself, and was so terrified by singing that she put off the songs longer and longer by chatting, until the whole act was chat.

She never wanted to appear on *New Faces*: "It were a Friday and Friday was when I did the shopping and cleaned me windows." But she did go on, and won, and got her own television series, then six more series and her own sit-com. The marriage broke up when her husband fell in love with another woman: "He always liked the ladies. It were his hobby, and I always think a man's entitled to his hobby.

"I've always been attracted to men who like women. The King Penguin mates for life, but most of the rest of us are at it like knives whenever we get the chance. Certainly most men."

"Does that apply to your second husband?"

"I think they settle down after 45. But given half a chance …"

When I ask why she doesn't get frightened or panicky or angry about the cancer she says: "I don't think I've really accepted it. I still think I'm the one who will slip through the net and live to be a thousand. And I believe in God, which makes the thought of death more bearable. Mind you, I also believe in Father Christmas."

"Does it make you live more intensely?"

"You do initially, but complacency sets in. You start by watching daffodils and end up watching *Neighbours* – which is healthy enough I suppose."

"Do you have any ambitions you'd like to fulfill?"

"Well, like I said, I was never really ambitious. I just wanted mince on Monday, liver on Wednesday, fish on Friday. All my life I've just been trying to get back to that place where I was when I was seven."

The Daily Telegraph, 29 December 1993

Home

Politicking in Labour's backyard

One of the best questions to ask Parliamentary candidates is where they live. This is hardly ever in the constituency and somehow they always get embarrassed and start blustering about how their aunty lives down the road, or how they used to deliver papers in the next borough-but-one.

Harriet Harman, the civil rights lawyer and Labour candidate for the south London constituency of Peckham, lives in up-and-coming Kilburn in north London, but says she does "a lot of work" in Peckham and plans to move there in January. Tory John Redwood, who looks like a young pension fund manager, which, astonishingly, is exactly what he is, says he lives "ten minutes up the road". This turns out to be Lower Thames Street in the heart of the City, which might be ten minutes away by Harrier jump-jet but is more like 15 in a Porsche Turbo.

SDP man Dick Taverne's biography says he lives "at Vauxhall Bridge, just 15 minutes away". Aha, chronologically exact, but which *side* of Vauxhall Bridge? It turns out to be the north bank, near such proletarian gathering places as the Tate Gallery, the Chelsea Flower Show and Dolphin Square.

There is no real need for all this coyness either. Parliamentary candidates apart – or perhaps included – no-one in their right mind would actually *choose* to live in Peckham. It is a hideously ugly slice of south-central London with some of the nastiest social conditions in Britain. Natural Labour territory you might think and, complicated by a few boundary changes, the area has been represented by Labour MPs with thumping majorities since the war. Freda Corbet for '45 to '64; Minister of Labour Ray Gunter form '64 to '72 and Harry Lamborn up until his death this year, when he bequeathed a 10,811 majority – 60 per cent of the vote – to his anointed successor Harriet Harman. Peckham is, quite literally, Labour's backyard – with the national party headquarters in Walworth Road and a formidable structure of co-operative societies and trade unions based within the constituency.

So what is Dick Taverne doing in Labour's backyard? He has been talking centre party politics almost since he entered Parliament as Labour member in 1962, No tormented soul-searching in Kentish Town or Limehouse; no blinding light on the road from Brussels. Taverne was urging Roy Jenkins to form a new party as early as 1971, during the Labour battles over entry to the EEC. Taverne is, in short, the kind of authentic SDP Mr Clean who would stand a good chance in any of the Alliance "winnables"; and yet has chosen, apparently, to chuck it all away on Peckham.

Closer to, however, things look a bit different. For one thing, Taverne knows how to win elections. His original by-election victory at Lincoln in 1962 was a tremendous upset for the Tories, through rather overshadowed by the Liberal victory at Orpington a week or so later. After defying a three-line whip by voting for EEC membership in 1972, he resigned his seat and fought it again as an independent, winning a sensational 13,000 majority over the official Labour candidate.

His Peckham HQ is a giant converted mission hall, buzzing with formidable middle-aged ladies and cheerful young men in anoraks. An earnest lady in spectacles asks cryptically if I have been "filtered through yet", but is deflected by Taverne himself, a springy, greying athletic figure in Observer-offer Guernsey, red check shirt and those smart casual trousers that used to be called slacks.

"No I don't live in the constituency," he replies to the first question. "I've no connection with it at all", which gives him an advantage that he proceeds to press home. He says he dropped out of the short list for Cambridge and decided to fight Peckham because it was a "challenge". More specifically, Taverne thinks the Labour vote is soft. "Labour has taken it for granted that this is their natural territory. At the last election there was a 56 per cent turnout. This time we'll be lucky if it's a 40 per cent poll. It's an area of *utter* disillusionment."

So far he has made most of the running. He has focused on housing as his main issue and has sent out questionnaires to 25,000 council tenants to hear their complaints. Fairly ineffectual in practical terms but a good PR stunt. He was first to react to news of a National Front march on 23 October by firing off a demand for a ban to the Met and a request for prosecution under the Race Relations Act to the Director of Public Prosecutions, who he addresses as "Tony". Harriet Harman belatedly followed up with a request to the Home Secretary for the ban to be made selective, but it was Taverne who got the headlines in the local press.

A *Daily Mail* poll last week gave Taverne a 21 per cent share of the committed vote, but, as he points out, Roy Jenkins climbed from 17 per cent at Warrington to 42 per cent on polling day. In theory, Taverne could just scrape home if the Tory did really well, but he won't. Even allowing for the fact that he does not like the *New Statesman*, John Redwood seems an extraordinarily unsuitable Conservative candidate for this sort of area. A PhD in philosophy, Fellow of All Souls and investment adviser to Rothschilds, he responds to questions like a preoccupied suburban bank manager being asked for an overdraft. Blank incredulity followed by tolerant amusement at the sheer idiocy of the request. You have to prise his jaws apart with a car jack to get a three-syllable answer.

"What do you think of the proposed National Front march?"

"No 'pinion on it."

"You don't care about a racially provocative demonstration taking place in the constituency five days before an election?"

"Matter for th' police."

Probably some joker at Central Office thought they'd give him a hard time before sliding him into the House for somewhere like Brentwood or Chelmsford.

Conversation with Harriet Harman is equally fragmented, taking place mostly at about 70 miles an hour in a succession of brightly coloured X and Y registration hatchbacks, tearing through the red lights of Peckham to one late appointment after another.

"We want a campaign that will really mobilise ordinary people – turn left here – it's not just getting in a Labour member – Can you pull back to let him through?"

"A significant defeat for a leading member of the SDP could destroy them – Please don't run over any of my constituents – We are talking about welcoming black and brown people to the community – I think we're here."

"Here" is the Carib centre, a hostel for homeless black youths where the welcome for the Labour campaigners is polite but not exactly ecstatic. "Why do you ask blacks to vote for you when all the nationality and immigration laws were initiated by Labour?" asks one leader. Harman, the NCCL lawyer, steers the conversation around to her pet subject of legal rights for arrested young blacks but the Carib people are not overly impressed. "I read a lot about you in the *Guardian*," says one, "but most people around here don't read the *Guardian*."

Later, in a school playground a young mother tells her cheerfully: "I am a racist. I'm sorry, I know I shouldn't, but I just can't stand them." She is still unmoved after a few minutes earnest lecture on solidarity with oppressed ethnic groups, and Harman retreats nonplussed.

She also has the disadvantage of defending the record of Labour councils, which have presided over much of the present decay in housing and services. Not surprisingly, she has chosen to make unemployment her main issue, but the answers are all a year or two away in Labour's *Plan For Jobs* and don't have the immediacy of Taverne's relentless hammering on the housing question. She has also allowed herself to adopt some of the "Peckham belongs to me" attitude of the local party machine and seems over-concerned with talk about mass mobilisation and consciousness-raising. She won't lose the election. She can't lose the election, unless she does, in which case she might do worse than to hang on to the house in Kilburn.

New Statesman, 22 October 1982

Where are the Marxists in 1983?

Highgate cemetery is the nightmare garden of London. Oddly articulated angels and cherubs lurch drunkenly from behind gloomy, creeper-laden trees; there are giant rugged crosses and intricate grottoes of tufa rock where pumice pets lie at the feet of dear departeds.

Most grotesque of all is a giant rectangular box, cheaply plated with modern compound marble and studded with concrete bosses. The box is surmounted by the massive grizzled head and shoulders of a cross old Victorian gentleman looking, for all the world, like grand-pa, left buried in the sand for the tide while the children scamper off for ices and macaroons.

"Karl Marx," says the inscription, "1818-1883", and beneath, picked out in fresh gilt is the eleventh *Thesis on Feuerbach*, chosen by Engels for his master's epitaph: "The philosophers have only interpreted the world in various ways," it says. "The point is to change it."

At university a dozen years ago, that sounded like a call to arms. In the damp gloaming of Locke and Hume and John Stuart Mill, which was still the basic climate of philosophy faculties, the vivid mechanisms of classical Marxism and its appeal to action, were powerful intoxicants. "It's all there," we told each other excitedly, "everything explained."

So we occupied the Senate to protest against files; and we went on rent strike to oppose the Thatcher cuts (remember *those* cuts?); and we boycotted the lectures of behaviourist psychologists; and we picketed the dining halls in support of puzzled catering workers. And more thrilling still was that pervasive myth of the vicar's daughter, or was it the stockbroker's son, who kept a .22 under the bed, "for when the day came".

Sixty-eight, which, of course, means 1966-74, is not a bad starting point for a thumbnail sketch of Marxists in Britain today. It was one of those watershed moments for Marxism, though here you immediately have to start being careful. There are only about 24,000 people belonging to Marxist parties now (about 18,000 of these are in the Communist Party), and few of those are really active. Perhaps the same number again would profess to Marxist views of one kind or another. Like any small, somewhat beleaguered group, they are very introspective and tend to the over-generous use of words like "watershed", "epochal" and "seminal".

Nevertheless, '68 *was* important in several ways. Up until that year the history of British Marxism was largely the history of the Communist Party. The British CP, founded in 1920, lost a lot of members after the collapse of the Popular Front movement and the Nazi-Soviet pact of 1939, but managed to survive, in semi-dormant form, the worst years of the Cold War. Then, with the Russian invasion of Hungary in 1956 and Khrushchev's denunciation of Stalin at the 20th Party Congress, 10,000 members left, and many others, including a number of dissenting intellectuals like E.P. Thompson, were expelled.

Thompson, with a group of like-minded intellectuals and academics, which included names like Stuart Hall, Perry Anderson, Doris Lessing, Eric Heffer, Lindsay Anderson and Robin Blackburn, helped set up what would now be called a "dissident" Marxist journal – the *New Left Review* – which became and remains very influential. It is mainly a theoretical journal – "too theoretical," Thompson was to say later – but its "line", insofar as it had one, was basically that of a liberalised CP, only with clean hands and a clear conscience.

Then '68 came along, with the anti-Vietnam movement, the student revolt in Paris, the "siege" of the Democratic convention in Chicago – all signalling, so we were told later, the rise of a new radical consciousness in a new mass intelligentsia.

True or not, it was a consciousness with an ideological hole in the middle, with texts ranging from Che Guevara to *Chariots of the Gods*. The Communist Party and the "old" New Left were largely indifferent if not hostile to the student movement. E. P. Thompson – according to Stuart Hall, who's now Professor of Sociology at the Open University – was of a mind that the revolting students should all be doing National Service, or conscripted into the Young Communist League, until the row over personal files at Warwick University won him over to the cause.

Hall himself, while more sympathetic, regarded the movement as "pre-figurative" and "top-down". "There was something incongruous," he says now, "in the spectacle of the flower of western intellectual life dressed up as Che Guevara and waiting for the workers to come over the hill to rescue them." Many other Marxist academics, dismayed at their promotion to the role of oppressors, took a lurch to the right from which they never recovered.

The political organisations that *did* arise – the International Marxist Group (IMG), the Socialist Workers Party (SWP) and the International Socialists (IS), to name but a dozen – were Trotskyist or Marxist-Leninist in orientation. That is, all-out admiration for the Soviet Union stopped in about 1926. Marx was okay, Lenin was okay, armed insurrection was okay, but Stalinism was "mistaken". Okay?

Hard-line Stalinists in the CP called these new groups "revisionist". Liberal CP members called them "adventurist", "workerist" and "vanguardist". The New Left academics asked them nastily why their essays were always late.

But the Trotskyist alphabet soup was only one product of '68. Round about 1971, I remember a friend who belonged to IMG bursting into my room, white with anger, and shouting about how IMG women were setting up a discussion group and *wouldn't let men in*! It seemed funny then. It seems funny now, but in a completely different way of course. The skids were under the new-New Left.

Leninist doctrine states, somewhere or other, that before the revolution *there is only one struggle*. That is, for the orthodox Trot, the blacks, women, gays, ecologists etcetera are just going to have to wait for *the day*. Lots of blacks, women etcetera couldn't be bothered and took their custom elsewhere.

The seventies witnessed a general decline in the taste for alphabet soup. The IMG has virtually vanished into the left wing of the Labour Party. IS was absorbed into the SWP and the SWP itself, the only party to adopt racism as a major issue, is shrinking.

Single-issue groups, by contrast, have grown apace in CND, the women's movement, and the various ecology groups. The only party that has established successful links with the new fractionist left is the CP, which was fortunate enough to rediscover a chap called Gramsci. He was the Italian communist, imprisoned by the fascists in the 1930s, who decided that it was no longer necessary to seek outright revolution, but to construct a broad alliance (key phrase) or "hegemony" of left-wing groups to bring about change through peaceful, gradualist means.

So in the 1980s the Marxist geography of Britain looks something like this. On the extreme right is the extreme left wing of the Labour Party, technically Marxist in some cases but no talk of extra-parliamentary activity allowed (see Bermondsey). Moving leftwards we have the Communist Party (parliament, broad alliance, plus some mass struggle) followed by the New Left (less parliament, more struggle) followed, on the far left by the unreconstructed Stalinists, Marxist-Leninists and Trotskyists (lots of struggle, no compromises and sod parliament). Cutting horizontally across these groups you have the single-interest pressure groups, probably with a bias towards the CP and Labour.

The toings and froings of British Marxism in the last 20 years look terribly complicated even in thumbnail versions. But all the various strands *can* be seen from one viewpoint, which is the attempt to come to terms with the actual experience of a fairly successful, fairly stable, bourgeois, democratic state. Revolution *hasn't* happened in the west. Classes have *not* become polarised in the way predicted by Marx, and most western states seem, through conscious policies of social and fiscal intervention, to be able to control capitalist crises.

There are lots of different arguments advanced for this apparent failure of Marxism, but the most fundamental is the critique of *economism*, which is shorthand for the classical Marxist view that economic processes form the *base* of society and shape all its other aspects like laws, institutions, state apparatus and so on, which are known as the *superstructure*. If the economic base is sick, as Marx thought capitalism was, then the superstructure must eventually die.

The Gramscian view, which is now the orthodox view of most of the CP and New Left, is that in advanced capitalist societies the superstructure is able to tinker with the defective economic base to keep it chugging along indefinitely. Therefore communism is not inevitable, but can only be brought about by broad alliances working for gradual change within the existing structure of society.

Stuart Hall puts it like this: "Marxism is no longer a single set of protocols with a built-in guarantee that the formula is right and that the laws of history will make it come right. It is no longer a recipe for life that you can consult on whether you should go out tonight."

Most Marxists would now describe themselves with Hall, as "a Gramscian first and Marxist second." It is a tenable and coherent viewpoint that takes account of political realities, and it is also a convenient one for people no longer in the first flush of youth and with a stake in the status quo. It means that it is no longer necessary to go to lots of boring meetings that interfere with your social life, or to dress up as Che Guevara of a 19th century Manchester mill hand. It doesn't matter if you drive a Lada, a Moskvitch or a Ford Escort, and you don't have to worry about the morality of a mortgage or a job at the BBC. All you have to do is to participate in some vague fashion in the broad alliance for ultimate hegemony.

The main popular vehicle for Gramscian views is the magazine, *Marxism Today*, a glossy, smartly-produced monthly owned by the CP and circulating an astonishing 16,000 a month. Its editor, Martin Jacques, is a small, dapper man with owlish Andy Warhol glasses and one of those luxuriant moustaches with which nature compensates the prematurely bald. A life-long CP member and a former lecturer at Bristol University, Jacques is enthusiastic about introducing Marxism to the mainstream of British political culture. "The last crisis produced Keynes and Beveridge," he says. "An open-ended, pluralistic Marxism could achieve the same influence after this one."

The effort to legitimise Marxism has involved a series of articles, interviews and "round-table" discussions featuring people as unlikely as Peter Jenkins of the *Guardian* and father figure of the SDP, Shirley Williams, Walter Goldsmith (Institute of Directors) and Peregrine Worsthorne (*Daily Telegraph*). It makes for stimulating reading, but more traditional Marxists disapprove.

Robin Blackburn, current editor of the *New Left Review*, admires *Marxism Today* but describes it as "a curious journal". As a former IMG member who was sacked from a lectureship at the London School of Economics for supporting student occupations, Blackburn retains some traditional suspicion of the Communist Party. *Marxism Today*, he argues, aims not so much as legitimising Marxism but legitimising communism. "They don't want to change the *terms* of political debate," he says, "and for a socialist that is quite wrong. You don't interview people like Peter Jenkins in that passive way."

Blackburn is about 43 now and prematurely grey, but disarmingly boyish: "Don't you go writing about the colour of my jumper," he says, so I don't. He left IMG because of "the high input ... meetings every night," and "schematic politics". He is now mainly interested in the impact of ecological, feminist and peace movements on Marxist programmes and the traditional Labour movement. "The trouble with the CP is that they are embarrassed about being outflanked by the Labour left."

He is less apologetic about "actual socialism" (key phrase) in other countries that the CP tends to be. "China is a far more humane society than somewhere like India." The main change in Marxism over the last 20 years, so far as he is concerned, is that "there is now a very serious body of Marxist work in print."

Neither Eric Hobsbawm nor Raymond Williams had published much before 1960, and Lawrence & Wishart were just about the only publishers of Marxist work. Now, Blackburn points out, most large firms run Marxist lists, even establishment names like Macmillan, Heinemann and Routledge. What about some names? He reels them off: Andrew Gamble on economics, Ian Gough on the welfare state, Michele Barrett on the family and women, Peter Fuller on art, Barbara Taylor on early socialism.

Business certainly looks pretty good at the publishing headquarters of Pluto Press in Tufnell Park. It's a big converted factory done out in Richard Rogers hi-tech style with grey, dimpled rubber flooring and lots of red gloss ironwork everywhere. How long before industrial chic becomes as kitsch as coach lamps and cartwheels?

The managing director, Richard Kuper, is the first 1983 Marxist

I've met who *looks* like a Marxist, with beard, Trotsky glasses, tousled grey curls and shabby cords. Unfortunately he's not a Marxist at all, but a happy capitalist, thanks very much, turning over £750,000 a year. Yes, Pluto did start up for ideological reasons. Yes, they are unionised. No, there's no profit-sharing. Main areas in the current list are women's movement, third world, trade unionism, ecology, black struggle. Very little Marxist theory. This is sounding *very* familiar.

The trouble with these Marxists is that they're all so moderate and ordinary. There's the historian, Eric Hobsbawm, with his Birkbeck study full of pipes and books and his home in Hampstead; there's Robin Blackburn with his Pimlico flat and dry Martinis and oozing charm; there's Stuart Hall with his Ivy League outfit and Open University chair; and there are feminists like Anne Sassoon with her house in Clapham and "*taramasalata*" on the memo board in the kitchen. What this article needs is a bit of colour: a couple of raving loonies.

Derek Robinson, better known as Red Robbo of British Leyland seemed like a good bet, but didn't turn up for his interview. Peter Carter of the construction union UCATT, who substituted for Robinson as token Marxist trade unionist, was terribly sane.

"We've never argued for insurrection," he says. "The trade union movement must find a way to join forces with a broad alliance of people outside its ranks in the peace movement, ecology groups, the women's movement ..." Sound familiar?

Last chance for a good loony was the Assembly House pub in Kentish Town where one of the very few, hard-left, unreconstructed Stalinist groups still gets together after its party meeting on Thursday to erode the base of capitalism by drinking vast quantities of draught Guinness and Lowenbrau. This is the Communist Part of Britain open brackets Marxist-Leninist close brackets.

"I think there's a real possibility that if Thatcher wins the next election there won't be another election," says Phil Vernon, an USDAW shop steward. Good, good, that's the stuff. Scribble, scribble. "We believe in protecting the British worker with immigration controls," says Phil's mate, Geoff Mount, a further education college lecturer. Terrific stuff this. Give me more. "Solidarity in Poland is a result of false consciousness among the workers." War is peace, black is white. Got it.

But Phil and Geoff are too good with their tongues, and produce the most quotable and redeeming quote so far. "Look, mate," says Geoff, "for the odd Bob Dylan song, the odd highway and the odd sunset, all of this," he waves around him at the ruins of western Europe, "all of this just ain't worth it."

Outside the pub, under a wobbly moon, you can just make out the crest of Highgate Hill, where Karl Marx looks down over London, with that stern injunction to action chiselled over his marble breast. Geoff and Phil still believe it but does anyone else?

The reason why Marxist governments rule half the world, why every branch of social, political and economic science is illuminated with Marx's insights, why everyone, in a sense, is a Marxist now, was the powerful claim of Marxism to scientific validity. But the test of scientific theory is its ability to accommodate new information and discrepancy.

If the weight of new knowledge becomes too great then the theory can retreat from reality and become a species of religious faith or dogma in which mysticism and ferocious discipline replace empiricism.

On the other hand, it can become so diffuse and disparate in its attempts to incorporate new knowledge that it loses its power as a practical analytical instrument and becomes just another intellectual diversion in the academic toybox. Which is preferable? Most British Marxists have already made their choice.

New Society, 10 March 1983

A school for men

The school is old, probably 1860 or thereabouts, but rechristened after a 20th century socialist. Outside, it is a gladiatoral, tarmac playground, a jagged cliff of cinder-coloured brick and high ladders of small window panes. Inside are corridors of rattling parquet and smells of sick and Jeyes Fluid and wet ashes that clutch at the stomach with their familiarity.

Our group is one of many. Yesterday evening was *Assertiveness Training* and *Recorder Playing for Beginners.* Tomorrow is *20th Century Woman Writers* and *Effective Reading.* Our class, this

October evening, is *Men's Sexuality and Masculinity: an awareness group for men*. Organised by Islington Council and run by a pleasant, bearded young man in jeans and check work-shirt, who says his name is Dennis.

Dennis is 30, a part-time gardener, driven indoors by the weather and the shrinking evenings. He is studying psychotherapy part-time. He lives with a companion who is very involved in the women's movement and this has made him interested in how men are to redefine themselves in relation to the changing role of women. They have a new baby girl that he is very thrilled about. He is a bit nervous about how the class is going to work out.

We know all these thing because he tells us. We spend most of the evening telling each other about ourselves. There are 16 men, average age about 30, though there are a couple in their teens, and two or three in their late forties. Only a handful appear to have jobs. A graphic designer, a civil servant, a computer programmer, a social worker. Three or four are divorced. One or two seem to be gay.

The first thing we have to do is to split up into pairs and to spend two minutes introducing ourselves to our partners. No questions, interruptions or deviations allowed.

My partner's name is Julian. He is pale, thin and bony with a red short back and sides. There is a gold hoop in one ear and a turquoise star in the other. He wears flat-earth shoes and turmeric-coloured socks. His orange shirt and green corduroys are a little jaded, like a couple who have spent too many Sunday afternoons together at the launderette.

He comes from Southampton; a middle class family; dropped out of some sort of community work course. Now getting himself together in a house in Finsbury Park with a 16 month old son called Reg and a radical feminist companion who won't sleep with him. I can't remember any more about him, because the first thing he asks me is why I'm being so defensive, and I'm trying to find an answer that doesn't make me even more defensive. The art of being sympathetically vicious.

Julian seems like a shit to me, but I strike out such stereotypically combative male thoughts. It is my turn to do the intro now and I tell Julian a complete pack of lies, which makes me feel a lot better.

Back then into the larger circle where each partner introduces the other. Someone called Neil begins: "Ewan is 34 years old. He comes from an Irish working class family. He went to a local grammar school and then to university to do economics. He got interested in acting and ended up joining the Irish National Theatre. He played the lead in the West End production of *Hair*. Recently he was stabbed by some men and then raped. He now finds it very difficult to relate to other men and felt very nervous about coming here tonight." Phew.

The circle of men, crouched on miniature chairs of gaspipe and plywood, gaze intently at the dusty light fittings of the classroom ceiling, and at their feet. One pair of tan Trax lace-ups, two pairs of trainers, one of white Olympus Counties, one of Kickers and one of Timberland topsiders. Not a polished toecap in sight.

After a long silence, Ewan takes his turn. He is a handsome young man with a denim jacket and curly dark hair. "I had no idea," he says, "that when we were telling each other about ourselves it was going to be repeated in front of the group." There is another, even longer silence.

The next thing we are supposed to do is to look at some photos and cuttings we have collected from newspapers and magazines. "Okay, who's got some photographs?" says Dennis. No one has brought any photographs, but Dennis has a pile of *Daily Mirrors* and colour supps that are spread out on the floor. There is Cliff Richard, Clive Jenkins, Yuri Andropov, Steve Ovett, Neil Kinnock.

"They're all so *macho*, aren't they," says Julian.

"There's a lot more pictures of men than women in the papers," says one of the teenagers hesitantly.

"We'll put a stop to that *right* away," says someone, and there is the first, blessed laugh of the evening. "What do you think of this?" asks Dennis, producing an advertising photograph of a moody young man in an ugly zippered pullover, leaning against an alley wall.

"He's a potential rapist," says Julian, unhesitatingly. "The advertiser is selling his clothes by exploiting male violence towards women."

"Oh, I don't know ..."

"It's a *horrible* cardigan ..."

"What if he was wearing a pipe and slippers then?"

"Equally exploitative," says Julian. "The question you must ask yourself is who *bought* him the pipe and slippers."

If Dennis ever had a lesson plan it's getting recycled now as we split up once again into pairs for another little confessional, but this time for an excruciating ten minutes. My new partner is Paul, a 38 year old civil servant with a grey goatee and collarless purple shirt. We are supposed to tell each other things we don't like about our roles as men, so we make a list. We don't like being expected to be: breadwinners; sensible; responsible; brave; leaders; wheel changers; sexually adept; sexual initiators; sports mad; serious; humorous; smartly dressed; shabbily dressed. The list, as is the way of abstract lists, rapidly becomes self-cancelling.

Paul is particularly keen to talk about the sexual initiator thing, and tells me about a woman he met after his wife divorced him three years ago:

"She was a very unusual woman. Continental. And continental women *are* different. After a party, when everyone had gone to bed, she'd just go into one of the single men's rooms and climb into bed with him. Perhaps someone she'd hardly spoken to all evening.

"Perhaps that was what I liked about her. She always took the lead. Always knew what she wanted. It was a real change from my wife. But after a couple of years you start to get fed up with it. You want a bit of a rest."

It's all very interesting and we whizz through our ten minutes, swapping stories about women who made the first move. But is any of it true? Perhaps even the man who starred in *Hair* and got raped and stabbed … The group of 16 earnest men suddenly takes on a slightly different colouring. Candour is a conversational technique, which is not at all the same thing as truthfulness.

At the close there is a summing up where we say how we felt about it all.

"I feel a lot closer to other men," says Ewan.

"It was a real buzz to talk intimately with another man," says Paul.

"I was a bit freaked out by the competitive atmosphere of an all-male group," says Julian-the-shit.

We troop out through the darkened playground without talking to each other, embarrassed by the normality of chalked cricket stumps and netball hoops. Tomorrow little boys will play here, shouting about knickers and jostling over a football. Little girls will do salt, mustard, vinegar, pepper, and handstands against the wall.

You can go back to school to learn about woodwork, or German, or those new skills of enforced idleness: *Self-Presentation, Facing Unemployment, Effective Reading*. You may even be able to learn the tactful vocabulary of sexual equality. But, a dangerously portentous and gloomy voice seems to argue, even if there *is* anything really amiss with these pleasant and anxious young men, aggressive in their humility and deceitful in their candour, it takes more than a spasm of renunciation to excise a past.

New Society, 13 October 1983

Below the city streets

W e're a very *regular* nation," says water worker John Diplock, as we gaze into the foaming orange torrent of Brighton's main sewer. "Every morning at seven o'clock, up comes the level two or three feet. You could set your watch by it."

You can see the morning surge on graphs of the sewer levels. And there are smaller blips for lunch, tea, bedtime, and even commercial breaks on the TV. A very regular nation. And there must be other sociometric clues, too, in that sluggish rise and fall of detergent, turd, toilet tissue, hair clot, diaper and condom. For those with the nose for it.

Neville Chamberlain was always being attacked for it, but you certainly get a new view of things from the wrong end of a municipal drainpipe. You can see, for one thing, the terrible frailty of social systems that lean so heavily on these despised and invisible mechanisms. And there is a sharing, too, in the power of the doctor and the priest, with their insight into the democracy of decay. A sewer, Victor Hugo said, is a cynic. It sees all.

And the sewermen turn out to be natural cynics, and natural democrats. Bill Holden, the sixtyish labourer leading our official tour, ticks off a young schoolteacher for taking photos of her kids while he is talking: "You wouldn't like it if I did that in your classroom."

"Har, har. Norty Miss!" says Darren or Tracy or Dean, and there is much blushing and tittering and shuffling of feet. But he's quite right, everyone nods.

And the sewermen are very cynical about their industrial muscle. The manual water workers' unions, NUPE, GMWU and TGWU, are balloting members on the first-ever national water strike after rejecting a 4 per cent pay offer. They are asking for 15 per cent to bring them into line with gas and electricity workers.

"If we did go on strike," says Holden, "what would happen? Nothing … These sewers are self-maintaining. If someone got *very* militant they could drop a gate and stop the flow but an engineer would soon put that right."

They are all very proud of the Brighton sewer system. John Diplock, the most articulate of the gang, is a sort of sewer poet. "Look at that brickwork," he says, "never been re-laid or even re-pointed in 100 years." He pats the immaculately meshing runs of bricks appreciatively. Which is, of course, directly contrary to our safety lecture, as Tracy or Dean points out.

Don't touch the walls of the sewer, we have been told, and whatever you do *don't* touch your mouth or your face with your hands. They get a lot of rats from the town, coming down the sewers at low tide, searching for crabs and shellfish, and they coat the sewer walls with the bacteria of their excrement.

"Yeearchgh!" squeals Darren or Tracy or Dean. "We gonna see *rats* down 'ere then?" Could do, nod the sewermen soberly: but the rats hardly ever bite. So off we go, a crocodile of yellow hard-hats, following a bobbing flashlight up the main storm sewer: an eight foot pipe, empty now but for a trickle of seepage.

Although it is a cold, windy December day outside, with big grey breakers smacking on the shingle below the Palace Pier outfall, the atmosphere inside the sewers is warm and clammy. "It's like this all the year round," says Diplock. We are walking in the combined latent heat of thousands of bed-warm bodies and morning bathtubs. An oozing claocal slime coats the walls like a snail's trail and collects beneath iron handrails and ladder rungs in chilly dribbles to frighten an over-confident grasp.

We pause in the echoing vault of an overflow chamber to wipe our hands on paper towels that are thrown into the sucking current of an open sewer trough. There is not the blatant barnyard stench you might expect, but more the sweetish, butcher's backroom smell of over-ripe meat.

Diplock turns his flashlight on the stream of sewage. "See that pink colour?" he says. "That's from the slaughterhouse. When they flush out in the mornings it runs bright red."

"Yeearchgh!" says Darren/Tracy/Dean. And we plod on in the flashlight, coughing steadily from the damp. If there is a sudden downpour, the sewer spills into this overflow chamber, and out to sea through the storm sewer. This means everyone out of the sewer system double quick, and a couple of days clearing up acres of soggy toilet paper, seaweed and worse.

The men are casual about the risks, but the visitors bunch closer together as they move further up the sewers, and begin to feel the remoteness of the place, for all its manholes and escape passages. There is a definite sense of potential panic in the claustrophobic brick labyrinth of chambers, tunnels, ladders and pipes, with upstairs a dozen lurking clouds that might deliver an inch of rain at any moment.

Is anyone ever hurt? "Someone *did* break his leg a while back," says Diplock.

"It was a bone in his *foot*," says Holden firmly. The dirt doesn't worry them much, either. They'd rather work down here than on the dustcarts anyday. That's really *filthy*.

In fact, more than half their work is on the surface, hauling silt and sludge, repainting manhole covers and tracing lost sewers. The main work underground is clearing up after overflows, and digging out the silt traps which catch the road grit. This is a job for barrows, buckets and winches at the moment, but it is eventually supposed to be done by machinery.

For this Holden, who has worked on the sewers for 30 years, takes home £75.80 for a 39-hour week. When he started, he says, it was £4.60 for a 47-hour week. After some thought he says yes, he is probably better off now, in some ways. It's not a lot of money for the nastiness of the work, and work moreover that is done cheerfully, with care and even with pride.

What if there was a union strike call in the New Year? Would they come out then? Yes, says Holden reluctantly, after even more thought. Then there would be no choice.

When the water workers called a one-day strike in October there was 100 per cent support. If the National Water Council is abolished, as planned, next April, it will be the last chance the unions have to fight for comparability on a national basis. So if the employers do not come up with an improved offer before January a strike looks certain. What is more, the workers know there is more money in the pot. The National Council was ready to offer 6.4 per cent in September until the government stepped in, which led to the resignation of the council's then chairman, Sir Robert Marshall.

The clean water workers at reservoirs and pumping stations are more militant than the sewermen, but they lack the same clout. Most clean water supplies are automated enough to keep running almost indefinitely. But three days of raw sewage into the Thames would kill off most of the 90 species of fish it has taken 20 years to nurture there. A couple of weeks of raw sewage and the doctors would be looking up cholera in the medical textbooks.

It is not a prospect that pleases the Brighton sewermen. "A strike would hit our families like anyone else's. People always seem to forget that," says Holden gloomily.

We have been standing at the back of the party, listening to Diplock holding forth on Victorian masonry again. But the crocodile is growing disconsolate. "We've been walking mi-iles!" says Darren/Tracy/Dean. "Mi-iss! Donna wants to go to the toi-ilet!"

"Tell her she's come to the right place," says Holden mercilessly, and stumps on to the next ladder.

But this time a manhole grates and light explodes at the top, and suddenly we are standing, blinking in the sunshine of the Old Steine Gardens in the middle of Brighton, just a few hundred yards from the seashore, with people shopping, eating sandwiches, getting on a bus.

Someone replaces the manhole cover, slots a section of railing into place above it, and the sewer is gone. The bus driver looks suspiciously at the crocodile of schoolchildren and adults in hard hats that has just materialised in the middle of the park.

"Another world," someone says, inadequately, and someone else repeats it, foolishly, like a toast. The sewerman snorts. "Another world," he says.

New Society, 16 December 1983

A little bit illegal

S mall, hairy and lightly stoned, Keith sits on the sofa opposite, discoursing on the world of drugs. An eloquent and measured speaker, his paragraphs are punctuated by thoughtful jokes – *sssscccchhhh … haaaa* – on a giant hubble-bubble pipe, ingeniously constructed from a fruit-juice jar.

"You know, one good thing that's come out of this McCartney bust is that he's gone on record as a doper. The Legalise Cannabis Campaign were on at him years ago to come clean."

"Another good thing," says Sue from the corner, "is that Linda can apply to the *Guinness Book of Records* with the fastest two busts in history."

An immoderate giggle comes from the shadows next to my chair, followed by a joint in a bodiless hand. "Pakistani black," says the hand. "Lots about at the moment." *Sssssccchhh ... haaaa.*

There are three people in the room apart from me – though it's hard to be certain as the only light comes from one of those four-watt bulbs that only heads seem able to buy. They are Keith, the dealer; Sue, university graduate and market stallholder; and the hand in the corner. A possible fourth person slumped against the far wall turns out to be an amicable Labrador, who shambles up later for a slobber.

It was very *odd*, everyone thinks, after all these years, to see that familiar old McCartney moon-mug, surfacing sincerely once again on the TV screen, to field all those same old, silly old press questions about drug addiction and corrupting the fans. Fifteen, or was it 17 years ago, after the Beatles' first bust, it all seemed a bit of a giggle. Just a matter of time really before the anti-cannabis laws simply *dissolved* in the general march of enlightenment, along with the royal family, the short-back-and-sides and Petula Clark.

Yet here we are, with the Legalise Cannabis Campaign practically defunct, and all the beautiful people who signed the famous letter to *The Times* in 1968 publicly recanting in the *Daily Mail*, and here is Keith, 17 years a smoker and four times busted, *still* having to be careful with the press. "I haven't dealt for three years now," he says. "Only the occasional half ounce for friends and that sort of thing." *Sssssccchhh ... haaaa.*

Back in the 1970s, Keith was shifting three of four "weights" (ie, pounds) a week out of the back of an ice cream van around the Birmingham suburbs, along with John Preece and Alston "Smiler" Hughes. Preece owned an ice cream factory and would sell cornets out of one window while Keith sold grass out of the other. Preece and Hughes were eventually sentenced to four and eight years apiece for their part in the "Operation Julie" LSD ring, and Keith moved to London, where he helped found the Legalise Cannabis Campaign.

His last bust was at a squat off the Essex Road in Islington in

1980 when four carloads of police turned up at 10 pm to smash down the door, break up the kitchen, tear down the ceiling tiles and eventually to arrest Keith for the possession of four ounces of grass and half a gram of cocaine. "I don't know why they didn't do me for dealing. The place was full of scales and wrap-bags and stuff. I just got a £70 fine for the hash, £50 for the analyst's fee and six months suspended over two years for the coke." *Sssscccchhh ... haaaa.*

Even at its busiest, though, Keith's dealing was small stuff. "A friend of mine used to drive a container full of dope off Manchester docks every week. Smiler's consignment used to be as long as that table and up to here." Keith draws a line at chest height. "And *that* would be gone in a week. And *he* wasn't a big dealer."

But most dealers aren't in it for the money, these people tell me. Of course there are a few criminals at the top, but that's the fault of the law. Most people just make enough to keep themselves in rent and dope. A kind of public service really. "Of course there's money to be made," says Sue, "but then people are taking a risk, aren't they?"

Sue first got into dope at Bristol University. "The people who smoked just seemed a whole lot *nicer*, you know? There was never any uptightness like you get in a pub." She doesn't smoke herself, but produces some hash-oil fudge, which starts Keith off on another reminiscence.

"I went to a party a while back where the lady running it met everyone at the door with a glass of mulled wine and a piece of naughty-cake. Don't use her name 'cos she's a solicitor. Anyway, she'd got the dope and the chocolate in the recipe the wrong way around, so there was a quarter weight in 15 of these little cakes ..."

The hand in the corner starts giggling again and passes another joint. "Th-at's s-ome ... really ... good Rocky," it says. "Very hard to get anything good from Morocco these days," says Keith. When it's around, it costs £56 an ounce, compared to £64 for Lebanese, £88 for black, and £11 a gram for oil. Keith probably gets through about half an ounce a week. "There was this *beautiful* Kerala a few weeks ago ... that's Indian grass."

"I ... thought ... Ke-ra-la ... came ... from Kat-man-du," says the hand in the corner. "India," says Keith firmly, and passes the joint on. *Sssscccchhhhh ... haaaa.*

Police seizures of cannabis (resin and grass) in the United Kingdom have grown steadily, from 10,223 seizures in 1973 to

21,446 in 1982, or in terms of quantity, from approximately nine tonnes to about 17½, Keith says even the biggest seizures have had practically no effect on the market. "I've had no trouble getting hold of dope at any time in the last five years," he says. And in spite of the image of cannabis as an over-30s drug for fading hippies, usage appears to have almost doubled since the early 1970s. Of the 20,319 people cautioned or convicted for drugs offences in 1982 17,410 were for cannabis; 54 per cent of the total were under 25 years old, and 78 per cent were under 30.

Keith doesn't worry about getting busted any more. "If I get caught walking down the road with a joint in my pocket it would be a very zealous copper who turned me in." Fines at Marylebone magistrates court, for a first offence of possessing marijuana, are between £3 and £5 and some police areas like South Yorkshire now just let people off with a caution.

Even so, outside London, you can still get a big fine for a first offence, or get sent to prison for a third or fourth offence of simple possession. In 1982 1,738 people were jailed for cannabis offences in the United Kingdom, and the proportion of cannabis convictions to all drug convictions has risen steadily from 45 per cent ten years ago to almost 88 per cent now.

"The ... po-lice ... are ... just ... a ... bunch ... of ... fuck-ing ... gangsters," says the hand in the corner. *Sssssssccccccbhhhhhhh ... haaaaaaa!*

And they go on some more about pigs and fuzz and stop-and-search, and they're absolutely right of course, and 20,000 arrests a year is an enormous and stupid waste of public money, and 1,700 people in jail is no joke, and there's no evidence that moderate use of cannabis does any harm, so why is it hard to take entirely seriously?

The answer has something to do with the asinine smirk of Linda McCartney as she waved her peace sign at the Heathrow photographers. It's still us against the straights. The McCartneys are probably rich enough to *buy* Heathrow Airport if they wanted to. So why are they getting busted in the customs hall like a pair of penniless heads back from Katmandu? The only answer seems to be that in some obscure way they *wanted* to be.

And for the dope smokers at large, though they'd deny it to the last toke, their relationship with the cannabis laws is a symbiotic one. Just as the police need the cheerfully inept dopers to keep up the arrest rate, so the heads need the law in order to *be* heads. To fuel all the giggly anecdotes about scores and highs and munchies; of busts and near-busts. To remove the wrinkles from a poor-quality lifestyle and to provide a satisfactory sense of persecution. To keep at bay the straight world of jobs and unemployment and old age.

Of course they should decriminalise cannabis, though it's hard to imagine a government with the balls to do it in the face of the Fleet Street reaction. But perhaps they should keep just a *little* law against it, to keep it just a *little* bit naughty.

New Society, 26 January 1984

The animal rights brigade

John Stuart Mill, an intellectual father of animal rights, once wrote: "All great movements go through three stages: ridicule, discussion, acceptance." So let's start with some ridicule.

In the reception area of the British Union for the Abolition of Vivisection is a carrier bag of tinned dog food and an ideological confrontation. The tins are being collected for miners' dogs, apparently suffering as much as their masters from the effects of the pit strike. But some BUAV staff disapprove of meat-eating dogs and are boycotting the carrier bag. Others disapprove of pet dogs *per se*, as an anachronistic and humiliating master/slave relationship. Still others disapprove of miners because they tend to be fond of fox hunting. The bag fills slowly.

In another corner is a poster of a shapely model girl trailing a mink stole behind her. "A hundred dumb animals died to dress one dumb animal," says the caption. Is this sexist? The staff of BUAV are divided.

There is much about the animal rights movement that mirrors the broader political left, with its welter of blinkered factions, snapping over the dry bones of rival orthodoxies. Much of the same conviction that can turn all grapefruit eaters into agents of apartheid, all mortgage payers into crypto capitalists, and all men into rapists.

A pursuit of compassion that expresses itself in petrol bombs, and an advocacy of equality that leads to a Calvinist elitism of the saved.

Emma Peel, a 24 year old activist with the Animal Liberation Front, is trying to be a fruitarian. "You can eat apples and pears and husks of corn but you leave the plant to grow. Potatoes and onions are out of course." And yes, her name is a joke, for they are not without wit, the ALF. The latest slogans of the movement are Dig Deep for the Duke of Beaufort, and Dig for Victory. The forthcoming trial of the Hunt Retribution Squad members who attempted to exhume the unfortunate peer is, inevitably, the Duke Box Jury.

I should say at this point that the separation between the ALF, which claims to avoid "serious violence" against people, and the more shadowy, avowedly violent groups like the Animal Rights Militia and Hunt Retribution Squad, seemed to me to be one of tactical convenience. They are clearly often the same people flying different flags.

Anyway, today Emma Peel is eating beans and chips with a Bacardi and Coke, as the best compromise vegetarian meal you can get in this sleazy Hammersmith pub. She is fashionably dressed in black beret and black drop-waist frock. Quite attractive, quite likeable, and quite, quite dotty.

Her family are decayed German nobility: father a dog breeder and mother a secretary. she went to a posh Kent grammar school but dropped out before 'O' levels. "They were pushing me toward a future I didn't want – that whole Oxbridge mould of things." She worked in hunt kennels, stables and vegetarian restaurants. She joined Amnesty and CND but left those quickly. "Everyone wanted some sort of reform within the system while keeping the system basically as it is." She tried suicide. "Before the ALF I was in hospital three times. I can't understand a life that isn't lived to the full in terms of commitment and passion. The alternative to the ALF would just be to kill myself."

Emma was not involved in any of the recent big ALF stunts: the Mars bar hoax, the Christmas turkey scare, and the petrol bomb attacks on the homes of employees of the Wellcome research labs in Kent. "But I did deal with the press for that. The *Daily Star* quoted me in a headline, saying 'We Don't Care If People Die'. I thought of complaining to the Press Council."

The ALF does not approve of killing people except in self-defence. Ronnie Lee, the leading figure of the movement, told me:

"I think using guns might be justified, but it would be wrong for the ALF as a movement to do it." Emma explains that it is a matter of public relations rather than scruples. "I tend to despise the life of Joe Public. Most people are animal abusers of one kind or another. The only reason I don't approve of killing them is because we need more people in the ALF – and they have to come from the public." On the other hand, she says, if a majority of ALF members decided it was time to start killing the public then that would be okay by her. Some of this must be taken with a grain of salt. The ALF consistently exaggerates the scale and ferocity of its attacks in its press releases, which, of course, are eagerly echoed by the newspapers. So far as I can discover, nobody has ever been even slightly injured by the ALF. Emma Peel is a fan of the Situationists of the 1960s. "We want to create situations that jog people into thinking about the everyday condition of their lives." And certainly there is some born publicist within the ALF with a natural talent for touching off the fuse of respectable outrage, whether by digging up dead dukes or poisoning the Christmas turkey, that central symbol of family order, ritual and unity.

The ideology of the Animal Liberation Front is simplicity itself. A total end to animal abuse, including all commercial farming, all animal experimentation and all forms of hunting. When would they feel their campaign had succeeded? "The ALF would continue until meat eating was made illegal worldwide," says Emma. And even then, she adds wistfully, there would probably be a black market that would have to be dealt with. This would be achieved solely through direct action. "If we thought people could be persuaded we would just hand out leaflets. It's because they *can't* be persuaded that they must be forced."

All this would mean, Ronnie and Emma both acknowledge, a complete social revolution, "far greater than any socialist revolution". The eventual shape of the future society is a little hazy but would probably involve things like intermediate technology and small, anarchist collectives. "Human beings would have to withdraw to pre-exploitation boundaries," says Ronnie. "Probably with compulsory vasectomisation to reduce the population," says Emma.

So much for the ridiculous. What about the discussion stage of John Stuart Mill's formula? How far has animal rights entered into the arena of respectable public debate? A recent leading article in the *Guardian* demanded to know the basis for animal rights. "Rights," it said, "are a human invention, derived from the system of laws for the regulation of human societies, and ... other species have no part in them. The same laws have laid down duties, and it is hard to see how the two categories can be separated. What are the duties of animals?" The ALF, it concluded, "will have to call themselves to order and present a coherent case if they are to carry any conviction".

The leader writer seems to have decided to substitute lofty tone for some modest effort, since libraries are stuffed with books on animal rights. It is one of the hottest topics in philosophy departments these days, with an impressive academic backing, including Tom Regan, professor of philosophy at North Carolina; Peter Singer, professor of philosophy at Monash University in Melbourne; Stephen Clark, professor of philosophy at Liverpool; Mary Midgley, the philosopher author of *Beast and Man*; and so on and so forth.

The justification for animal exploitation has always been based on the claim that there is clear, qualitative distinction between man and animal. This was expressed most radically by Descartes who maintained that animals were no more than machines, like clockwork automata, without soul or reason, and unable to experience pain, fear or hope.

The development of the life sciences, and particularly of evolutionary theory, has eroded this position considerably. Many people now accept that man is a very clever kind of animal, rather than a different order of being. The vital difference between us and them is now variously held to lie in things like language, transmitted culture, or that elusive quality we call "consciousness". A man, the argument goes, has awareness of the past and plans for the future, so his death is a more dreadful thing that the death of a gerbil, which is assumed to have no plans.

The problem, as animal rights philosophers like Tom Regan and Peter Singer point out, is that all these "unique" qualities can be shown to be present in some degree in animals. Some primates have a limited ability to acquire language and transmit culture. Even a dog, waiting at the door for its master to come home, can be argued to have some consciousness of the future. What is more, say the philosophers, there are plenty of humans who *don't* have these essential human qualities. Babies, so far as we can prove, don't have any more language, culture or plans than a gerbil, though they could be argued to have a *potential* for these things. Severely mentally subnormal humans do not have any potential so why don't we experiment on them, or even eat them? "Whatever test we propose as a means for separating humans from animals," says Singer, "it is plain that if all animals fail it then some humans will fail it too."

The gulf between us and animals may not be as wide as we would like to think, but it is wide enough to make it impossible for animals to play a part in the reciprocal system of rights and duties which we call society. It is a popular view of society, known to philosophy as contractarianism, the idea being that we are signatories to some invisible social contract. My duty not to hit you is your right not to be hit. Since animals cannot sign the contract and cannot carry out any duties, therefore they can't have any rights.

Singer's reply to this is that contractarianism is an inadequate description of a moral society. It is possible to have a contract which oppresses a minority, or even as in South Africa, a majority of the population. Apartheid is a social contract yet we do not hesitate to condemn it, so we must be referring to some higher notion of what is "right". This higher notion of right Singer describes as the "inherent value" of humans and animals. So far as I understand him he seems to argue that animal rights are a kind of squatters' right – the right to freedom from gratuitous persecution, the right to space – which is derived from the simple fact that animals were *put here* by whatever agency that put *us* here. If they have no rights to the world then neither do we.

The arguments and counter-arguments go on, but it is enough to say here that Singer and Regan at least make out a respectable case. It didn't stop me eating a bacon sandwich while writing this, but it did give me cause for thought.

It is Singer and Regan, in particular, who have provided the intellectual ballast for the enormous growth in animal rights campaigns in the last ten years. The degree of commitment to *pure* animal rights also tends to serve as a rough-and-ready yardstick to the degree of violence or direct action the various animal groups are prepared to contemplate. The Hunt Saboteurs, who were founded in 1971, and the Animal Liberation Front, which appeared around 1976, are wholeheartedly committed.

Older, single-issue groups like the British Union for the Abolition of Vivisection and the National Anti-Vivisection Society were founded in the late 19th and early 20th century, often as splinter groups from the Royal Society for the Prevention of Cruelty to Animals. In recent years, these older groups have been stimulated by an influx of radicals, and will usually maintain a modified commitment to animal rights with a support for non-violent direct action. The more conservative political lobbying and welfare groups like the League Against Cruel Sports, (founded 1924) and the RSPCA (1824) tend to avoid the animal rights debate altogether and to condemn any extra-legal action, although both groups have animal rightists among their leadership. The League was effectively taken over by former hunt saboteurs a few years ago, and even the RSPCA has now adopted an anti-blood sports policy, in spite of the activities of its royal patrons.

"The big move in the last ten years," says Angela Walder, scientific officer of the British Union for the Abolition of Vivisection, "is the shift from animal welfare to animal rights. It seems that men especially don't find animal welfare so exciting, and there is a lot of doublethink. You know, the old lady with 20 cats and two fur coats." The cat 'n' dog loving, anthropomorphic, Disneyish attitude to animals is something the radicals are desperately anxious to discard. "We strongly dislike the term 'animal lover'," says Walder. "It is a derogatory term like nigger lover." Though most radicals will admit to keeping pets, it is not politically kosher. Even conservationism is regarded with suspicion. "I'd rather there weren't any animals left on the face of the earth," Walder says. "When the last whale is dead, it will be the last one they can harpoon."

Ridicule, discussion – acceptance. How much acceptance has been achieved for the ideas of animal rights, and what may it achieve in the future? Surveys by National Opinion Polls show that around 80 per cent of people in Britain are now opposed to hunting with dogs. John Bryant, wildlife officer of the League Against Cruel Sports, says he feels it is only a matter of time now before fox, stag and hare hunting are made illegal. Factory farming continues to flourish, but even the most dedicated carnivore tends to feel queasy about veal these days, and to buy free-range eggs when they can be found. It does not seem inconceivable that we may one day regard a steak with the same distaste with which we now regard the Elizabethan habit of eating songbirds.

The most bitterly contested area, and the one, accordingly, where the ideological conflicts are in sharpest relief, is the use of animals in research. The government will shortly be introducing a revised White Paper on animal experiments (a first version was published last year). The aim is to replace the Cruelty to Animals Act, 1876, which originally outlawed vivisection in its literal sense of "cutting up alive". All animal experimentation projects will have to be licensed by the Home Office in addition to the present system of licensing the scientist himself. The White Paper will also include a "pain clause", which will attempt to ban the causing of pain for trivial purposes, by measuring pain against the importance of the experiment.

The White Paper has the general approval of reformist groups like the RSPCA but is bitterly opposed by radical groups, who have formed a joint organisation, known as "Mobilisation", to oppose it. They argue that it will actually weaken the 1876 Act by allowing animals to be subject to more than one experiment and by allowing surgeons to practice microsurgical techniques on living animals. Furthermore, it will not ban experiments in the tobacco, cosmetics or armaments industries. Tests like the outdated LD-50, which gauges the toxicity of a given substances by administering it to a group of animals until 50 per cent are dead, and the Draize test, which involves squirting things like shampoo into the eyes of rabbits, will still be allowed.

The defenders of animal research, like the Research Defence Society (which is heavily funded by drug companies), argue that animal experiments have already fallen from 5.6 million in 1976 to 3.5 million today: less than 0.45 per cent of these are experiments on cosmetics; and an even smaller percentage are for tobacco. The overwhelming majority, about five sixths of the total, are for medical research. As for the LD-50 and Draize tests, these are still required by foreign governments for the export of drugs, and are in any case falling into disuse.

Tim Biscoe, professor of physiology at University College, London, has been cutting up mice for the last ten years and expects to be doing it for the next five. He is investigating a particular mutant strain of spastic mice. It might be useful in treating human spastics or it might not. He doesn't particularly care either way. "I believe scientists advance knowledge because they are interested in the natural world. That is sufficient in itself. It is a cultural activity because it improves and expands the mind."

He sounds harsher than he is. A slight, boyish-looking man of 50 or so full of enthusiasm for his work; impatient with those who, as he sees it, want a return to the Dark Ages. Of course, the research often does turn out to be useful. "In 1950, when I was at med school, there was no proper treatment for TB. By the time I left, the TB wards were emptying, and that was all animal-based research." And he reels off some of the medical advances that depended on animal experiments: polio and smallpox vaccines, renal dialysis, transplants, microsurgery, safe anaesthetics, blood transfusions, practically every drug in the British Pharmocopoeia. Every batch of some established vaccines like polio is still tested on animals to spot "wild" batches.

What about the anti-vivisectionist argument that science should look for alternatives, like computer modelling and tissue cultures? "We do use alternatives where appropriate," Tim Biscoe says. "Who wants to use animals? They're a bloody nuisance, and expensive. But to treat the body you need to look at whole bodies." I try the Martian argument on him. What if a race of super-intelligent Martians invade earth and decide to kill, eat, and experiment on humans? "Show me a Martian," says Biscoe.

Then what about experiments on mentally disabled people? If you can experiment on animals, why not on them? "It's because they have relationships with other people – family, nurses, whatever. You don't experiment on pets for the same reasons."

Tim Biscoe would cheerfully chop up 1,000 animals on the basis of scientific curiosity alone. Emma Peel wouldn't kill a hamster even if it was certain to save a dozen human lives. These are irreconcilable moral positions. Of course the Situationists of the ALF will never get anywhere near their ideal world of compulsory vasectomy and fruitarian collective, but it is a measure of the acceptance already won by the rag-taggle brigades of animal rights that it is the superior disinterested world of the scientists that is on the defensive now.

New Society, 31 January 1985

Kith and kings

'Di's thighs surprise" was the front page headline in the *Daily Star* the other day, over a picture of Princess Diana showing an inch or two of knee as she climbed from her official Daimler. So "hopping mad" is "our Di" at attempts by Fleet Street snappers to get a crotch-shot as she clambers from her car that she is reported to be spending £60,000 on a new, peep-proof motor.

It's a classic royal "story": a homely touch, a dash of sex, a flash of wealth and a dollop of malicious envy. Not an ounce of truth in it, I would imagine, but mostly undeniable or not worth denying. Pure candyfloss, spun around the most usable picture of the day. This Princess of Wales has little to do with a body called Diana Spencer. It is more a kind of communal daydream amplified and authorised by the newspapers.

Two years ago the *Sunday Express* magazine published a series of articles on a "week in the life" of the royals, loftily claiming to be a corrective to this kind of thing. A portrait of the royals as ordinary, hard-working and so forth, though of course it ended up as yet another orgy of fascinating "personal" revelation.

Did you know, for instance, that the Queen's car has no handles on the outside? Or that she is the only person in Britain not required to have a dog licence? Did you know the Queen Mother has a bookmaker's wire service "blower" in Clarence House? That the royals carry a full set of mourning clothes wherever they go in case one of the other ones dies? That Highgrove has a steel room for the Prince and Princess of Wales to retire to in case of terrorist attack? That Sandringham produces most of the blackcurrants for Ribena? That Prince Haakon of Norway is 38th in line to the throne? That Buckingham Palace is believed to have a secret branch line to the London Underground?

No, I didn't know, either, and didn't particularly want to. But for some reason they stick in the mind like a burr. A special kind of non-information, both fascinating and unilluminating.

People like me who grew up in the republican 1960s are still angry and baffled by the whole royals phenomenon. They were hardly a presence in, say, 1965. No twinkly, heartwarming royal story at the end of every newscast. No feverish speculation in the tabloids about this one's love affairs or that one's hat. The royals were obscure folk in fantastically out-moded clothes, who performed mildly comic, but apparently necessary ceremonial functions, much as Black Rod knocked on the Commons door every November, or the Druids assembled at the solstice. Nobody could have made a living impersonating the Queen or Prince Charles on television.

Something happened, but what? Many argue it was the TV film, *The Royal Family*, in 1969 which started the rehabilitation by showing the royals as an ordinary family, arguing, eating a barbecue, breaking a cello string and so on. My only memory of the programme is of Prince Philip tending a barbecue in a dark lounge suit and poking disgustedly at a sausage. But there may be something in it, not because it showed the royals as ordinary – they aren't – but because this showed they could command television to wait upon them, and he who commands television commands attention.

Another view is that they provided a kind of bastion of tradition and continuity after the turbulence of the sixties. Right wing commentators like Paul Johnson go so far as to credit them with responsibility for what he sees as our current moral revival, as if they had somehow staved off the moral and social collapse promoted by people like Mick Jagger and Roy Jenkins, simply by dint of continuing to keep corgis and to wear unfashionable dark lounge suits, side partings and flowery hats.

Not that "tradition" and "continuity" are politically neutral terms. Such notions were at the heart of the recent miners' strike, and it was often the most fervent royalists who were the most savage critics of the miners. Tradition and continuity are admirable in some contexts, but in others they become "out-moded", "wasteful" – even "uneconomic".

Once again, though, there must be something in this idea. The decade of anachronism – of the urban squirearchy of the Sloane Rangers, the synthetic gentility of Neo-Georgians and ersatz rurality of Laura Ashley is also the decade of the revival of what Edmund Leach called the "irrational theatre" of monarchy. Not a real return to "traditional values" because the royals behave no better than the rest of us, but the creation of a kind of public fantasy as comforting as Winceyette pyjamas.

The royals are simply too symmetrical to be real; the firm mother, the irascible father, twinkly gran, naughty aunt, earnest son, his delinquent bachelor brother and bossyboots sister – plus a string of marriages, births and minor scandals. Too real to be real they can only be seen as a kind of avatar, a projection of national fantasy life.

For all the dozen of reporters who pursue them, and the titbits of information they obtain, we do not really know anything about the royals at all. Their personae are castles of meringue built on cobwebs. Prince Edward scrapes into Jesus College on three poor 'A' levels and he is "Educated Eddy" the intellectual royal. Prince Charles diffidently unwraps some public bar clichés about modern building and he is anointed an architectural savant. Princess Diana bulk-buys half of Harvey Nichols and she is a leader of fashion. She admits to listening to Capital Radio and she is Disco Di, the Dancing Princess.

A piece of real, publicly available information like Princess Michael's Nazi father can lie unnoticed for years, while inconvenient facts which do not fit, like the Royals' passion for blood sports, or Princess Diana's fondness for Rachmaninov, simply slip down the memory hole of the media and are ignored.

Some years ago a book appeared called *Dreams About the Queen,* which described the various forms in which the monarch appeared to her subjects in their sleep. It seems that such dreams are almost common as the archetypal Freudian ones: flying around the house; appearing naked in a public place; sitting an examination unprepared; having all your teeth fall out and so forth. Like the Freudian dreams, too, they tend to express both fear and desire.

Fear and desire characterise our conversations about royalty also – our waking daydreams. In these we may swap anecdotes of the royal family's wealth, power and privilege – placing ourselves in their roles. Or we may play the envy game, demoting them to ordinary life by discussing their sexual irregularities, their stuffiness, arrogance and good fortune – speculating where they would be without the accidents of birth or marriage.

Princess Diana, for instance, because of her looks and rather dim academic record, would have to be a check-out girl – but in a rather superior supermarket like Waitrose or Sainsbury's. Prince Charles, agonisedly dutiful and sober, would be a social worker – perhaps a probation officer. Princess Anne – a farmer's wife. Prince Andrew – a bingo caller. The Duke of Edinburgh, with his vehement opinions, mechanical aptitude and short fuse, would be a taxi driver. The Queen's stately demeanour and renowned efficiency would make her a first-rate sub-postmistress. The Queen Mother would have married a successful publican or bookmaker, and would fulfil much the same social role as she does now, albeit on a more local scale. Princess Michael of Kent would have, indeed *has* risen whatever her social background. In a republican Britain she'd be married to a rock star.

It's a good game, but is it good for us? Whether we are imagining ourselves among the great, or the great to be among ourselves, such fantasies have always existed. The difference from the fantasies of the 1960s, which centred on film stars, pop idols, models and sportsmen, is that they were, however remotely, achievable fantasies. Michael Caine, George Best and Twiggy were at least in principle imitable whereas royalty is not.

Princess Diana is plucked from obscurity to become a world celebrity but it is a magical transformation; not something you could emulate, only dream about. It is for this reason that royalty is hated as well as worshipped. (Look out for the undertow of malice in any tabloid story.) However envious you might be of George Michael you have to allow him his talent. Princess Diana's sudden elevation is more pure and more thrilling because of its adventitious nature, but this sense of pure fortune also makes us more spiteful. We envy the millionaire tycoon, but we envy *and despise* the millionaire pools winner.

Some of the more intelligent royals, like the Queen and Prince Charles, seem to be conscious of this, and to worry about it. The way the press turned so savagely on Princes Michael over her father's Nazi past *is* just a hint of what could happen to a real icon like Princess Diana if, for some reason, the wind began to change, as change it eventually must. We need the fantasy family of royalty in these uncertain times, but everyone grows up and leaves home sooner or later.

New Society, 20/27 December 1985

The garden bug

' **A** igh aargh ungh obrergig gargigger," says Geoffrey Smith. He swallows the piece of very dry Gala pie that is causing the problem, and tries again.

"I am an obsessive gardener. Far more so now than 10 years ago. As you get older it just gets worse."

He is older, and stouter than he looks on *World of Flowers*, his hugely popular television series. A tall, florid man with a silver slashback and military shoulders. He has one of those relentless, high-pitched Yorkshire voices that is the ballast to a passionate, poetic involvement in plant life which would make any less formidable man sound like a pansy.

A one-time gardener's boy and head of Harlow Car Gardens, he is also a panellist on Radio Four's *Gardeners' Question Time*, which is why he is sitting here today in Weston Rhyn village hall in Shropshire, poking at a pie and lettuce leaf that is naked of a drop of salad dressing. "Very acceptable at this time of year, a good salad," he says gallantly, and the tiny, shrivelled old ladies who are pouring tea and buttering bread, flutter with pleasure like dry leaves.

Further along the table is Clay Jones, the chairman and vegetable expert, stoking up a pipe the size of a coal scuttle, and further along still is Dr Stefan Buczacki, a bearded gnome, arguing intensely about the wild garden and ecological balances.

They are all here to record the 1,691st edition of *Gardeners' Question Time* in the hall next door, where even now the audience are shuffling to their seats, while I am here, well, to find out about gardening. No, I am here to find out why all my friends are suddenly interested in gardening, and why I, who used to sneer at my father, browsing among his brassica, suddenly find myself spending hundreds of pounds in the local garden centre, and suddenly able to remember the absurd Latin names of plants that were once as forgettable as knitting patterns.

What is Geoffrey Smith's diagnosis of this strange disease, I ask him. "You're a peasant," he says brusquely, then adds with the smile, and the timing of a professional raconteur, "and I am a peasant. Scratch anybody and you find a peasant. When the chips are down we all turn to the soil."

All right, but what has that got to do with growing roses and house plants and flowering shrubs that are food only for greenfly? "Ah," says Smith, "There's a Chinese proverb. If you have two yen you should spend one on a loaf of bread and one on a rose."

Which leads us on to China. "An unopened treasure house of plants," says Smith. And then on to "Chinese" Wilson, the greatest plant hunter of all time, who persuaded the ferocious Boxer rebels to find plants for him; and then to the plant hunter Robert Fortune, who founded the tea industry in Sri Lanka and India; and then to the Tradescants, father and son, who explored Muscovy in the Elizabethan age, and have left us their names in a hundred common plants. "When you hold a plant, you hold the threads of history in your hands," says Smith, and the rest of the table is silent, listening to him.

When they do finally get up to troop into the hall next door, Smith's eye falls on a bowl of fresh carnations on the tea table. He carries it tenderly up to the stage and places it next to his microphone, stroking the petals from time to time during the broadcast.

The hall, of fumed oak hammer beams and dusty mullioned windows, is packed with a sea of green tweed and grey permanent waves. About 200 members and friends of the Weston Rhyn Gardening Club have turned up. They have waited ten years since they invited *Gardeners' Question Time* to pay them a visit, and nobody is about to miss it.

Many of the faces are familiar now, after two days of touring the gardens of this quiet Shropshire village. There is Jack Hirst, 75, the chairman of the club and a former Mersey Tunnel policeman (specialities: fuchsias and ash trees); there is Jack Draper, 78, a retired cobbler from the Old Mill House (apples, daffodils and dahlias); there is farmer's widow, Louise Beddows, from Chirk Bank area (conifers and a prize bougainvillaea) and there is Myfanwy Davenport, the harpist and church organist from St Marton's (rhododendrons and forsythias).

It is the fortieth anniversary of *Gardeners' Question Time* next year. The old team of Professor Alan Gemmell, Bill Sowerbutts and Fred Loads, are all retired, or dead now, after 30 years continuous service together, but the format has hardly changed at all: questions from the audience on the ailments of tomatoes, dahlias and yuccas; technical answers from Stefan, flowers from Geoffrey, and veg from Clay Jones, all seasoned with a gentle trickle of intimate bickering and earthy anecdote.

First questioner is George Wright who, appropriately enough, is the local carpenter. He produces a very sad looking tomato plant, which Stefan promptly slits open with a penknife.

"You didn't want your plant back, did you Mr Wright?" asks Clay, mildly.

"Where do you get your soil from?" asks Geoffrey.

"We've got fields all around us," says Wright.

"So you pop out at night and pinch some soil, do you? says Smith with mock severity. "You've got brown root rot from infected soil."

"Our market gardener didn't think so," says Wright stubbornly.

"He wants to sell you more tomato plants," says Smith. "It's root rot."

"I think it could be a virus in your rainwater butt," says Stefan the Scientist.

"It's root rot," says Clay Jones. So root rot wins, two to one.

When *Gardeners' Question Time* was launched, in 1947, Britain was in the middle of its first post-war gardening boom. *The Times* even printed a special weekly gardening supplement, which remarked, in 1950, that "the popularity of gardening varies inversely with the prosperity of the nation." The drabness and austerity of post-war Britain made people turn to their gardens for food and for colour, and so too, perhaps, today, with the oil crises and inflation of the 1970s, followed by the unemployment of the 1980s.

According to *Gardening Which?* there certainly has been a boom in the last 10 years. Plant sales are growing at around 20 per cent a year and this year alone are expected to reach £850 million. There are now between 1,200 and 1,300 garden centres in Britain, most of them established since 1970.

Not that many of the gardeners of Weston Rhyn would set foot in a garden centre. They grow everything from cuttings which they get from other club members and from seeds they buy at Dobies in Llangollen.

So there is a class divide in gardening. The young urban gardener who frequents the garden centre (let us call him YUG for short – he's a Yuppie in wellies) sees a garden as something to be *done up* as he *does up* his house. It is an outside room to get finished, so it can be viewed from the French windows, or used as a setting for Sunday drinks parties. The more traditional gardener, let us call him the Weston Rhyn Gardener, or WERG for short, sees his garden as a continuing pastime, as an end in itself, which goes on until he drops.

These different attitudes produce different styles. The typical WERG garden is highly labour intensive: a large rectangular lawn, to be mowed each week into jailhouse stripes; straight beds of turned earth, like fresh graves, that need constant weeding, and masses of tender plants that have to be bedded out each season in *Champs Elysées* of red, white and blue.

The YUG garden, on the other hand, should need no gardening at all. Trees and shrubs are evergreen and slow growing, beds are covered in ground cover plants so there is no weeding, and there is most definitely *no lawn*. There may be cobbles, granite sets, yorkstone flags, graded pebbles or hardwood decking, but under no circumstances a *lawn*.

In the YUG garden, slashes of colour are out, and muted symphonies of grey, green, silver and brown are in. The only really acceptable flowers are creamy white, like Mexican orange blossom, or palest pastel, like dwarf narcissi. Favoured plants are snowdrops, cyclamens, helebores, hostas and castor oil plants.

WERG gardens, by contrast, are a riot of colour with spring bulbs, wallflowers, aubretias, roses, and perennials. Favourite plants here are mop head hydrangeas like old ladies' hats, brilliant floribunda roses like tarts' tea cosies, and big yellow King Alfred daffodils like poached eggs on sticks.

I express no preference for these competing orthodoxies, but merely note them in passing. Like the English house, the English garden is a vernacular hotch potch made up of inherited prejudices, borrowed influences and stolen cuttings. WERG style owes something to the formality of *Le Nôtre* at Versailles and the stiffness of J. C. Loudon's Victorian villa gardens. YUG style borrows from the austerity of Capability Brown and the simplicity of Gertrude Jekyll, but they are both bastard children, unloved by their parents.

Until 1800, there was no official style in gardening, apart from the large, country house garden, which evolved from the formal, geometric fashions of the 16th and 17th centuries, through the bleak "natural" landscapes of Capability Brown, which relied entirely on grass and trees, to the more colourful landscapes of Humphrey Repton in the 1790s.

These gardens were *big*. "Even the smallest garden," says the handbook of the 1800s, "*must* have at least three acres of rough woodland." A big garden these days is a quarter of an acre, but the influences are there if you look hard, through the corner of an eye: the handkerchief of lawn, descended from the vast parkland which once proclaimed "I am so rich I do not need to grow turnips"; the geometric flower bed that mimics the great formal *parterres* of Versailles; the shrubberies that hint at ancestral woodlands; and the vegetable patches that echo arable empires.

The nearest thing to a great garden in Weston Rhyn, is Stella Jones' three acres in Chirk Bank, which, although the house is a tiny bungalow, is a pleasing sweep of lawns and fruit trees and informal beds merging, in good Reptonian style, with the surrounding countryside. The only discordant note is Alfie, a totemic sculpture in the middle of the lawn, painted crudely in the likeness of a face, with a pipe in its mouth and a plaque hanging from one ear, which reads, simply: "F. C. Glover", and which marks, Miss Jones explains, the grave of her former gardener, Fred. "Old Fred always used to talk to Alfie, and say 'Alfie, I'll be down there with you one day.' So now he is."

Miss Jones' new gardener, Bill Evans, is a sprightly 76, from Criccieth in north Wales, who claims he was wheeled in his pram by Megan Lloyd George, daughter of David. He has quite the most erratic shaving pattern I have ever seen, and a Welsh accent so strong it sounds like German. Like Fred before him, Bill works in the garden every day for no money: just his dinner and his petrol and the love of it, and I leave, wondering at the power Miss Jones wields over her gardeners.

Small, suburban gardens as we know them hardly existed before the 1840s, but alongside the great country house was always the cottage garden, though it went mostly unremarked until "discovered" by William Robinson and Gertrude Jekyll in the late 19th century, and revived as a suburban style.

Jack Draper's acre or so of vegetables and flowers and fruit in Weston Rhyn is a perfect example of the unplanned, higgledy-piggledy style. Not that it is untidy. Jack's house, which was once a water mill, is semi-derelict, but, at 78 years old, and with a grumbling prostate, Jack keeps the garden immaculate.

He comes from Wallasey on Merseyside, and lived here first as a lodger, in 1928, when he courted and married the miller's daughter. He served in the war and in the Normandy landings. "I loved Normandy. There were apples everywhere." When he came back he planted his own apples over the dried up millstream, and they are still his favourites, along with dahlias and daffodils that line the banks of the lane. "All flowers I like. Anything real showy."

The Victorians liked showiness too, but not in the chaotic, cottage style. Victorians invented the suburban garden, and it was typical victorian product: formal, restrained, educational, and very hard work. Its prophet was John Claudius Loudon, a high minded and ferociously energetic Victorian whose great, and now entirely unreadable work was *The Suburban Gardener and Villa Companion.* This divided gardens precisely into first, second, third and fourth-rate gardens, and decreed a style you can still see in some big suburban gardens today. My own grandfather designed one in the suburbs of Swansea for his employer, a local doctor, and there are traces of it still. It had winding gravel paths, geometric beds of tender plants, isolated "specimen" shrubs set out in lawns of cropped velvet, sombre laurel hedges and gloomy monkey puzzle trees. Hardy "cottage" plants were despised, and daffodils were weeds.

Myfanwy Davenport's elegant bungalow garden in Weston Rhyn is the closest thing locally to Loudon's "gardenesque" style. It has shaved lawns, with edges cut clean as a cheese; central, geometric beds, choice shrubs, and a wall of dark holly. It even has the Victorian death motif, in the form of a brick garden shed, that was once the mortuary for a local colliery, Myfanwy's husband Sid shows me the mortuary slab, that is now part of his garden path, with its sinister central gutter and drainage hole still visible. "I used to be a medical pathologist," says Sid cheerfully, "so it doesn't bother me."

Myfanwy tells how she recently found a dead man. She was in the hairdressers' when a husband failed to arrive to collect his wife, who was in the next chair. Myfanwy and the hairdresser set off to find him, and discovered him locked in his garage, stone dead at the wheel of his car. "The hose pipe from the exhaust had slipped from his mouth and was lying on his chest," she says. "He was 82. No reason to do it at all."

We had to leave *Gardeners' Question Time* before the end, I'm afraid, so I can't give you the answer to Jack Hirst's question about propagating gel, or Gladys Bason's query about pruning a Prostrate Juniper. That will all be broadcast on 8 June in any case. On our way to the motorway we asked directions from a pretty teenage girl, and the photographer with me remarked that she was the first person we had seen in three days with her own teeth.

Looking back on all the images of death which seemed to cluster around our visit, from Fred the gardener's bizarre interment under his totem pole, to Myfanwy's mortuary, there does seem to be something gloomy and stoical about the business of gardening. The word itself is a metaphor for turning away from the world and coming to terms with its conclusion: hoeing your own row; tending your own cabbage patch; watching your garden grow. So perhaps that is why it seems such an appropriate activity for a period of decline and pessimism.

New Society, 16 May 1986

Chaps in frocks

Why should women priests split the Church of England? As the opposition to the idea illustrates – from crypto-Catholic to tambourine fundamentalist – the Church of England is already a wonderfully heterogeneous body. Who would notice a few girls among all the eccentric chaps in frocks.

I am much more interested in the Bishop of Durham's views on laser beams. We should not, says the bishop, expect God to do miracles like a celestial laser beam. But if He cannot outdo a simple laser beam, what on earth is the point of Him? A God who cannot turn water into wine is not going to hold out much hope of eternal life.

If the Church and Christianity are no more than a moral framework with some spiritual uplift thrown in, there are plenty of secular alternatives – like existential humanism – which don't require you to spend Sunday morning getting sore knees and singing Victorian doggerel.

Dr Runcie, the Archbishop of Canterbury, says he is frustrated by the amount of time being devoted to ecclesiastical and doctrinal matters when the Church could be getting on with things that really matter.

Why? If the Church has no foundation then it can hardly be mine. The Church is not an anti-apartheid movement, or an inner city monitoring unit or a women's rights organisation. Neither is it a bring and buy sale, an architectural preservation club or a "bring back the Prayer Book" society. If it is about anything it is about the awkward question of belief, which the legendary Reverend J. C. Flannel contrives so adroitly to avoid, but of which the Bishop of Durham disturbingly reminds us.

New Society, 11 July 1986

Sex stereotypes

A reader writes to complain about the number of sex stereotypes in this column. She is right, I know, and one is not supposed to notice any differences between men and women these days, apart from the obvious ones in the matter of wedding tackle, but I find it a difficult habit to break.

I am convinced, for example, that men are much dirtier than women, but make up for it by being tidier. A man living on his own, or any man who is not closely watched, will get into all sorts of disgusting habits. He will blow his nose on the sheets, pee in the sink, pick his teeth with used tube tickets and leave surreptitious bogeys on the underside of cinema seats.

On the other hand I have never met a woman who did not have a passion for collecting plastic carrier bags, for stuffing them inside other carrier bags and hanging them untidily on door handles. I have never met one either who is able to close a drawer or open a cupboard door fully and without a sock hanging out; who can empty a draining board completely of washing up, or who can see a gap between furniture and wall without wanting to stuff it, at once, with rubbish.

In our house for instance, The Powers That Be will not notice a coat that has been lying on the floor of the hall for three days, but will fret over the layer of dust that is minding its own business on top of the kitchen units. I kick the coat resentfully every time I walk through the hall but can put up with any amount of dust so long as the objects on which it rests are neatly arranged about the place.

Men never clean the lavatory but they do put a new roll of paper in the holder instead of on the cistern. Men make beds but never change them. Men throw out empty shampoo bottles from the bathroom but cannot help cutting their toenails in the bath and leaving the clippings in the waste trap. Men put soiled laundry in the washing machine, but women will always take it out and dry it.

I try to make deals with The Powers That Be. I will rinse the razor stubble off the soap dish if she will throw out the carrier bags. She tries to make deals with me. She will throw out the bin liner full of sixties clothes if I will never again tap cigar ash in the plant holder. It is no good. We know we are creatures of free will, but still carry on, clinging to our stereotypes, mindlessly as honey bees.

New Society, 5 September 1986

Concordes for all

You are supposed to be very cool on aeroplanes. You do *not* read the leaflets on escape procedures; you do *not* peer out of the window to check the wing rivets, and you *never* read the in-flight magazine. The correct procedure is to refuse all free food and booze, to order a glass of Perrier, an aspirin and to go to sleep with your mouth shut.

Well, to hell with that. Here am I sitting next to Neil Kinnock at 55,000 feet, Mach 2, in Concorde, with one of the best breakfasts I've ever eaten under my belt, and it's amazing. Give me some more of that free champagne. Pass the Concorde chocolates.

I've been pretending to interview Kinnock, on his way to Washington to meet President Reagan, but it has more or less collapsed now into a conversation about south Wales and the sixties and giving up smoking. Kinnock is as excited as I am, to judge by the way his knees keep jiggling and his pipe keeps falling to pieces, and the way he keeps rummaging through all the free gifts and goodies you get on Concorde.

There are Concorde flight socks (tasteful dove grey); Concorde chocolates (just three pralines in an exquisite pale grey box) and Concorde leather luggage labels. "They should put these things in a time capsule," says Kinnock. "What would people in 2,000 years make of a society that produces leather Concorde luggage labels?"

While most wide-bodied jets are getting more and more like the squalor of a cross-Channel ferry, Concorde cossets you in the way airline passengers used to be cosseted, in the days when Imperial Airways took three days to get to Cairo. Your coat is hung and brushed, your hand luggage stowed, your brow mopped with steamy lemon towels, your face is stuffed with caviar and smoked salmon and asparagus and scrambled eggs and champagne. And all for a mere £1,500, one way.

I ask Kinnock if, in a democratic socialist society, there would still be a place for Concorde. "In a socialist future," says Kinnock, dreamily mopping his face with another hot towel, "We'll all have one each."

New Society, 3 April 1987

Against the grain

This is my last regular column for *New Society*. I leave entirely from motives of personal greed rather than discontent. This is a delightful slot to write for and I shall miss it, although I shall continue to hold forth in a similar weekly column for *The Daily Telegraph*.

Several readers have written to ask me how it is possible to work for a left-wing paper like *New Society* and a right-wing one like *The Telegraph*, so perhaps I should explain. In the first place, *New Society* has never been especially left wing. Its first editor, Timothy Raison, later became a minister in Mrs Thatcher's government, and its second, Paul Barker, is probably best described as a Tory anarchist. Its readership seems to be predominantly leftish, but that is probably because it has always welcomed sceptical and radical attitudes, which until fairly recently were the prerogative of the left.

In the second place, *The Telegraph* is no longer the citadel of reaction it once was. It is a Tory paper but an independently minded one, which has differed sharply with the government on issues ranging from South Africa to the Wright affair.

At *New Society* I wrote from a position slightly to the right of most of the readership, and at the *Telegraph* I write from a position considerably to the left, but it is always good for a journalist to write against the grain.

When the present editor, the blessed David Lipsey, and I chose the title for this column, which is, or course, pinched from George

Orwell's famous feature in *Tribune*, I felt distinctly uneasy at treading on the grave of a personal hero. Orwell's column was a model to countless journalists: quirky, penetrating and based on a lifetime of extraordinary experiences and exceptionally wide reading.

To set up in any kind of competition, with my own short and placid career through school, university and journalism, seemed the height of hubris and, indeed, I don't feel that I have ever attained the same blend of lightness and seriousness which seemed to come so effortlessly to Orwell.

But the title of the column is too good to be allowed to languish, permitting, as it does, something between the relentless levity of a conventional "diary" and the po face of a leader. I hope it continues to provide a kind of haven for writers who occasionally chafe at the orthodoxies of their own newspapers or at the drab demarcations between features, news and opinion. Orwell, who to this day resists classification into right and left, journalist or novelist, prophet or clown, would certainly approve.

New Society, 21 August 1987

Bashing the buskers

B usking must be a fairly easy way to scrape a living, I've always thought. Get out of bed at lunchtime, and head for the Tube station. Bash out a Bob Dylan three-chorder and watch the guitar case fill with silver. If I ever got the sack, and my wife left me, and the house was repossessed, busking was one of those things I could always fall back on, like house-painting or writing for the tabloids.

Well I have to tell you it's not so easy. I busked for 20 minutes this week at Finsbury Park Tube, which is all that my fingertips could stand of guitar strings these days, and I made 12p, and that was all from *The Sound of Silence*.

The pros make more, of course, like Bongo Mike and Extremely Frank Jeremy, who have been in Westminster County Court this week, suing British Transport Police for wrongful arrest and false imprisonment. Bongo and Extremely do not just have a lawyer: they have an accountant; they have income tax returns; they have a professor of music to testify to their prowess, and they have taken their case to the European Court of Human Rights.

Busking on the Underground is "strictly illegal" according to London Transport, though in fact it is not. What the relevant by-laws say is that you must not cause an obstruction, you must not play music "to the annoyance of any other person". A busker can get around the obstruction rule by moving on when asked, but the "annoyance" clause is more tricky, because LT argues that "any other person" includes members of its own staff. Effectively, if LT says a busker is annoying, then that busker is breaking the law.

The ban operates in a random and senseless way. About 100 people a year are prosecuted, with fines of up to £200, but buskers can also perform all day under the noses of station staff. Certain places, like the long, cloacal underpass at Finsbury Park, have a more or less permanent population of buskers. They are shy creatures of the tunnels and burrows; hazy about their origins, reluctant to emerge into the harsh daylight of addresses and surnames.

Sylvanus, for instance, who plays the pan-pipes, tells me he is a white witch, a weekend courier of coach trips to Innsbruck, and the former deputy town crier of Chester, but he won't tell me his real name. "I can't write Sylvanus," I tell him reasonably. "*Daily Telegraph* readers won't believe it."

"Then call me Earthspoon," he says graciously.

He is a vivid, faun-like creature, with a witch's hat, satyr's beard and mascara'd eyelashes. Around his neck are hung a piece of rock he calls his "bog off" stone and a silver ankh, the Egyptian symbol of immortality. Earthspoon says he believes in resurrection, which makes him a more orthodox Christian than the Bishop of Durham. "I met a guy recently called Michael, who was an angel, though he didn't have his wings on. He gave me this Swiss Army knife."

Earthspoon/Sylvanus is busking, he says, to raise the Tube fare back to Clapham, where he plans to open a teashop with friends. It is to be called The Magic Teashop, in case anyone wants to avoid it.

At the bottom of the escalators at Tottenham Court Road I meet the classier end of busking in the form of the César Franck violin sonata, performed on the flute, and in schoolgirl's navy skirt, by Dorothy, aged 17. No surname, no detention: "If my mother found I was busking, she'd kill me."

Dorothy, who studies at a comprehensive in St. Albans, comes to London once a week for music lessons, and supplements her pocket money with the £10 or £15 she can make on the escalators. "It's actually only my fourth instrument," she says apologetically though it sounds fine to me. No trouble getting into the Royal College of Music, where she is bound next year.

Compared with the three-chord guitar bashers, who average about £2 an hour, the classical musicians do well, but the stars are the saxophone players. It is a fashionable sound at the moment, and carries well without amplification. A good sax player like Gary Reader, performing this week at Leicester Square Tube but more usually with the One-eyed Jacks R&B Band, can make £20 an hour, and with a band T-shirt it is all good advertising.

"Try to mention that we're playing at Dingwall's this week," Gary says.

Camaraderie is one of the chief attractions of busking. Swapping gossip, songs and legal hassles. Popular pitches operate a rota system of hour-long slots, handed on from one busker to the next, though there are some snakes in the Underground Eden.

"I used to think it was all Bohemian bliss," Gary Reader says, "but there are people who will throw away the list and write false names on it. Some will even get up at six o'clock to claim the pitch, and if you get up that early I can't see much point of being a busker."

When I eventually pluck up the courage to busk for myself at Finsbury Park, I choose the opposite end of the tunnel from the established pitch.

String-picking on a classical guitar vanishes completely in the echoes of the tunnel. My rusty Leonard Cohen repertoire is sucked into the air conditioning. I am as invisible to the passing commuters as an Aids poster, and after three songs I am sweating cold embarrassment.

A sympathetic hippy called Penny in a man's trilby and kaftan tells me it has to come from the heart, so I bellow out *The Sound of Silence*, thrashing the strings with a Barclaycard as a makeshift plectrum. Six 2p coins have clinked into my guitar case by the third repetition, and I am ready to escape. Point made.

Busking, especially if it is busking properly, is a professional job, which some professionals do very well indeed. Most people seem to enjoy it, and if they don't enjoy it they can walk past it in a moment.

The London Transport arguments about causing obstruction and annoyance are gossamer-thin. Buskers can't operate in very crowded spaces anyway. They look for the empty corners and the dead spaces between escalators. And if music is so annoying, then why does LT have the right to annoy me with piped Muzak on the platforms of its central London stations?

In France, Holland and the enlightened open spaces of Covent Garden, buskers are licensed and even encouraged, as something which relieves the grimness of city life. Only in the dim netherworld of London Transport are they abhorred, moved on and prosecuted.

Extremely Frank Jeremy and Bongo Mike, I am glad to report, won their case against the Transport Police. They got only 20p damages, it is true, but that was 8p more than I got, and I feel a lot more damaged.

The Daily Telegraph, 8 July 1988

The Rushdie affair

A petition of support for Salman Rushdie, from my fellow authors at Penguin Books, arrived in the post this week, so I must make up my mind about *The Satanic Verses*. I have avoided writing about it so far – largely because it meant I would actually have to read it, and the wretched thing is 550 pages long.

I've never been a big Rushdie fan. I got through three chapters of *Midnight's Children*, and only one of *Shame*. "Magic realism", which is the Rushdie speciality, is a lot of old toffee in my view. It means over-long books full of characters who walk through walls, catch bullets in their bare hands and, whenever the writer gets bored with them, turn into angels and fly out of the window.

Novels work by creating sets of rules which more or less resemble the rules of the real world. This is even true of fantasies like *Gulliver's Travels*. Gulliver's world is absurd, but it does obey its own internal rules. Gulliver can turn into a giant or a midget, but you know that he could not turn into an angel and fly out of the window. It is the fact that he is bound by rules which makes his predicament interesting. If you create a world where, at the whim of the author, *anything at all* can happen, then nothing at all is interesting.

Another reason I don't like Rushdie's work is that he writes 227-word sentences. All right, I know Henry James wrote 300-word sentences, but Henry James wrote them for a reason, while Rushdie only writes them because he thinks full stops are unliterary.

I also get cross with these idiots who keep comparing Rushdie to Joyce. On a single random page of *The Satanic Verses* (page 341, if you want to check) are the phrases: "contributed in no small degree"; "plied him with delicacies"; "long-standing pre-eminence"; and "something of a legend himself". They are not resounding cliches, but they are all stale, shop-soiled expressions, which a writer of real stylistic compunction, like Joyce, would never use with such frequency.

The Satanic Verses is a large, baggy book, whose sub-plots include the mid-life crises of two Indian actors; the experiences of an immigrant family in the East End; the foundation of Islam; the religious possession of an Indian village: a Khomeini-like Imam, exiled in a Kensington flat; the ascent of Everest by a girl mountaineer with flat feet; and much, much more. The whole never really coheres.

Leaving the book itself for a moment. I have also been irritated by the attitude of writers like Antonia Fraser and Norman Mailer, who seem determined to see the Rushdie affair as proof of state hostility to literature in general. Why are they posturing about, holding meetings and organising petitions as if the lunacies of the Ayatollah constituted some general threat to free speech? My guess is that the death sentence on Rushdie has allowed the normally disregarded ranks of the writing profession to feel *important* for once, and they are enjoying every minute.

I don't much like this Government, but I've been rather impressed by its readiness to support a writer who has been consistently hostile to it, to protect him and his wife and to take the fairly drastic step of cutting off renascent relations with Iran. I only hope Rushdie has the courtesy to thank them for their trouble and expense.

A death sentence for what is in the end only a fictional entertainment is monstrous madness, but the novelist clearly has only himself to blame for much of the trouble he's in. Last summer the Indian editor of Penguin, Mr Khushwant Singh, predicted mayhem if the book was published unabridged, but his warning was ignored.

Even without the crackpot intervention of the Ayatollah, violent reaction could have been expected – and it is worth remembering that the deaths of six Moslems in Islamabad *preceded* the Ayatollah's sentence on Rushdie.

At the core of *The Satanic Verses* is the proposition that the *Koran* is not divinely inspired, a proposition which attacks the central tenet of Islam, as Rushdie, an ex-Moslem, *knows perfectly well*. Whatever we sophisticates think of it, Islam is a great world religion which gives meaning and hope to the lives of tens of millions of poor people around the world. In the West we do not take religion seriously any more, but it is a great arrogance to suggest that others should do the same.

So what can one say in defence of Rushdie? In the first place *The Satanic Verses* is not an awful book. Quite funny in parts, and with some nice set pieces. Chop the showy stuff about angels, demons and miracles, cut out all the intrusive bits on the history of Islam, and you are left with a decent 200-page novel about a character rather like Salman Rushdie, divided between his Bombay roots and adopted English culture.

As a British citizen, Rushdie has the right to say whatever he likes about Islam, and has been unlucky to attract the attention of a vicious old bigot who has exploited it for domestic ends. If Moslems find the book offensive they don't have to read it. There is more devastating critique of the divine inspiration of the *Koran* in the *Encyclopaedia Britannica*, and nobody is burning that.

But the only question that matters now is whether the novel is good enough to justify the continued violence of riots and demonstrations, the threat to the lives of Rushdie and his publishers, and the freezing of relations with Iran, where the British businessman Roger Cooper is still in jail. Some novels which have created great controversy, like *Ulysses* and *The Gulag Archipelago*, are so good and so important they deserve to be published no matter what the consequences, but is the Rushdie book among them?

The writer Roald Dahl has advised Rushdie to "throw the bloody thing away. It would save lives," and I agree. There is no great issue of principle at stake. It can be quietly withdrawn, and reissued in a few years' time when everyone has forgotten about it. There are very few books which are worth a human life, and *The Satanic Verses* is not one of them.

The Daily Telegraph, 3 March 1989

Groomed for TV

I am terrible on TV. I slouch, sneer, stammer, fidget, forget my lines and swallow the ends of my words. It rankles, because I know inside I am scintillating, sensitive and sincere. Television can make Anne Diamond look like an intellectual. Nicholas Witchel contrives to look nice, and even Alastair Burnet can seem sensible, but I come over as a blue jowled, shifty subversive.

The single television programme I have presented was so awful that even my mother couldn't find a good word for it. After a catastrophic radio show last year when I addressed the interviewer by the wrong name throughout, I swore I'd never do broadcasting again.

Until now, that is. I have my first novel out next month, which is called *Do It Again* ("scintillating and sensitive" – *The Daily Blurb*) and the PR people tell me you just have to get out there and promote it. Radio Orkney one day, Bodmin Community Broadcasting the next. It's going to be hectic and I have to get my act together.

Which is how I find myself in Chester being scrutinised for televisual potential by two svelte creatures from Public Image Ltd, while cameraman Alastair tight-focuses on my open pores and trembling upper lip.

"He blinks a lot, doesn't he?" says Diana, the speech specialist, studying my image on a video monitor. "And the crossed legs look defensive. But the voice isn't bad." Jeannie, who is introduced to me as Public Image's "charisma consultant", takes a step backwards to study the general posture: "Needs to get his bottom back in the sofa. And the jacket makes him look a bit deformed. Where does he get his clothes from?"

"Shop called Blazer actually. In Covent Garden."

"Paul Smith might be better for someone your shape."

"Oh. Right."

Public Image is the outfit which has been teaching MPs how to appear on TV, in preparation for the televising of Parliament this autumn. They also groom executives from ICL, American Express, Shell and British Airways in everything from corporate presentations to handling broadcast interrogation, but as far as I am concerned, if they can make politicians look like people, they are good enough for me.

Diana is Diana Mather, a BBC newsreader in Manchester, while Jeannie France-Hayhurst is a former barrister and general media person. The third member of the team, Peter Wheeler, another newsreader, is off somewhere in Granadaland, dubbing the funny voices on *What The Papers Say*. They run their courses all over the place: in Westminster, at Manchester University and on the House of Commons mock-up set at Granada. But today we are in Jeannie's house, a formidably immaculate villa, done out in the High Cheshire Suburban style of brass-rimmed tables, glazed chintz sofas and opal globe standard lamps, fringed with white porcelain leaves.

"Honesty is the most important thing," says Diana. "We don't want to turn people into actors. We want to bring out the personality. And of course speech is most important too. Lots of MPs don't breathe properly, so they have to shout, like Neil Kinnock. Give themselves sore throats and polyps on the vocal chords. Breathe from the diaphragm and you can speak quite loudly and for quite a long time without strain. Then most importantly there are the three Es: Energy, Enthusiasm and Enjoyment. And do try to stop blinking."

And so, as I breathe from the diaphragm, clench my eyelids apart, and desperately try to project honesty as well as all three Es at once, the camera rolls. "Today we are visiting the home of Martyn Harris," says Diana dishonestly. "A journalist who has recently published his first novel, *Do It Again*. Tell us a little about the plot, Martyn."

"Umm ..." A long pause. "Errr ..." A longer pause. "Tee, hee, hargh ..." An asinine giggle.

"All right, Alastair," says Diana patiently. "We'll try that again."

We try it again, many, many times, each time chipping away at another tic and mannerism and gaucherie. On the second run-through, my crossed legs keep bobbing up and down which makes me look as if I want to run away (I do, I do). On the third run they are uncrossed, but my hands are clenched in my groin like those of a little boy who wants to go to the lavatory. On the fourth I have wrenched my hands from my lap, but now they are fiddling with my ears, which means I've heard enough of this (I have, I have). On the fifth I'm throwing away the ends of my sentences, which sounds as if I think my audience is thick (I don't, really).

Between takes, Diana and Jeannie fill me in on the general stuff.

Dark jackets are best for men, with pale blue shirts and bright ties, dark patterns tending to disappear on screen. Avoid reds, Harris tweeds and small checks, which wobble disconcertingly. Women look best in clean, bright colours, simple lines and high round necks. Female newsreaders such as Sue Lawley often use a big brooch to soften the austerity and large round earrings to catch the lights and draw attention to their eyes.

Television does curious things to your face, dragging it towards the edges of the screen. People with wide cheekbones look like Eskimos, while if you have a long face, as I have, it makes you look like a cadaverous mule. It emphasises the darkness of lipstick and eyeshadow, so make-up should be minimal, and used mainly to soften facial shadows. Does Diana think it is wicked, I wonder, to mould politicians in this way?

"As soon as anyone gets on telly these days we expect them to be as good as the professionals, because that's where we get our standards from. It's unfair, but that's the way of the world. As for the ethics, I leave that to others and get on with my job."

And it's a job she does very well, because on the final run-through, after three hours or so, I really don't look too bad. Steady gaze, breathing from the diaphragm, no twitches, no blinking. Not Melvyn Bragg or Barry Norman, but not bad. I'm brimming with honesty, energy, enthusiasm and enjoyment and I'm talking a lot of twaddle, but you'd hardly notice. Over the next few months, from the House of Commons chamber, you're going to see a lot more just like me.

The Daily Telegraph, 15 September 1989

Cow now

Following the *World in Action* report this week on mad cow disease, I found myself visiting a dairy farm, where I learned that the modern cow can now produce 16 gallons of milk a day, a staggering figure compared to the five or six of 20 years ago, or the one or two gallons of a century before that. These cows, which go under picturesque names like Number 456, spend half the year indoors, and produce more milk on winter silage than they do on grass. In fact there seems little reason to put them out to grass at all, apart from stopping them getting depressed. The modern cow is nothing more than a hugely efficient converter of vegetable protein into milk, and this is exactly how some farmers refer to them – as converters. One of them told me proudly that he had fed his own herd of converters for some weeks on a container-load of spoiled Jaffa Cakes and another time on a lorry-load of cheese-and-onion crisps. I don't know if he took the wrappers off, but I imagine not, for the modern cow will, as he told me, "eat bloody anything", – including, as *World in Action* points out, dead sheep. It strikes me as curious that while we must be told exactly what ingredients went into a Jaffa Cake, we don't need to be told exactly what went into a cow. Of course it is typical urban humbug to complain about the treatment of cattle on the one hand, and the price of milk on the other. If animals were not treated like machines then hardly any of us could afford to eat them, but all the same, I haven't been able to abolish the faint odour of cheese and onion that has hung about my cornflakes for the last few days.

The Spectator, 3 March 1990

Visiting the toiledau

News that the Inland Revenue in Wales is to employ a special team of Welsh speakers arouses little criticism. Perhaps it is because English journalists are shy of sounding racist, so as a non-Welsh speaking Welshman let me do it on their behalf. Every time I go home to Swansea I am enraged by the spread of the solemn idiocies of bilingual policy; of "toiledau" for "toilets", of "ambwlans" for "ambulance", of "tacsi" for "taxi" as if, as Kingsley Amis once remarked, no Welshman had ever seen the letter "x". There is no Welsh person alive who cannot read English, so what is the point of it all? It costs a fortune, and the only visible result, after 45 years of compulsory Welsh in schools, is that Welsh-speaking has declined from 23 per cent to around 17. Outsiders assume Welsh authorities are responding to popular demand, but in fact the opposite is the case. Ordinary Welsh people could hardly care less about the language, but it has become a semi-official requirement for a range of establishment jobs: education; local government; BBC Wales and the like. It would be a pity if Welsh disappeared completely, but I can't see much point in permanent life-support. The real reason governments pander to it, though, is not sentiment but the nationalist vote, which was condemned to eternal impotence by the final defeat of devolution in 1979, but which is always able to swing a few marginals.

The Spectator, 10 March 1990

The diary of Sarah aged 10¼

Do you two want to go to the pantomime, Dad says, so Tom does his Herman Munster moan, and I say, oh God, you're going to put us in another article in your newspaper aren't you? And my teacher's going to read it out in class and I'm going to just *die* in front of Julie and Rachel. Why can't you just *hire* some kids or something?

And Dad says, oh dear, I suppose you think you're a bit too grown-up to go to the panto now. And Tom says he'll go, but only if we can go to McDonald's first and have an ice cream at half-time, and if he can have those binocular things on the back of the seat. So Dad says then that going out to the theatre is not supposed to be an ordeal, Tom. It's supposed to be a *treat* for you both, where you *enjoy* yourselves. And I say, I might go but only if it's to see Jason Donovan in *The Amazing Technicolor Dreamcoat*, and Dad says but that's not a proper pantomime, that's just stupid old Andrew Lloyd Webber and some Australian soap star who can't even sing.

So I say right then I'm not going at all, and Tom starts crying like he always does when he can't get his own way, and Dad says now see what you've done Sarah, like he always does. So in the end I say I'll go, but only if I can have one of those spangly bra tops from Father Christmas and my ears pierced in the New Year, and Dad says absolutely *no way*, categorically *no*, but then next day he says oh all right then ...

So on Thursday we go down the West End in a proper black taxi, which Dad usually says are Far Too Dear and what's wrong with your legs? But he says it's all right this time because it goes on expenses, and I say that I thought taxis went on petrol. And Dad says you're getting that sharp you'll cut yourself one of these days, and I say that's a cliché, Dad, and he says OK, Dorothy Parker, you write the rotten article.

At the big McDonald's in Sharfsbryavv we sit in the basement on slidy benches with our feet in a puddle of dirty milk shake, and Dad has to go back upstairs three times to fetch ketchup and straws and napkins and a spoon.

I'm not hungry after the bouncy taxi and Tom says he feels sick, and Dad says there are Poor People living out there in cardboard boxes who are starving, and it's criminal to waste food. So Dad eats my burger and Tom's chips and says he hates McDonald's food. We think it is brilliant.

On the pavement there are people with clown masks and a man in a gorilla suit and people lying about everywhere being Drunk and Disorderly. Dad says some of them are Poor People and Tom says we could have given them my chips if you weren't so greedy Dad, and Dad says look here's the theatre. And there's a big sign saying *Jack And The Beanstalk* with Cilla Black, and Tom says who's being Jack? And Dad says Cilla Black, and Tom says don't be stupid dad, she's a girl. And I say I love Cilla Black and I want to go on *Blind Date* when I'm as big as Julie's sister Susie and wear my spangly bra top, but I'm not going on dates with any stupid boys.

So we go and get our tickets which the lady calls comps, and Dad says that means they are specially good tickets, but they are right at the back so Tom has to sit on Dad's knee all the way through and wriggle. I have to use the special binoculars, and the man in front turns round and says can you *kindly* tell your child to stop snapping the opera glasses in and out of their case? And Dad says all sarky that he is *terribly* sorry, he didn't know we were at Covent *Gahden*, and I have to pretend I am Not With Him.

In the seats next to us there are two men holding hands and I say to Dad look there's two gays, and he says do you know what gay means and Tom says I know, it's when a man thinks he is pregnant, so I have to say don't be stupid Tom, it's when two men go to the loo together, which makes Dad choke, so I have to pretend to be Not With Him again, and concentrate on the panto.

This is quite good in the bits when Simple Simon comes on with his dog called Spit, who spits on the audience, and I like the Giant Rat who runs up the aisle though he doesn't run up as far as us, and I like Cilla Black, though Tom says she doesn't look like a boy and has a fat tummy like Rory's Mum. And at the end we all sing a song called *If I Had a Hammer* which Dad and Cilla Black know the words to, but nobody else does, and Tom falls asleep and has to be carried out to the taxi.

Did you have a good time, Dad wants to know on the way home, and I ask him if he meant it about the pierced ears and he sighs and says yes, and I say I had a great time, thanks Dad.

The Daily Telegraph, 21 December 1991

Can we see a future in tea leaves?

Tea accounts for 45 per cent of all liquid drunk by the British people, according to a Tea Council report. They are leaving out tap water, of course, and although the figure is a good deal smaller than 30 years ago, when James Bond inspired a generation to switch to coffee, it is still impressive – on the face of it.

The trouble is that the Tea Council is referring to a seriously-debased beverage. Almost three-quarters of tea drunk today is tea-bag tea – made with a kind of dust, sealed in muslin bags and dunked perfunctorily in tepid water.

This is a foul and lazy practice originating in offices, which at least have the excuse that there is seldom anywhere to dispose of tea-leaves or to rinse a teapot. Personally I find the nest of dessicated tea bags, growing beards of mould in the bottom of the office waste-paper basket, every bit as disgusting as the streaks of tea leaves on office windows from people on the floor above emptying their teapots, medieval-style, into the courtyard below.

In the home it is far more unpleasant to pick soggy tea bags out of the waste trap than to empty the dregs of a teapot on a nearby flower bed, where it can build up into a useful mulch.

Tea bags, for me, taste of boiled J-cloths and sawdust, which is effectively what they are. To get tea fine enough to dispense into the little bags it is necessary to macerate the leaves to such an extent that they lose most of their oils and aroma to the atmosphere. A tea leaf is quite a big thing in nature – about the size of one of your finger joints – and was never intended to be reduced to the consistency of snuff.

The automated tea dispenser has been another source of decline. Like computers, these are very popular with senior management who, you notice, never have to operate them or consume their murky output. Tea-machine tea is made with an even finer kind of dust, manufactured, I understand, by some heavy industrial process which involves making tea in the conventional way, freeze drying it, and then blending it with ground zinc and bath cleansing powder. It is now almost universal in offices, motorway cafés and British Rail catering establishments.

Proper tea, like proper mayonnaise or proper gravy, is the easiest thing in the world to make. You need tea-leaves (Assam in the morning and Earl Grey in the afternoon, or sometimes a mixture of both) in proportions of one heaped teaspoonful per person and one for the pot. You need a warmed china teapot (the Brown Bessie variety sold in Woolworths is fine) and you need fast-boiling water. Milk and sugar are a matter of argument; I like both, but the tea must be drunk from a thin china cup, not one of those misshapen pottery mugs covered in a warty glaze. They make the tea cold and they make people dribble.

Why we don't make tea properly is as much of a mystery as the reason we use salad cream and gravy granules. A Tea Council spokesperson mumbled vaguely about "speed" and "convenience" and "the pressures of modern life". Yet surely life is, if anything, becoming more leisured for most people, especially old age pensioners with whom tea bags are most popular?

It is very odd that something which is the epitome of relaxation and leisured reflection should need to be fast and "convenient", unless it is merely that people need the time saved by drinking bad tea to grumble about the decline in civilised standards generally.

The Daily Telegraph, 15 April 1987

A brief history of Hawking

In a week's time from now Stephen Hawking's book, *A Brief History of Time*, will have been on the bestseller list for a record 183 weeks, displacing the current champ, *The Country Diary of an Edwardian Lady*. It has sold 550,000 copies in the UK and between 5 and 12 million worldwide – when I asked the publishers, Bantam, they were joyfully uncertain.

"And will there be a paperback?" I inquired.

"Oooh, *well*. We *did* have one scheduled for March 1993, but it does keep getting postponed. You can understand why." At £14.95 a copy for a 200-page book, you certainly can.

It is the publishing sensation of the last decade and a deeply mysterious one. As a *Daily Telegraph* survey found last year, hardly anyone who bought the book has read it, and hardly anyone who has read it understands it. After a "dawn of time" style beginning, and a few chapters of chatty, everymannish science history (Newton's apple, Galileo's balls etc.) it plunges into the oceanic abstraction of space-time singularities, charmed particles, superstring theory and the finite universe which has no beginning or end. Throughout the book Hawking lurches disconcertingly between the levels of *Blue Peter* commentary and postgrad seminar, so that at one point, for instance, he tells us "an ellipse is an elongated circle", then a few pages later is going on about undefined terms such as curved space and antigravity, which do not even appear in the skimpy glossary.

I have driven my eyes through it two and a half times now, and though I think I catch Hawking's drift it is only in the sense of being able to repeat his assertions rather than paraphrase them, or manufacture my own metaphors. Nobody but a trained physicist could understand half of it, and the trained physicists I asked said they knew it all already. So why are people buying it? In the first place incomprehensibility itself is probably a selling point. If a book tells you the answer to everything is 42, you feel cheated, but if it tells you it is an unbounded, multi-dimensional universe you can gape and pass on. Like the Bible in the bookcase in days gone by, you may not understand it but at least you have the feeling that *somebody* does, and that you possess his understanding, even if you are not clever enough to share it.

Then there is the image of Hawking himself, as pictured on the book's cover: the lonely, indomitable genius progressively crippled since the age of 23 by motor neurone disease. This was initially forecast to kill him within two years, but has left him with control of two fingers, which he uses to operate his wheelchair and the synthesiser which generates his unearthly, Speak and Spell voice.

The fascination of Hawking is in what an *Observer* profile importantly called "the fundamental contradiction" of a physical body increasingly enslaved by gravity, and a mind that probes the furthest secrets of the universe (add Star Trek-type phrases to taste). In fact, of course, there is no contradiction: physical feebleness often goes with great mental energy – one only has to think of Milton's blindness, Beethoven's deafness, Keats's consumption and so on. But the fact remains that people like a genius to be handicapped – if not as dreadfully as Hawking. It brings him closer to the human, and reinforces his claim to greatness by casting it in relief. It is now almost a condition of scientific glory to be flawed, which is why, whenever a new star emerges, from Albert Einstein to Edward Witton, the newspapers set off on a hunt for his endearing eccentricities, absent-mindedness, early failures and odd socks.

A third factor in the book's success must be the title, which is catchy (who hates a short book?), paradoxical and hugely promising. A history of *time*, and one which tells the reader, "Our project is a complete theory of the origins of the universe." You have to think, Well, that's not bad for £14.95. Hawking introduces himself as "Lucasian Professor of Mathematics at Cambridge – the chair formerly occupied by Isaac Newton" and in case there are any residual doubts as to his credentials, he was "born on the anniversary of Galileo's death". We then trot briskly through Aristotle, Copernicus, Newton, Einstein, Heisenberg and on to Hawking with a few nods to contemporaries such as Roger Penrose, though not, oddly, to the outstanding theoretical physicist of the day, Edward Witton, whose name does not even appear in the index.

The vanity is understandable, and perhaps unintentional, but does Hawking in fact measure up to these weighty names? His reputation is largely based on two major papers. The first, published in *Nature* in 1974, and known now as "Black Hole Evaporation", outlined a baffling contradiction – that black holes are not black. Essentially he proposed that black holes, which are collapsed stars too massive to let even light escape, can still emit some kinds of radiation. The argument was of marginal scientific importance but had implications for the understanding of the first few seconds of cosmic history after the Big Bang. More importantly, Hawking carried out this work by apparently combining two previously irreconcilable branches of physics: quantum mechanics and relativity. The second paper was even more esoteric – proposing a universe which had no boundaries in space and in which time had no real existence at all, but could be dealt with, mathematically, by means of "imaginary numbers" derived from the square root of minus one, which, as we all remember from school, has no square root.

One highly improbable consequence of this improbable sounding notion was the break-up of Hawking's marriage, at least if one goes by the account in Brian Appleyard's marvellous new book, *Understanding the Present.* Hawking met and married his wife, Jane Wilde, shortly after the onset of his disease. A language specialist and Christian, she nursed him for 25 years, bore him three children, and during the writing of *A Brief History* served as what Hawking called his "lowest common denominator", putting a red pencil through passages she did not understand. "I wanted to find some purpose in my existence," she would humbly say, "and I suppose I found it in looking after Stephen."

When they split up "spiritual and religious differences" were cited, but more specifically it was the direction of Hawking's work which was to blame. When Appleyard met her in 1988 he records: "She was distraught and even in the formality of this first and only meeting began to pour out her doubts about the direction he was taking. She was a devout Anglican but he cared nothing for religion. This did not matter, she explained, so long as he adhered to the Big Bang theory of creation. A single event at the start of time clearly left room for God. But Hawking had moved on to his "no boundary condition" view which implied no beginning and no end ... "God was unnecessary."

The separation gave a new meaning to the term "physical differences" and more bizarre still was the news that Hawking had not retired to college digs but to the bed of one of his nurses, Elaine Mason. She, moreover, happened to be the wife of the man who designed Hawking's mobile voice computer, which must surely be the only case ever of someone who has literally engineered his own wife's seduction.

Some readers will be cross with me by now, for it is a convention that disabled people should receive a special reverence, but this is patronising. The disabled are entitled to consideration in everyday life but not to any moral exemptions, still less to exemption from the dispassionate standards of their chosen field. Hawking is brave and clever and good-natured, but that has no bearing on his scientific stature, and nor would he want it to have. So, once again, is he a genius in the Einstein, Newton mould, as he himself has sometimes seemed to suggest? Or is he a run-of-the-mill physics prof with a gift for self-promotion?

The broadest objection to the hagiolatry of Hawking is also one that applies to cosmology as a whole, and was summed up by an applied physicist I spoke to: "You have to understand that first there is speculation, then there is wild speculation, and then there is cosmology." Modern cosmological theory is based on the tiniest scraps of evidence about the way the universe works, and on suppositions which will never be testable in the foreseeable future. Nobody has yet seen a black hole, still less an evaporating one. Nobody has ever observed a "string" or a "superstring", nor – given that they are required to exist in 10-26 dimensions, and are smaller than an atom to the same degree that the earth is smaller than the universe – are they ever likely to.

More detailed objections to Hawking's status come from his own colleagues, such as Michael Green, Professor of Physics at Queen Mary College, who describes "imaginary time" as "a trick for avoiding complications" employed for years in quantum mechanics. "But Stephen Hawking takes it much more seriously. That is difficult to understand." John Barrow, Professor of Astronomy at Sussex University, is similarly sceptical of Hawking's use of imaginary time, and of the lasting value of his work: "Black hole evaporation and his singularity theorems were really the more interesting aspects of his work – mathematically correct – but it is now doubtful that they apply."

Barrow's use of the past tense here is significant, for Hawking is now in his 50s, and it is a general rule that most theoretical physicists will have shot their bolts by their mid-30s. Einstein was 26 when he published his major paper on relativity, and by 34, with his first paper on general relativity, his life's work was effectively done. Barrow says: "To compare Hawking to Newton or Einstein is just nonsense. There is no physicist alive who compares to Einstein or Bohr in ability. But those rather grottily researched little biographies of Galileo and Newton in *A Brief History* do rather invite you to put Hawking in the same sequence. In a list of the 12 best theoretical physicists this century Steve would be nowhere near."

The broadest and perhaps most important objection, set out in Brian Appleyard's book, is that Hawking is running counter to the main philosophical thrust of 20th-century science, which has been dominated by the theories of quantum, relativity and chaos. In terms of the history of science he is a "hard classicist" – that is, someone who takes the 19th-century view that there is an objective world outside ourselves which is completely accessible to observation and reason. At the end of the 19th century it seemed to many people that human knowledge was within sight of completion. If Newton was right and Darwin was right, then all that remained was filling in the details.

Within 20 years this confidence was overthrown by quantum mechanics and relativity. Quantum revealed that our perceptions of the very small were wrong, relativity that our perceptions of the very large were wrong too. Matter was no longer a game of Newtonian billiards ricocheting about in predictable patterns, but something that at the deepest level was inherently random. The universe was no longer a giant version of the same billiard game but an illusion of our homocentric view, with the same relationship to "reality" as the pixillated vision field of the house fly. In the last 20 years chaos theory has contributed to this undermining of classical precepts by showing that even quite ordinary phenomena such as animal migrations and weather patterns are inherently unpredictable. More worrying still, the quantum view of a universe which was discontinuous and random seemed to be in fundamental contradiction to the Einsteinian picture of a smooth continuum.

The work of Hawking's life, and of similarly inclined classicists, has been to try to combine the two theories in a "Grand Unified Theory" which will enable us, famously, "to know the mind of God", but it is an aim which Green and Barrow question, and which Appleyard describes as an "ahistorical arrogance". Green's view is that a comprehensive theory of the origins of matter and energy will always be elusive: "I think we shall just push back the question and turn it into another question. The lesson of physics has always been that just at the moment when people think they understand everything they realise they understand almost nothing."

The idea that life, the universe and everything is "algorithmically compressible" also seems at odds with Karl Popper's dictum and all scientific theories must be inherently falsifiable. For although Hawking approvingly quotes Popper in *A Brief History*, how can a theory which purports to explain everything also accept its own intrinsic impermanence? There is a conundrum here like the riddle of an omniscient God who must be able to create a stone which He cannot move. A conundrum which seems to point to some inadequacy in our language, which is to say our thought processes, driven to reach conclusions about our condition, but also sensing dimly that there is something in our condition which denies the possibility of ultimate insight. "The universe," as J. B. S. Haldane said, "may not just be queer to imagine, but queerer than we *can* imagine."

All of this, by the way, is not to supply some back door to religion or obscurantism, through which clergymen and New Agers can creep. It is only that we may have to learn to see science, for all its immense effectiveness, as a provisional, cultural construct rather than a superhighway to the absolute. The millennialist arrogance which drives scientists to insist on the opposite is described perceptively by Appleyard as "an essential working tool. To ask a scientist to accept the possibility that in relative terms the world will be no nearer the truth at his death than at his birth is probably to ask too much." Any scientist needs the consoling spectre of ultimate truth if he is to continue. How much more must Steven Hawking, with death at his elbow for 30 years, be in need of that elusive ghost?

The Spectator, 27 June 1992

The ace game

In the second week of Wimbledon the queues on Church Road are a mile long and there is guilt in the press taxi as we cruise past, clutching our passes, and ducking the envious gaze of the real fans.

I was queueing for ground tickets myself 20 years ago, so I

shouldn't really wonder, but why *do* they do it? Jan Marshall from Bridgend does it every year, every day of the tournament that she doesn't have a ballot ticket. And she queues all night. "It's the only way to be sure of a Centre Court ticket – and there's this very nice lady down the road who lets us use her shower."

It was Alan Sillitoe, I think, who said there was nothing in the world worth queueing for, but the Wimbledon queue, with its camaraderie of rotas and tea-runs and queueing clubs, *is* the world for some people.

It's an eccentric place, Wimbledon, with an atmosphere halfway between a royal garden party and Gatwick airport, and every year it irritates and thrills in equal measure. Cross little notices forbid advertising, while commercial logos blaze from clothes, rackets and umpire's stand.

Fans drop from heat-stroke in the queues, while the corporate tents and press centre watch matches on TV monitors, too weighed down by the ennui of privilege to claim their seats. Three hundred thousand tickets and £30 million pass through the hands of a private club which doesn't even publish its accounts.

In the royal box, serge suits droop in the soupy heat of Centre Court while brown, half-bare girls sprawl below on the public benches. The suits sit in carefully graded seats, from padded thrones in front, to the single-cushion seats behind, to the bum-breakers at the rear. Players make £10,000 for *losing* in the third round, court coverers make £32 for a 12-hour day; army stewards work two weeks for nothing at all.

On the table of the press cafeteria I find this little notice: "The following are not permitted: No photographic equipment, no card playing, no use of Tandys or typewriters". The fusspot mentality, the other-ranks condescension, and illiterate double negative are all entirely typical.

Everything supposed to be glamorous is disappointing: the Tea Lawn is cement; the Pimms is served in beer mugs; the strawberries are huge and Spanish and tough as turnips – trying to carve one with a bendy plastic spoon I managed to plunge the spoon through the soggy cardboard carton and empty the lot in my lap.

Contrariwise, the unsung aspects become addictive: like the gas-jet heat of a player's body brushing past on his way from the court. Or the tiny cockpit of Centre Court with its brilliant rectangle of grass set against the thunderous drab of the stands. The thrilling proximity of magnificent athletes spraying sweat and spit and terrible oaths. The accelerating drum roll of a close match where a tiny edge suddenly turns into the yawning pit of defeat.

The real draw, though, is that tennis is an absurdly simple game into which it is possible to parachute for two weeks every year and become an instant expert. The rules can be grasped in minutes, the gladiatorial structure is self-explanatory, and the personalities of the players – they are usually young, inarticulate and ignorant – are two-dimensional.

They are empty screens on which it is possible for the media to project their simple fabulations: "The facts about Agassi's hair transplant", "The truth of Monica Seles's pregnancy". There is nothing like the density of strategy, lore and personal relations which characterise football and cricket.

There is a chapter in Martin Amis's novel *London Fields* in which the hero decides to learn darts, but finds after a few lessons that there is, in fact, nothing to learn. You throw the darts, walk to the board, pull them out, walk back and throw them again. You must learn to discipline your arm into the same mechanical arc every throw – but that's it. No strategy, no tactics, no tricks.

The one thing that marks a great darts player from a mediocre one is his nervelessness: a complete absence of introspection which makes his throw immune from mental twitches.

I was reminded of this passage by Jeremy Bates's repetition of Olhovskiy's remark, early in the second week, that "The difference between the top guys and the guys around 200 is in the head". In Bates's final match against the Frenchman Guy Forget he proved the point by showing himself to be just as fit and committed and to my eye more skilful. Forget's first serves averaged a shattering 116 mph against Bates's 104, and he served 31 aces – the equivalent of eight games, but Bates more than compensated with his touch and placing. The key difference showed when Bates was serving for the match, and a place in the quarter-finals, at the end of the fourth set – and his concentration visibly evaporated.

The Centre Court was as quiet as the asteroid belt; play paused on other courts as spectators listened in on their radios; even the strawberry eaters in the concourse stopped sawing at their turnips and froze, with eyes on the scoreboards, Bates bounced the ball once, twice, threw it up – and then let it drop. He said later that someone had sneezed or maybe a camera motor-drive had whirred. I heard nothing, but in any case players serve all the time through the noise of aircraft and crowds.

The total tennis pro keeps the nerveless, ingrained arc of his serve intact through a lightening strike, but Bates had lost it. He served a fault, then a flabby second service which Forget smacked past him – and the match was effectively over. The last set took barely 20 minutes, but poor Bates will be replaying his match point in mental slow motion for the next 40 years. "If you could have one gift, what would it be?" a journalist asked later, and Bates said sadly, "A *huge* serve."

Some writers suggest these crises of concentration and aggression in British players are down to the cosy social structure of the game here. Nice middle-class youngsters rise through local clubs and counties to the level where they can make a decent professional income – and then stop.

At 113 in the world rankings, Bates makes enough money from opening rounds at big tournaments to afford a house in Wimbledon and a Porsche with a personalised numberplate. He will never have the fire in his belly of a poor girl from Czechoslovakia, or an American boy weaned on the ideology of winning, who will settle for nothing less than a personalised Gulfstream jet. There is some truth in this, but just as important, I'd say, is Bates's obvious intelligence. For as in darts or golf, or acting for that matter, the important thing in tennis is not insightfulness but its opposite – a kind of unselfconscious grace.

Unchallenged by inbuilt complexity, players and coaches try to reduce tennis to a still more protean level – witness the growing dominance of the serve and volley. Twenty years ago the crisis was power tennis: all those Australian and American players with butterfly-swimmers' shoulders, who could burn the paint off the baseline with nine returns out of 10.

The only response to this game was to develop piano-wire wrists and stand yards behind the baseline, waiting for a mistake. With baseline warriors like Borg this could take years. But to risk a run up court for a fancy shot was to risk getting a hot tennis ball through the thorax.

Then came the thigh rethinks in the mid-'80s, where players like Becker suddenly acquired massive packs of muscle on their legs, like Christmas turkeys, which could fire them up and down the court faster than the electronic scoreboard winked. I wrote then that "like pre-1914 Dreadnoughts constantly outstripping each other in armour and firepower, players now have the armour to match the guns, at least until a bigger gun comes along". And now, of course, we have the bigger gun – the 130 mph serve – which on the slippery Wimbledon grass, with its low, sometimes uneven bounce, is virtually unreturnable.

To create this serve, players have bought bigger rackets but also seem to have grown taller and acquired longer arms, whether by hanging from bars for months on end, or by attending those mythical West Coast clinics, specialising in graphite elbows, Kevlar wrist extensions and neoprene ligaments. These may be installed permanently or donned before the game – hence the sudden ubiquity of long wrist bandages, worn to conceal the joins. Look out for players like Ivanisevic and Courier, who appear on TV with normal arms, but emerge on court next day with two feet of bandages, and knuckles that trail along the grass.

Years ago a player might hit 10 aces in a match and be rewarded each time with a polite round of applause. In the modern game it is not uncommon to see 30 aces, and the applause is becoming uncertain. The time it takes to win a point is down from a 1970s average of 3.8 seconds to 2.7 seconds, and in the Bates-Forget game I did not register more than three decent rallies – generously defined as anything over five shots.

Various solutions are suggested: smaller rackets; longer grass; softer balls; a deeper base-line; a reintroduction of the old foot-fault rule – even a two-tier tournament with one trophy for the lofties, and one for the shorties. Come to that – with Krajicek's remark about women players in mind – why not a third tier for the fatties?

The most controversial suggestion, striking at the heart of Wimbledon's eccentric pre-eminence – is to follow the other Grand Slam tournaments and get rid of the grass.

The argument, mooted this year by David Lloyd among others, is that it makes no sense in a country where there are only 200 grass courts, and fewer every year, for the pinnacle of the game to be represented by 18 hugely expensive, labour-intensive strips of rye and fescue which can only be played on for three months.

Chris Gorringe, chief executive of the All-England Club leaps to the defensive at this idea: "Grass is unique … an idyllic surface … the essence of the traditional game", etc etc. All of which is true, though much the same arguments of uniquenes, tradition, mystique, etc were used to keep out professional tennis in the 1960s – until it came close to threatening Wimbledon's existence.

H. G. Wells once wrote that, "In England we rely on a time lag of 50 years between the perception that something ought to be done and a serious attempt to do it." My own guess is that Wimbledon is smart enough to move faster, and in 20 years' time will be a very different spectacle. There will be bigger courts, more public tickets, less class flummery, and probably hard courts. Though it will still be called Wimbledon, it could even be in Milton Keynes. The tournament, for all its tradition, is always willing to bend when it has to – from the acceptance of professionals to the introduction of the "TV tie-break". "Tradition," as Chesterton said, "is the democracy of the dead," and I don't think Wimbledon is interested in being dead yet.

The Daily Telegraph, 4 July 1992

When language is mind bending

I first encountered PC when I applied for a teacher training place at London University, 17 years ago. "How would you motivate a class of students?" the interviewer asked (the word "children" was already frowned on). I had absorbed enough education babble to know that "group" was a key word, so I said I might divide a class into groups so that could compete with each other.

"Compete?" said the interviewer, and I was done for. No amount of flannel and recantation could cover it up. I was in favour of *competition*, which meant 11-plus, grammar schools, Thomas Gradgrind and kids down coalmines. They rejected me, and when I did find a place in another college, had to search hard for a substitute word. It was some awful formula like "co-operative dialectic", which kept the education thought-police off my back.

This wasn't called PC, for the term Political Correctness had still to be coined. It was called cant, small mindedness and stupidity, which have always been with us, and I didn't take it seriously. After all, who would want to be educated by people like that? In the past 10 years, however, PC has become a big issue, at least in America.

University lecturers have been fired for political incorrectness;

DWEMs (Dead White European Males) have been cut from college reading lists in favour of right-on black women writers like Alice Walker; seminars have become "ovulars"; the able-bodied have become "temporarily abled persons" – and so on.

Hilton Kramer, editor of the US monthly *New Criterion*, describes PC as the culmination of that "long march through the institutions" that leaders of the New Left called for in the 1960s. The PC tendency is, says Kramer, well established in Britain.

When it comes to finding examples of PC closer to home, the whole subject becomes curiously slippery. The BBC seems a likely hotbed of PC attitudes, but the worst I can extract from John Wilson, controller of editorial policy, is a section from the Producer Guidelines, titled "Sensitivity To Others".

Reporters are encouraged to say "ambulance crews" rather than ambulancemen" and "black and Asian people" rather than "blacks". There should be no mention of a crime suspect's colour unless police are calling for witnesses – "These are guidelines rather than rules," says Wilson – hardly the stuff of cultural revolutions.

Children's books are a favourite area for PC-sniffers, who like to fret over the suppression of *Little Black Sambo* and the more violently racist pages of *Biggles*. Liz Attenborough, the head of Puffin books, confessed she had cut four "niggers" from *The Jungle Book*: "But Kipling had no intention of being derogatory at the time, so leaving them in now creates a misleading impression."

So, out of their historical context, formerly commonplace attitudes can become offensive. There are few parents, for instance, who would read to their children, on grounds of its literary integrity, the charming Grimm's fairy story where a magic fiddle is used to drive a man to dance himself to death in a briar thicket. Expurgated from most editions now, it is called *The Jew In The Thornbush*.

Looking back on the colourful newspaper yarns of PC in America, some curious patterns emerge – like the fact that it is always the same three academic dismissals which are quoted. And that all the amusing examples of PC speech, like the ones quoted above, seem to trace back to half a dozen comic columns and a handful of half-serious student discussion papers.

The argument of PC sniffers – that there is something uniquely sinister in leftist attempts at language control is patently silly. All significant social groups try to bend language to their ends and it is government, the military and the commercial corporations which are the worst offenders.

Think of Norman Lamont's "acceptable unemployment", meaning "acceptable to those with jobs", or "equity retreat" for stock market crash; or "period of economic adjustment" for slump; of "deferred maintenance programme" for no maintenance; "collateral damage" for dead civilians; and "inoperative statement" for lies.

If these seem more "natural" and less ridiculous than the nonsenses of PC, it is only a measure of the authority behind them.

PC has emerged at a suspiciously convenient moment, as an alternative bogeyman to the collapsed threat of communism. The term itself is an invention of its critics, an instant way of marginalising people with whom you disagree.

The Daily Telegraph, 12 December 1992

Crime immemorial

'Crime in England this century has increased 400 per cent, in Ireland 800 per cent and in Scotland above 3,500 per cent." It has increased because "the restraint of character, relationship and vicinity are lost in the urban crowd"; because high wages and strikes have induced "a confusion of moral principle and habits of idleness and insubordination"; because "the employment of women has destroyed the familial bond, emancipating the young from parental control". These conditions are generating "a dismal substratum; a hideous black band of society from which nine-tenths of crime and nearly all professional crime flow".

Thus reported *Blackwood's Magazine* in 1844, and a little research in social histories and newspapers will find a similar quotation for every generation since. In 1863, in the wake of a series of "garrotting" attacks in London, *The Times* reported: "The dangerous classes seem to be getting the better of society ... under the influence of philanthropic sentiments and hopeful policy we have deprived the law of its terrors and justice of its arms." The Great War was accompanied by an apparent upsurge in juvenile lawlessness which "spread through the country like a plague" (C. Leeson, *The Child and The War*) and which was blamed on working mothers, absent fathers, the cinema and well-paid war work.

In the 1950s, in the wake of the Teddy Boy riots, the Conservative Party conference rang to complaints about "the leniency of this country", "the lack of parental control", "the sex, savagery, blood and thunder" in films and television, and "the smooth, smug and sloppy sentimentalists who contribute very largely to the wave of crime".

The key elements in each period of respectable fears, as Geoffrey Pearson observes in his book, *Hooligan*, are an apparent increase in crime statistics coupled with some new, or newly-noticed form of crime. It was mob violence in the 1840s; "garrotting" in the 1860s; infanticide and sexual abuse in the 1870s; "hooligans" (a new word) in the 1890s; cat burglary in the 1920s; black marketeering in the 1940s; Teddy boys in the 1950s; mugging and rioting in the early 1980s. The current moral panic, which has managed to conflate the hideous murder of James Bulger with joy-riding, "home-alone" children, the trade figures and the death of Bobby Moore, is more comprehensive than most, but the rhetoric is familiar.

There is a "tidal wave" of crime, caused by an unreachable, subhuman underclass, which threatens the traditional, peaceful, British way of life. It is blamed, variously, on urban life, working mothers, absent fathers, family breakdown, erosion of deference, weak sentencing and soggy liberals.

There are calls for the birch, for short sharp shocks, and for clampdowns on the corrupting popular media. In the '20s and '30s it was Hollywood films, in the 1890s it was music hall and "penny dreadful" magazines, and in the 1840s the essayist Thomas Beggs felt it was "the cheap theatres, penny gaffs and dancing saloons which are an incitement to crime. The daring enactment of the outrages of Jack Sheppard, Dick Turpin and Claude Duval ... exhibit to admiration noted examples of successful crime and attract the attention and ambitions of these boys." *Plus ça change*.

The sense of fall from a golden age is a universal delusion: a chronocentrism which holds that your own era must be more special and more scary than any age before – because you happen to live in it. The serious question is whether things really have got worse. Is the second half of the 20th century in Britain really more violent, more criminal, more immoral than, say, the last half of the 19th century? Like most serious questions, it is hard to answer and is really several questions in one.

The first is: has crime really increased? In 1978 James Anderton, then chief constable of Greater Manchester, said that "crimes recorded in England and Wales in 1900 stood at 77,934; by 1976 that figure had reached 2,135,713". There had been a 20th-century crime wave of cataclysmic proportions.

Or had there? Victorian and Edwardian police stations were much more casual about recording crime than the police of today. Until the 1930s, it was common to record thefts from the public as lost property, and not to record incidents that could not be cleared up. Legislation this century has expanded the definitions of crime, so that, according to the Police Federation, of the 5,100 most common offences that its members have to deal with, 3,560 have been created by Parliament in the past 20 years.

To give one example of this inflation: after 1977, the distinction between major and minor damage (set at £20) in cases of vandalism was abolished. This had the effect of adding one-sixth of a million indictable offences to the criminal records – which alone was four times the total of criminal convictions in 1900. An instant crime wave was created at a stroke. "Criminal statistics," writes Geoffrey Pearson, "are notoriously unreliable as measures of the actual extent of criminal activity, to such a degree that it is not unknown for historians to disregard them altogether."

Before 1901 the Home Office did not even have a centralised criminal records system, so we have almost no idea what was the general rate of crime in Victorian England. The evidence, as historians say, is "reconstructive and anecdotal", which means newspapers, court records, guesswork and gossip.

The only reasonably reliable figures are for serious crimes such as murder, and these will surprise most people. In the 1980s the average homicide rate for England and Wales was 634 a year. In the 1870s it was 389 a year and in the 1880s, 393. Remembering that population has doubled in the past 100 years and that 19th-century detection rates were certainly lower, it is clear we have a lower murder rate now than in the golden years of the Victorian period. Petty, casual violence of the kind police attend to has apparently declined as well. Prosecuted assaults were six times more numerous in the 1870s then a century later.

What about other contemporary anxieties, such as child abuse and child murder? The great scandal of the 1870s and 1880s was "baby-farming" and infanticide. As Lionel Rose describes in *The Massacre of the Innocents*, it was common throughout the Victorian period for unwanted babies to be "farmed out" to foster mothers who might look after dozens at a time, keeping them half-starved and stunned on "Syrup of Poppy".

"Fifteen shillings a month or twelve pounds to adopt" was the conventional wording of newspaper adverts, and there were reckoned to be at least 30,000 children "farmed out" in 1860s London. In 1867 the *Daily Telegraph* reported the discovery of a baby farm run by Mrs Caroline Jaggers of Tottenham. She had several decomposing babies in her attic and 40 more-or-less alive, several of them looked after by a three-year-old boy or "ganger". A raid on the home of Mrs Margaret Waters of Brixton in 1870 found five babies on a sofa, "filthy, stinking and stupefied with opiates" and five more in the backyard. One died soon afterwards at Lambeth police station and the other four died at Lambeth workhouse.

If children survived to the age of six or seven they were often sold into trades such as prostitution or chimney-sweeping, though some baby farmers short-circuited the process and saved money by murdering their charges. In 1865 Charlotte Winson of Newquay, on trial for the murder of baby Thomas Harris, boasted that she killed babies as a business, charging between £2 and £5 for "compressing the jugular vein". In 1861 *The Times* reported that the bodies of 278 babies had been recovered that year in London from rivers, doorsteps and dustbins. Given that babies are easy to dispose of, contemporary estimates of 1,200 murders a year in London and 5,000 nationally do not seem incredible.

Nowadays, or course, we kill our babies legally before they are born, but the examples above prove something, which is a greater indifference towards cruelty and violence among ordinary Victorians. Modern agonies over the Cleveland child abuse scandal or the Kincora Boys' Home abuses would be incomprehensible to them. For every modern tragedy like that of Jamie Bulger, it is easy to find a Victorian parallel, like the 1859 case of Constance Kent, the 16-year-old daughter of a factory inspector who was tried for murdering her four-year-old step-brother. Such horrors were almost too common to be noted, and we only know about Miss Kent because Wilkie Collins borrowed aspects of the case for his novel *The Moonstone*.

The prevalence of other offences, such as burglary and street crime, is harder to measure. From the pages of Dickens and Henry Mayhew it is clear that pickpocketing and bag-snatching were major, well-organised industries, but few victims would have bothered to seek out the police, who were in any case rather few and inefficient. Few burglaries were reported either, until the general advent of household insurance after 1918. (It is worth remembering here that insurance company loss-adjusters now estimate that two-thirds of burglary claims are fraudulent.)

Up to the mid-19th century, house-breaking seems to have been very common, as the multiple bolts, bars and shutters on houses of that period testify. The social historian James Cornford points out that most respectable streets had gates and guards, while the early Victorian square, like the modern American condominium, was designed as much for security as symmetry, with its limited access, fenced gardens and good visibility.

In wealthy houses it was common for a manservant armed with a pistol to sleep in the silver pantry, and many a lady would carry a tiny "muff pistol" in her carriage. People took more responsibility for their own security – and the relatively tiny apparatus of state allowed them to do so.

Middle-class people were three to four inches taller than the poor, which gave some advantage, but there were large areas of London, the East End especially, where they never went at all and which were too dangerous even for policemen.

In 1851 Charles Dickens recounted, in *Household Words*, a daring expedition to the infamous Rats Castle, the largest criminal rookery in London. He went with an assistant commissioner of police and several constables but was still clearly relieved to escape with his skin. Rats Castle stood at what is now the junction of New Oxford Street and Tottenham Court Road, barely 400 yards from some of the richest streets in London.

Even those respectable streets had a raffishness and squalor that is hard to imagine today. Kellow Chesney in *The Victorian Underworld* describes how, of an evening, Haymarket, Leicester Square and Regent Street teemed with prostitutes, many of them children, of either sex, plucking at the sleeves of gentlemen as they strolled to their clubs in Pall Mall.

In Mayhew's survey of London seamstresses, one quarter were part-time whores, while his study of costermongers, one of the largest working-class groups, records that fewer than one in 10 was legally married to his woman, who might often be swopped with a friend.

There was no drug problem: morphia, laudanum and other

opiates were freely available and freely abused. Violent assault was treated much more leniently than crimes against property. One of Mayhew's costermongers who attacked a policeman from behind, disabling him for life, was sentenced to 12 months, at a time when the penalty for stealing a few pounds' worth of goods was 10 years' transportation.

Rape was barely recognised except in the sense of an assault by a lower-class man on a woman of higher station. What an upper-class husband did to his wife was above the law and what the lower classes got up to in their stews was beneath notice. "The gals," said one of Mayhew's louts, "axully likes a feller for walloping them."

The great gulf between now and then is not so much in levels of crime and violence as in social attitudes to them. There has always been vastly more crime than is ever reported. Even today, criminologists calculate from self-reporting surveys that only around 15 per cent of crimes are ever recorded, and in Victorian times it was far, far less.

What evidence there is, coupled with common sense, suggests that human dishonesty, greed and violence are fairly constant. As the *Cambridge Social History of Britain* puts it: "For centuries in Britain, stealing from and hurting other people have been pursuits as common and traditional as drinking and fornicating."

What has changed is our attitude to such things, which in turn means readiness to confront and record the truth. Our crime waves, moral panics and hand-wringing are not measures of relative depravity but of a civilised willingness to look more steadily at something that has been there all the time.

The Daily Telegraph, 13 March 1993

Rock fans

"Hattie!"
"Toby!"
"Sophie!"
"Oliver!"
"But this is a-maaa-zing!"
"I don't beli-eeeve it!"
"Ab-so-lutely incredible!"
"BLOODY small world!"

Four young people who barely know each other have met in the public bar of the Mariners, a pub in Rock, Cornwall, much favoured by the young of the upper middle class. The first thing they do after ritual expressions of joy and disbelief at this modest coincidence is establish their credentials:

"Sophie's PRACTICALLY our next-door neighbour in Fulham."

"Oliver was at Stowe with my BROTHER."

"HATTIE was our CHALET GIRL in Val d'Isère."

The next thing is to announce where they have just come from:

"Cowes."

"Salcombe."

"St Trop."

And where they are off to next:

"Chamonix."

"St John's, actually."

"Some bloody awful crammer, I'm afraid."

And the last thing is to rush off and greet somebody else:

"Hattie!"

"Toby!"

"Sophie!"

"Oliver!"

"How am-aaaa-zing!"

Really it is the opposite of amazing, because the point of Rock, for parents at least, is to guarantee such encounters and to guard against meetings with other, less suitable types. These are, in order of unsuitability: sexually attractive yobs; sexually attractive blacks;

185

gold-digging bimbos; predatory married men; leftish intellectuals and artists; hard-drug dealers and journalists. There are none of these in Rock. Practically none, at any rate.

The Mariners is a dump, with aluminium-frame windows, a sullen barman with a poodle perm, and a ragged string of plastic Budweiser flags. The music is a tape of *Space Oddity, Love Me Do* and *This My Life*, endlessly recycled. The beer is warm and comes in scratched plastic skiffs; the pasties are cold and filled with minced rubber glove.

A gilded youth with his Circle One wetsuit peeled down to his waist, so the arms stick out from his thighs, sidles shyly to the bar. "No we 'AVEN'T got any bloody French mustard. Where do you think you are?" As with all enormously successful pubs, the staff of the Mariners are wonderfully rude.

By nine on a Saturday night it is wall-to-wall with rich and beautiful young people. The boys wear hooded Gap sweatshirts and back-to-front baseball caps; the girls wear cut-offs and vests, with grey-striped duffel jackets. There are touches of individuality, like the customised T-shirts: Rock '93 – This Is Not A Rehearsal; Rock '92 – Wrecked At The Mariners, but basically they all look the same, boys and girls. It is the washed-out colours of the clothes; the golden tans that go right into the armpits; the long blonde hair, picturesquely matted with seawater.

But the resemblance goes deeper: as if they all had a gene in common. Something to do with the way the skin is so taut on their well-fed faces that it pounts the upper lip, and tilts the tip of the nose, and gives the cheekbones a gloss. Many are cousins, but they look as if they all were.

John Betjeman gets them just right in *North Coast Recollections*: "Oh, healthy bodies, bursting into teens/And bursting out of last year's summer clothes." Those were Betjeman's childhood friends on his Cornish seaside holidays in this same village: "Ralph, Vasey, Alastair, Biddy, John and me" – and these are their grandchildren, 60 years on.

"Hattie!"

"Toby!"

"Sophie!"

"Oliver!"

"How am-aaaa-zing!"

Old and drunk, I ask one pretty girl if she knows where is the church of St Enodoc where Betjeman is buried.

"Who's Betjeman?" she says. Rock is a small village on the Camel estuary – a crooked nick in the coast of north Cornwall. Until the 19th century it was just a landing stage for the ferry to Padstow, across the estuary. From the 1850s the railway began to bring fishermen from London, then golfers, who knocked balls about among the dunes, and founded the famous St Enodoc club. A couple of small hotels were built along the shore, and mothers arrived, seeking sea air for their children at cheaper rates and in less plebeian conditions than Brighton and Southend. Regular visitors began to retire to Rock and, when the fishermen's cottages were all bought up, they built nasty bungalows.

It is not a pretty place; basically a long street with a Spar, a petrol station, a Post Office and a chip shop, and yet it has a summertime population that rivals Port Grimaud for smart. The Marquis of Zetland; the Duke of Norfolk; Lady Sarah Armstrong Jones; Field Marshal Lord and Lady Bramall; the writer Candida Lycett Green; the TV director Jonathan Stedall; Michael Bromley (of Russell and Bromley) – all own or regularly rent houses in Rock.

On a Saturday morning the pavements outside the Rock Bakery and Di's Dairy (Fortnum's-by-the-Sea) are lined with Range Rovers and Shoguns – four-wheel drive being essential for the 20-foot gravel driveway to the bungalow. Across the bay in Padstow, normal Cornwall, people play Krazy Golf, eat cream teas, go mackerel fishing, wear Jurassic Park beach pyjamas – but here we are not in normal Cornwall. This is Trechelsea, Penfulham and Kensington-super-Mare.

In Di's Dairy a 15-year-old nymphet in cut-offs is hovering at the deli counter: "Could you tell me please how much is left in the kitty?" The grey Cornish-woman behind the counter sternly inspects a bown envelope in the till drawer:

"Thirty-eight pound forty."

"Oh, phew, gosh. That's all right then," says the nymphet. "How much are those quails' eggs?"

The Dairy is an amazing place for a remote rural hamlet: pink peppercorns, black olive paste, vegetable ghee, Spanish turon, pistachio halva, whole black truffles, fresh lobster, crevettes and turbot and a good 50 cheeses running from Ski Queen Ejetost to Rutland Beer and Garlic. If they haven't got it then Di will order it from Anthony Rowcliff of London – next day delivery by Securicor.

The window of the Dairy is half covered with a lurid reproduction of a Posy Simmonds cartoon – for Rock is not just

Trechelsea but Tresoddit, the mythical Cornish village, created for her *Guardian* strip by Posy, who has a house in neighbouring Port Isaac. Di's Dairy is the original of Tresoddit Stores, infested by fierce old bats with Kensington accents, while Di's husband Tony Dunkerley is the prototype of that acquisitive cartoon Cornishman, Kevin Penwallet.

Di and Tony have 750 account customers – Sir Frederick Lawton, Sir Mark Patten and Edward Fox are names that come up at random. They also issue a Di's Dairy credit card – handling money is as infra dig in Rock as in any royal palace. I watched one old lady buy a scone from Rock Bakery and, when asked for 17p, declare, in ringing tones; "I DO have an account here, you know."

When an account customer is "down", a weekly grocery order of £600 is not uncommon, and when parents return to London, children not trusted with a credit card are left with a brown bag kitty, guarded by Di. "Before the credit cards," says Di, "a kid would give the account number to a mate down the Mariners, and the next thing half the kids in Rock would be charging up the stuff."

Hanging out in Di's Dairy is an entertainment itself on a wet morning as the air is cleft by the confident stridencies of a hundred thou a year: "Down Jasper, DOWN boy. He's perfectly harmless if you don't flinch" … "Now, you'll put those on the account for me, won't you" … "No, no, no. The APPLEWOOD smoked Ilchester" … DOWN Jasper" … "Just pop along to John Bray and get the tennis court key, would you Jums?" … "Oh Jasper you BAD dog."

John Bray is the estate agent who practically runs Rock, through a network of interlocking companies: John Bray and Partners sells houses, while John Bray Cornish Holidays lets them; John Bray Services cleans them and does their gardens, while the more modestly named Rock Electrical Services supplies TV sets and fixes their cookers. As one-time owner of Rock Water Sports he has even taught Sir John Junor to sail.

A large, affable man, he is a descendant of Billy Bray, the famous revivalist preacher, and of "Dandy" Bray, the Victorian swell who founded the *Cornish Times* and ran Bodmin's largest grocery. He has 190 houses on his books, all in a three-mile radius, of which 120 are let out to visitors and 70 looked after for their owners. Eighty of the owners live overseas and 25 have swimming pools – built, naturally, by John Bray Swimming Pools. "Oh, and we have had a field cleared so people can bring helicopters in. But you mustn't call it a heliport."

House prices here are incredible: £168,000 for a teeny slipway cottage with no garden and no living room, £250,000 for a three-bed house with a sea view. But Bray started by letting caravans in the '60s – one early customer was a nice schoolmaster called Harry Patterson who used to limp down from up north with his family crammed in a hopeless old banger. John used to help fix Harry's car, and sympathise with him over the book he was trying write and could never finish.

To everyone's surprise, it eventually was finished and published as *The Eagle Has Landed*, with a picture on the cover of a sinister chap in black leather and dark glasses called Jack Higgins. Another client was Betjeman himself – "SIR John," says Bray firmly – who stayed at the house owned by his mistress, Lady Elizabeth Cavendish. "They'd let it out to people. And he'd leave all his books and manuscrips lying about there, quite happily."

Bray decided to put payphones into all the houses, for visitors, "but Sir John, who was Poet Laureate by then, was very worried about phoning over a poem to the Queen and running out of coins. We took him and Lady Elizabeth on a special outing in a chauffeur-driven Rover to inspect one of the phones, but he wouldn't have it".

Bray is one obvious reason for Rock's success, but even he is puzzled by the glamour. "The basis is the golf club, I suppose, and the estuary, which is the only place in North Cornwall that you get sheltered sailing, a sandy beach, and the sun all day. but it is a very strange place." A man pops his head around the door at this point to return the key to the tennis court, with a brisk, "Cheers, John." "That's a typical one there," says Bray. "Former Lord Lieutenant of Kent. It never ceases to amaze me."

At the golf club bar I meet a man called Tim Harvey, a solicitor from Newbury who is the same age as me, but who already has teenage children.

"Where do grown-ups go at night here?" I ask him curiously, and he says: "Fish and chips. Bottle of wine. Watch telly. Go to bed early. We sometimes have a bridge four, or go to Rick Stein's seafood place in Padstow. But the great thing about Rock is you don't have to worry about the kids. There's only one place they can be, which is the Mariners, and if they can't walk back, the police will bring them eventually."

On the door of the golf club is a sign which says: "A reasonable standard of dress is required. This excludes denim jeans, collarless T-shirts, track suits, multi-coloured baggy shorts and beach shorts.

(Tailored walking shorts are permitted.)" The notice is new, and the exquisite pendantry of "collarless" and "tailored" suggest it is replaced frequently.

Locals are not as laid-back as visitors about the Mariners, which was the quiet little Rock Hotel 10 years ago. Andrea Jago, the village hairdresser, warned us off going down there, and said she never risked driving past at night, "with kids rocking the cars. But they're all MPs' children, so the police do nothing." Di Dunkerley takes the tolerant, motherly, "They'll grow out of it" line, but her husband Tony says, "I think there is a sinister side to it, with cannabis and other things. They sent 12 police down last year and they drove them off, throwing pint pots at the van."

Back in the public bar of the Mariners, I am wedged in a corner with Harry and Ollie and Toby, who are getting ratted on a vile babymix of cider, lager and blackcurrant. "Courshe thersh dope," says Ollie, thickly, "but not in the bloody pub."

"Shmoke dope at the beach parties," says Harry. "Or in the shand dunes," says Toby.

"Try under the 14th tee," says Ollie, and they all giggle. The big dunes under the 14th are a legendary spot for lost virginities.

At my left elbow a big blond berk called Jums is shouting about the estate agency business. "There's 10 per cent of people in this country will never work again. Call them the underclass if you like. What they are interested in is income, not capital, and that's where we come in …"

"That's Jums Greaves," says Harry, "He wash on the Campbeltown." I look blank.

"The *Duke of York's* ship," says Toby, pityingly.

A pretty girl called Emma with eternal brown legs comes up to scrounge a cigarette off Ollie, and walks back to the Jums group.

"God, I'd love to get inside her wetsuit," says Toby, suddenly full of despair.

"State you're in," says Harry, "you couldn't get into a bath."

"God, Rock is bloody boring," says Ollie, who is the intellectual of the group, with six GCSEs and a half chance of Exeter University in the autumn so long as he didn't totally screw up his sociology A-Level.

"You never get out of BED in the daylight," says Harry. "How do you know what Rock is like?"

But as usual in adolescent circles "Bloody boring" is a term of highest approval. Sailing round the beautiful estuary all day in

Lasers and Firebirds is boring. Getting 10 quid out of your parents to get ratted every night is boring. Getting stoned, and jostling cars, and chucking glasses at the odd police van, and going to all-night beach parties, and charging up foie gras on the parents' account at Di's and maybe even getting inside Eternal Emma's wetsuit – they are all bloody boring.

If I sound jealous, it's because I am jealous, but more of their youth than their privilege, which deprives as much as it bestows. These boys are more awkward with girls than kids in London comps; inarticulate outside their narrow grooves of conversational formula (Hattie! Toby! Sophie! Oliver! How am-aaa-zing!) and who's to say they will go further?

The poet Lawrence Binyon wrote *For the Fallen* here – which is recited every Remembrance Sunday: "They shall not grow old as we that are left grow old / Age shall not weary them nor the years condemn" – everyone knows it. It is that kind of melancholy which attracts me: of Betjeman's "salt and hot sun on rubber water wings", "the coconut smell of gorse" and the luxurious discomfort of beach picnics with "Sand in the sandwiches, wasps in the tea / Sun on our bathing dresses heavy with wet ..." It is the easy, gilded nostalgia of any place where generations have played as children and brought their children and grandchildren and which brings the Rock tribe back year after year.

But Rock is not for me, with its braying accents and Jeffrey Archer novels and golf handicaps and frantic uniformity. As we walked down the beach one day past the quacking encampments of Circle One wetsuits and hooded Gap sweatshirts my wife said suddenly. "God, it's like a penguin colony," and there seemed nothing else to say after that and we left, thankfully, for Padstow.

The Daily Telegraph, 21 August 1993

Gun lore

'**B**ooff!" Next to my ear the shotgun makes a dull smash like a hammer on a cabbage. Twenty yards away the bird stalls in flight, one wing high, and at the wrong angle. It was moving at 40 miles an hour, so the momentum carries it another 30 feet, in pantomime flight. But all vitality has gone. It flies like a beanbag. "Good shot!" says Robin.

My head replays the sequence from start. The grouse comes rocketing over the bank to my right – a simple black squiggle on the sky. "Two o'clock," says Robin Peel, an old grouse hand who is loading for me today, but my gun is already swinging up, in the groove that has eluded me all morning.

Weight forward on the left foot; stock snug against right cheek; a snick as the safety goes off. The triangle made by the twin muzzles and bead swings across the sky, *through* the bird just as the instructors tell you. Booff! Stall. The graceless pantomime flight. The beanbag thudding into the heather. "You'll always remember that," says Robin, and I think I will. The first thing in my life I have deliberately killed, apart from mackerel and mice.

The trouble is that I haven't killed it. The bird is a "runner", meaning it is sitting bleeding and fluttering in a stream, where we find it once the drive is over. "Shall I finish it for you?" says Robin, and I say, "No. If you're not ready to kill something, I don't think you should be shooting at it" which is a piece of tripe I got from Hemingway or somebody.

So I seize the bird and wring it's neck, which is something else you read in books. But this is a real grouse, which pecks me hard on the hand, and struggles free, and sits shivering on the stream bank, his black-jelly eye on mine. This grouse has clearly been on one of those seminars executives attend, on how to survive kidnapping and terrorist attacks. Do not come along easily, but if forced to, make eye contact with the terrorist; use first names; make him see you as a real person; break down his training; destroy his stereotypes.

The grouse's name, he mutely tells me, is Gary. He's two years old and happily married with eight kids in his covey (he produces

192

the photographs from under his wing). Gary the Grouse is a strict vegetarian (heather shoots, bilberry and the occasional catkin), with no political views except on blood sports. He has never done harm to anyone, but I kill him anyway. My training demands it.

My guide to grouse shooting suggests that a stubborn bird should be dispatched with "a sharp bite to the vertebrae. Do not shirk this unpleasant task – it is your duty." But before I can fall to gnawing at Gary's neck, Robin intervenes: "Index and middle finger around the throat and give a sharp tug and twist."

But it isn't as easy as that.

At 28 ounces Gary is only a hundredth of my body weight, but he's a tough old bird who knows how to fight, and there are moments in the mist of spray and blood and beating wings and pecking beak that I begin to wonder who will come out on top. I get my fist around Gary's throat in the end, and squeeze, which is inelegant but effective, and the wingbeats steadily slow, then stop, and it is just me standing in the stream with blood up to my elbows. He's dead. But then he twitches and I drop him in the stream again. "Only nerves," says Robin.

This is the bit the shooters don't like to talk about. They say they shoot because it is a force for conservation, which is true. They shoot because it is a way of having a great day out in wonderful countryside with your friends, which is also true. They even say they shoot because they like the social rituals and the smart clothes and the dogs, and that can be true too. But they don't say they shoot because they get a kick from killing things. This is difficult, but if you don't say it somewhere, you are a phoney.

There are two competing hypocrisies at the centre of the blood sports argument, both tedious, and worth getting out of the way early. The first is the shooters' pretence that they don't do it for fun. The second is the antis' pretence that they only disapprove of cruelty, whereas in fact they disapprove of people.

Most antis would ban all blood sports, including fishing; many want to ban meat; some, like the Animal Liberation Front, favour "withdrawal of human populations to pre-exploitation boundaries". They don't say it too loudly because people would regard them as nutters, and stop supporting them. I back the hypocrites who hunt and shoot, because they want freedom rather than prohibition, and because their view of human nature is more realistic, but I wish they'd be more honest.

Shooters don't talk of moral, but "sporting" behaviour, an

elusive and slightly absurd notion when we are talking of a contest between an armed man and a two-pound bird. But it is real enough, though the boundaries of "sportsmanship" vary.

Before 1850 it was unsportsmanlike for hired beaters to drive game birds towards hidden Guns (a gun is a weapon, a Gun the man who fires it). The invention of the pin-fire, breech-loading shotgun (by a Frenchman), the opening of the moors to railway and road and the gentrification of an impatient new business class changed all that.

The late Victorians swallowed their compunctions and shot everything that moved, then posed proudly for the photographer in front of their mountains of game. They shot 4,000 pheasants one day at Hall Barn in Buckinghamshire, and Lord Ripon shot 28 pheasants in one minute, using four guns. At Blubberhouses in 1888 the sixth Lord Walsingham shot 1,070 grouse in a single day – a record that still stands and will probably stand forever.

There arose, as the shooting historian J. K. Stanford writes, "an ineradicable taint of excess" and the boundaries of sportsmanship were tightened. Quality replaced quantity and the concept of "the sporting bird" was created – that is the bird with as good a chance of escape as the Gun has of killing it.

On August 12 this year, the opening day of the grouse season, I am standing up to my knees in freezing slurry in a grouse butt in Yorkshire with a dentist from Macclesfield called Steve. We have been standing here all morning, our boots filling with hailstones, our glasses and noses streaming, and our clothes turning to moulds of sodden cloth.

"Aren't you miserable?"

"It beats looking in people's mouths all day," says Steve. He has paid hundreds of pounds to be here, invested thousands in his equipment, and looked forward for months to this day – and there are no birds.

Late snows and strongyle, a parasitic threadworm, have seen off most of the chicks, and only a couple of dozen grouse have fluttered across the line of butts, well away from us. Then a black squiggle clears the skyline ahead and comes jinking a few feet above the heather in the characteristic flight pattern of the grouse. A few wingbeats then a glide; a few more wingbeats, another glide – dipping and swinging all the time with the ground contours below.

But this grouse is slow, and very low, and apparently short-sighted, heading straight towards us, until, at 15 yards even I could hit it, and Steve is a good shot. And he lets it go. Doesn't even mount the gun. The grouse positively *ambles* past, clearly wondering whether or not to take a rest on Steve's shoulder like Long John Silver's parrot.

"What are you DOING? Why didn't you SHOOT it?" I am hopping from foot to foot with thwarted urban blood lust.

"Not a sporting bird," says Steve.

He lets another bird go by a few minutes later because he says it's a better shot for a neighbouring Gun, though it looks about equal to me. Then he lets another one off because he likes the colour of its feathers or something, and I am beginning to think this whole thing is insane. That you stand in the sleet for hours and hours at crippling expense just to get your £295 David Ripper Balmoral jacket ruined, and your £158 leather-lined Aigle wellies full of water and to short-circuit your £120 Peltor electronic ear defenders. Madness!

And then a grouse comes in diagonally and very fast, from left to right and dipping like mad, and Steve's gun is up and swinging, quicker than I can follow. Booff! Stall. The beanbag flight. The thud into the heather. A sporting bird.

I don't shoot this day. I'm still taking lessons at the West Wycombe shooting ground; still banana-fingered with the shotgun when I pull it from the canvas slip. A shotgun is more organic than mechanical, with its snaky lines; the sensual hatching and engraving; the seamless merging of polished walnut and oily steel. You don't aim a shotgun so much as point it with your whole body, and it seems to call for an organic familiarity.

The instructions are so simple: weight on the front foot; stock into the shoulder; safety off; swing the muzzle *through* the bird – but also absurdly difficult, like the litany of "mirror, signal, manoeuvre" when you learn to drive.

I keep forgetting the safety catch; I fire the gun before it is properly mounted and bruise my bicep; I keep shooting behind the little clay discs.

"No, no. Swing *through* the bird." We lack organic unity, my gun and I.

I'm not ready, but Mark Osborne, the owner of West Wycombe, has invited me to join his syndicate in Derbyshire for the day. This is a kindness worth £600, in a year when grouse are scarce and one doesn't want to cock it up.

"Don't worry, you'll get a bird," says Robin Peel, my friend from the British Association for Shooting and Conservation. But I don't know. Before the day Robin runs through all the stuff you need to know: the right clothes, drawing lots for the butt, NEVER swinging your gun across the line, how to tip the keeper: "About 30 quid is normal; just tuck it in his palm as you shake hands at the end."

"Rather feudal, isn't it?" I protest. "A bit Bootsie and Snudge?"

"It's the way it is done," says Robin.

We meet at nine at a handsome National Trust house in a dark valley full of rhododendrons. There is the usual litter of Range Rovers and Shoguns; florid men in beautiful, dense tweeds; quiet spaniels and flatcoat Labradors. Everyone shakes hands: "Martyn, this is Tom; John, this is James; Lucy, this is Martyn ..." I recognise Mark Osborne and his partner Edward Dashwood from West Wycombe. Everyone is smiling, but it's quite formal and I am very nervous.

A group of beaters and keepers, some in jeans but mostly tweedy, sits off to one side with sticks and flags. One calls me "Sir", which reminds me of my father's story of serving with the RAF in Norfolk in the dark days of 1940. Weapons were short, so when, one day, the men were all issued with brooms, they thought the Germans must be landing at last. But they had only been detailed for a pheasant drive on the Sandringham estate, with free beer at the end, and my father says he knew then that Hitler had no chance. And we have gone from beater to shooter in one generation, which must be familial, if not social, progress.

In two groups we climb the valley to heather moorland, drying off in the morning sun, where a million bees are already booming, like a distant speedway track. Folds of ground recede in elegant gradations of colour: lavender and azure and purple. "Wonderful day!" people say to each other. "Quite enough to just be up here on a day like this, and never mind the shooting." But of course it wouldn't be here without the shooting, for I know now that what looked to me like wilderness a month ago is as carefully husbanded as any farm.

Grouse are wild birds, but with a fragile ecological niche, living almost entirely on young heather shoots. Left to itself, without regular burning or pest control, this moor would revert quite rapidly to bracken, which is poisonous to most animals and largely useless. More probably, if it were not let out to shooting, the owner would plant conifers or graze sheep, neither of which would support grouse or the 30-odd other species of bird that thrive here now.

Antis say the grouse moor is an artificial environment, and so it is, but as Robin Peel asks, "What is a *natural* environment in a country like England?"

The butts look different from the ones at the West Wycombe shooting ground, which has plastic greengrocer's grass and electric buttons for releasing the clays. These are little more than holes lined with stones, but at least they are dry.

I have drawn butt six, near the middle of the line, which is the best place to be, and I miss everything. I keep forgetting the safety; I break the gun with barrels up so the cartridges fall out in the heather. I forget to take my thumb off the lock lever, and it gets split when the gun recoils. I shoot behind the birds. My glasses begin to mist up with anxiety and the pain in my thumb. I get so excited I swing my level through the line of butts, which is the cardinal crime of grouse shooting, and which people have been sent home for, but which Robin is kind enough to ignore. I drop the gun on my foot.

Expensive grouse stream endlessly and healthily over my head while the other Guns drum their fingers in neighbouring butts.

They are very nice about it at lunch, which is game pie and cold chicken and scotch eggs and tomatoes and smoked salmon sandwiches and beer. Personalities emerge shyly in the gruff, smoky masculine atmosphere. One is heir to a title and large estate; another runs a gun shop in Lincoln; a third has sold his building company and is living well on the proceeds; a fourth has retired from the steel industry in Sheffield.

All are rich but none is especially grand. It's a fairly typical syndicate, according to Robin. Eight friends chip in, say, £6,000 a year each for six to 10 days' shooting, while one holds the lease and manages the moor. In this case it is Mark Osborne, my host, who is a chartered surveyor in St Albans, specialising in the leisure industry, and has two other grouse moors.

After lunch I kill Gary the Grouse, and honour is satisfied and the sun comes out again. My etiquette guide says: "Your contribution to the bag, and that of other Guns, is NEVER a topic to start discussing, though it is perfectly in order to give or receive compliments about marksmanship."

All kills go into a common bag, with a share-out of two brace each at the end. So is it bad form to confess I shot three grouse, while the other seven Guns accounted for 151? I don't care. I killed my second bird, flying fast and dipping from right to left, with a 50-

yard shot that Mark said was the best of the day. I drove home glowing, with Gary Grouse in the boot – or one of his cousins, at any rate. I plucked him and drew him and cooked him and ate him, with the reflection that his was probably the most expensive meal I had ever had – but Gary Grouse was very good.

The Daily Telegraph, 28 August 1993

No sex please, we're married

'Researchers have found that 95 per cent of teenage boys masturbate. The remaining five per cent are liars." So ran the old schoolboy joke, and I quote it here as a caveat for what follows. Everyone lies about sex and at every age. When I was 11 I was the only child in the world who didn't know how sex worked; at 18 I was the only virgin in the university; at 30 I belonged to the only couple on earth which wasn't doing it five times a week – and I never learn.

There is a married couple I know – call them Boris and Sophie – who I'd always known had a good sex life. She was one of those glowing blondes and he was one of those small, swart and hairy types who you know are frantically busy in bed. They have no children, and are very focused on each other – caressing in public and swopping mildly suggestive banter. They went to live in Italy recently, where I jealously imagined them romping naked in hay meadows, having candle-lit baths together, and doing creative things with linguine. it turns out they have been spending most of their time in therapy, and working overtime to pay the shrinks' bills. "They haven't done it in *18 months*," my partner told me after a long confession session with Sophie on the phone, and we glanced speculatively around at our other acquaintances.

"Do you remember what sex was like when we are at college?" a friend asked me dreamily a few weeks ago. "Pat and I used to get twenty Player's Number Six, a box of Kleenex and just stay in bed *all day.* For a daytime screw these days we've got to fly to a Greek island with a full-time nanny, and then I'd be lucky." In fact, this particular man says he hasn't had sex with his wife for over a year, and I know another man who hasn't had it for nine months. They are both in their early forties, healthy, and in apparently stable marriages. Neither of them thinks their circumstances are particularly unusual. Another friend, in his early thirties, has just separated from the woman he has lived with for six years. He told me in the pub the other night that they had only had sex three or four times a year for the last three years of their relationship. I told him it was about the same at the end of my own first marriage, which lasted some seven years.

"Do you think it's always like that after seven years then?" he asked me, and I said, "God, I hope not," thinking of my own six-year relationship (still 10 or 12 times a week, honest). According to the Wellcome Foundation's *Sexual Attitudes and Lifestyle*, which was published in January, men between 40 and 45 are having sex an average six times a month, but of the dozen men I know well enough to ask, only two are even claiming to have intercourse at this rate. In the public world of magazine surveys, tabloid features, and ice-cream commercials everyone is at it like knives. Windsurfers are doing it standing up; young farmers are doing it in their wellies; hang-gliders are doing it in their thermals, and every business tycoon is doing it seven times a night with his kiss-and-tell Karen. Zipless, guilt-free and athletic; everyone in the world is doing it, apart from you and everyone that you know.

Everyone lies about sex, and it is important to remember this in the face of the propaganda which pours from the news media and research bodies. In the 1960s, according to Masters and Johnson, men only averaged 11 seconds before ejaculation, while today, according to Hartman and Fithian, they are up to an heroic 15 minutes. In the 1940s the Kinsey Report found that 14 per cent of women were capable of multiple orgasms – a shocking revelation which sent shivers through male self-esteem and shattered the image of woman as Victorian angel, submitting herself to the filthy male libido. But by 1994 that 14 per cent had become a whopping 75 per cent. One woman was even recorded as having a Kalashnikov-like 134 orgasms an hour. To take a similar example, Hartman and Fithian recently found that 12 per cent of men were capable of multiple orgasms – a series of sexual climaxes without ejaculation – even though there were *no* men in this category 50 years ago. As the percentage is similar to the number of women who were once multi-orgasmic, it may be that in 50 years time men will be firing off 134 orgasms an hour as well. Sad to say, they offer no helpful road map to this Nirvana, apart from some vague talk about flexing the pubiococcygeous muscle – and stop that fidgeting in the back of the class.

The reason for these modern lies and fantasies is that, in the language of the sociologists, sex has become "commodified" in this century, which is to say it has become tangled up with marketing and advertising. In the 19th century it was social status that was used to add value to a commercial product – you smoked a certain tobacco because it was "By Royal Appointment"; you ate a certain anchovy paste because it was the "Gentleman's Relish". As outward differences between classes declined, the salesman's emphasis shifted from social to sexual ambition. If you want to belong to the new sexual elite (perfect bodies, multiple orgasms, guiltless coupling) you must eat Häagen-Dazs ice-cream, wear Levi jeans, use Calvin Klein's "Obsession" behind your ears, drink Volvic mineral water, drive a Renault Clio and fly Singapore Airlines.

Sex is now the free gift with every product, but to fit the packet it must be uniform. On the late-20th-century production line you can have any kind of sex you want, so long as it is perfect and three times a week with considerate foreplay, reliable erection, fail-safe orgasm and always with a condom. National economies depend on it, and there are whole industries of counselling, therapy, publishing, cosmetics and surgery urgently devoted to it. Language plays its part as the aseptic "bonking" becomes an acceptable euphemism for the sexual act across all levels of society. Even Aids has been recruited, as the necessary candour of health propaganda helps to license the increased blatancy of product advertising. The bachelor, the spinster and the celibate, once respected figures in the social landscape, are now treated as freaks – and in economic terms they are indeed a subversive element, requiring to be marginalised as efficiently as once was the 19th-century communist.

Sex as a commodity creates unreal expectations in people and at the same time fuels the fires of acquisitiveness for material products which make you too shagged for shagging in the first place. "Do you still have a good sex life with Christine?" I once asked a friend, and he said, "No, I've got a ten-and-a-half per cent fixed rate mortgage." Over the last few weeks I have asked 15 or so men and women friends, all married or cohabiting, if they believe in sex after marriage, and find I have acquired in the process a Dr Ruth Westheimer accent for dealing with the mild embarrassment that ensues: "So zen, tell me, Roger. How long haff you had zis problem mit talking about sex?"

The questions have been fairly standard. How often did you do it in the beginning? How often do you do it now? Why do you think it is less? (It always is less.) The respondents fall into two main groups. In the first are couples who have never done it more than twice in a day, and whose early average was about three times a week. In most cases, after seven years, they are down to twice a month or less. in the second, much small group, are the sex beasts who have done it up to five times in a day, and whose early average was six or seven times a week. (The champion couple claimed 24 times during a one-week honeymoon in Lanzarote, but the judges are willing to entertain other claims, suitably documented.) Members of the minority Group Two are still tending to average 2-3 times a week after the fatal seven-year period.

Very infrequent sex was almost invariably followed eventually by marital breakdown. "I always think that when it drops to below once a month, then a couple is in real trouble," one friend said. All the people I know who have been through divorces (over half my acquaintances) say sex had almost stopped in the last year or two of marriage, and that it was generally infidelity as a result of sex starvation which led to the final breakdown.

So, why is a busy start to the sex life so important? My friend Edward (Group Two), who is a freelance journalist, happily married for ten years, puts it well: "You break down such a lot of barriers in that period when you are just screwing your brains out. All that shyness and shame and reserve you have – about your body and your performance and your dignity – it just gets dissolved away. For sex to work properly you have to be very honest, but good sex also creates a climate of honesty between you in other areas." So sex is a kind of solvent in marriage that creates a collective experience of closeness, the mere existence of which can help to disperse tensions. "A difference is wide that the sheets will not decide," as I am fond of quoting to my partner, though she will ask, irrelevantly "Who washes the sheets?"

The enemies of sex, both groups agreed, were Sam and Joe and Kate and Sarah and Barnaby and Jack and Theo and Ellie – their children. My friend Michael, who is a solicitor, ten years into his second marriage, says its sexual side never recovered from the birth of his two children: "It tailed off after James was born, and then when Sian got pregnant the second time she had to have a very late abortion, which was awful. She couldn't stand me touching her afterwards, so we didn't do it for a year. And then she couldn't get pregnant again and we were doing all this precision screwing with a calendar by the bed and a thermometer up her backside, which was all pretty depressing as well. Sex seemed to be all about gynaecological disasters of one kind or another, so since Esther was born we've hardly bothered."

Obviously there are severe practical problems which come with the arrival of children – lack of sleep, lack of privacy, lack of money, but children also seem to expose more fundamental differences between men and women. Robert, who is a literary editor in his fifties, said he felt his wife's attention switch completely once their first child was born. "Which was quite a shock. I thought I had married *her*, and that it would be very nice for us to have a baby to look after together. But suddenly it was like she was married to the baby and I was the appendage." Eleanor, who is a doctor in her early thirties, had a similar experience with her first husband, "which made me wish he would just grow up. Couldn't he see that I was tired? Didn't he realise I could not put him first any more?" For the man a child can sometimes seem to rewrite all the rules of marriage in ways that have never been discussed or agreed. For the woman it can seem incredible that a man cannot grasp the shift of priorities that comes to her unbidden through the blood. At the root of the problem seems to be the generally unspoken male feeling that he has already *made* a sacrifice (of his promiscuity) by getting married in the first place, and that there was nothing in the contract about celibacy as well.

The relatively rare Group Two sex beasts tend to cope better with childbirth. "We didn't miss more than a fortnight" Edward told me, but even here children around the house are a powerful anaphrodisiac, especially when you like doing it on the dishwasher in the middle of the afternoon. Locks on the bedroom door are not much use: "They just regard that as an incitement, but we have found that a new Disney video can perk up our sex lives. They work through *The Jungle Book* and we get on with it." Sarah, a teacher in her early forties, said, "It's very hard for a working woman not to feel guilty about the children, but in the end it is your relationship with your husband which is the foundation, so making time for sex is not selfish." The other regular enemies of sex are long hours, two jobs, ill health, anxiety – all the usual culprits. But it was noticeable that while Group One often abandoned sex after a disaster such as a miscarriage or serious illness, the Group Two people seemed able to pick up the pieces again after a gap. Group One couples acquire that curious middle-class accessory – the dressing-room, "but only for when we are keeping each other awake of course", Group Two couples use the dressing-room for undressing each other.

All happy families, as Tolstoy said, are alike, and, as he did not say, all have similar replies to Dr Ruth's last question: "So tell me, vot is ze secret of a good sex life?" It is making time for yourselves; getting away for breaks without the children; being frank about your needs, however squalid or ridiculous you may think they are. Eleanor said, "It helps to become unfamiliar to each other, I think. To see each other as strangers from time to time." Edward's opinion was: "You should answer other people's demands and expect them to answer yours. You should not expect sex to be absolutely mutual all the time. You should even be able to treat each other as objects from time to time." Jennifer, his wife, who was listening to this conversation on the phone, shouted out: "And it helps to be totally incompatible." The most important strand, which came up again and again, was the sense of mutuality in sexual attraction: the assurance that they wanted you as much as you wanted them.

Dr Ruth's conclusion from all this was that there is sex after marriage, but that modern middle-class life is pretty heavily weighted against, and it helps to start from a fairly high level of engagement. Of course there will be people reading this who will be angry by now, and saying how crude, mechanistic and reductive to blame broken marriage on bad sex – as indeed it is. There must be many couples in the wider world who have virtually no sex lives and stay together 60 years in happy relationships. It's just that I've never met any.

Marriages do rely on love, friendship, sense of humour, shared interests – women stress these things particularly – but for the moment I am just talking about sex, and the people that I know. If a 25-year-old Janet and John came to me today and asked if I thought they should marry, now they had been living together for six months, the first thing I should say is: "Tell me zis, Chanet. Tell me zis, Chon. How often do you make luff?" And if it was much less than four times a week I would tactfully suggest that they forget it.

The Spectator, 20 August 1994

We are all disabled now

The starting point for this article was an argument I had years ago with a pub philosopher, who was complaining about all the wheelchair ramps which were just then being set into the kerbs at practically every road junction in our local borough of Camden. "Has anyone ever actually *seen* a wheelchair use one of them?" he demanded, and after some thought we confessed we had not.

"Ah, but people use them for buggies and prams," someone said.

"And how hard is it to push a buggy over a normal kerb?" the philosopher demanded, and we had to admit it was not very hard at all. So easy in fact that buggy-pushers (we numbered some among us) would ignore the ramps altogether if it meant taking the slightest detour from the shortest possible route across the road.

"And how much do the bloody things *cost*?" he wanted to know, and of course nobody had the faintest idea, but we made a guess, for the sake of argument, at not less than £50 for a granite kerbstone, cut to the appropriate angle for a ramp and installed with smart herringbone brick surround by council or even contract labour. There are eight such ramps at a typical crossroads, making £400 per road junction, and how many road junctions are there in Camden? If there were only 1,000, and there are certainly more, you are looking at half a million pounds worth of wheelchair ramps, which, so far as anyone in the pub could testify, had never seen a wheelchair.

Another point of departure occurred to me, symmetrically enough, when I was shepherding my family onto a plane at Heathrow this year. We were halfway down one of those interminable galleries between check-in and boarding gate, when my youngest child demanded the lavatory. The only one I could find had one of those little orange disabled signs, like a broken clock face, but as I reached for the handle an arm barred the way and a voice rang out, "*Thass* for wheelchairs." And it wasn't even some airport jobsworth, but a fellow passenger, in standard thuggo's holiday outfit of earring, tattoo, and three-day stubble.

"But, madam," I said (all right, I'm embellishing a little). "But, madam, I am about to miss my plane. My son is leaking. I am laden with baggage. I am wretched with the fatigue, anxiety and nausea inseparable from going on holiday. I effectively *am* disabled, and furthermore there is not a wheelchair user within *miles* of this lavatory, so why shouldn't I use it?"

"Because my *sister* has got a Down's Syndrome daughter," said thuggo with implacable illogic, and the stubbly, earringed, tattooed crowd which had already begun to gather murmured in sympathy.

"Yur, you tell 'im, mate."

"My daughter's bloke's girlfriend's youngest had that sickle cell whatsit ..."

"Why can't he wait like everyone else ... ?"

"Yuppie git ..."

I was rescued by my son. "Dad, I done it in my nappy ..." and fled the mob in favour of the 18-inch flip-down changing table in the aircraft loo.

Over the time it has taken to work up the nerve to write it, this article has become known to my friends as "Harris's kicking cripples piece" as in "When's the deadline for your cripple-kicker? I've got a story you might use ..." And then you hear the tale of how someone was wheel-clamped for parking in one of the 12 disabled parking spaces in a *totally deserted* Texas Homecare carpark. Or how someone went to this great bar in Cambridge, Mass, where they have go-go girls dancing in glass shower cubicles, but they have had to close it down because there is *no wheelchair access* to the cubicles. On grounds of common sense you do not believe half of these saloon-bar stories but what they do illustrate is an undertow of half-ashamed resentment towards the disabled industry: the sense that here is another sacred cow of the welfare state grown monstrously bloated, and sheltered from all criticism by the self-righteousness of truculent activists and dim telethon celebrities basking in the moral effulgence of their "cheridy work".

Sympathy and compassion for the disabled are natural and almost universal emotions, but they are emotions swiftly dissipated by the waspish reminder that it is *not* "the disabled" but "disabled people" we are talking about, as has happened three or four times in the writing of this. I am one of those who believe "political correctness" is a consciously fabricated media bogeyman, but there is no ignoring the fact that the disabled industry is packed with hairsplitting commissars of verbal correctness who are never happier than when reminding you it is *not* "blind" but "visually impaired"; not "wheelchair-bound" but "wheelchair user"; not "mentally handicapped" but "people with learning difficulties".

When I protested to Nigel Bull of the People First advocacy group about the clumsiness and silliness of this last prohibition, he told me solemnly that "handicapped" was demeaning because it derived from "cap in hand". The only effect of these euphemisms, it seems to me, is to alienate sensible people and to rob the language of evocative power – though language has a way of resisting this kind of manipulation. I have already heard my daughter and her friends refer to a scruffy-looking boy as "he looks a bit care-in-the-community", and to one of their dimmer classmates as "a bit special-needs, you know". It is worth noting, by the by, that the three seriously disabled people I know personally all refer to themselves cheerfully as "cripples".

When the Disability Bill failed in the last session of Parliament, there was great public rejoicing over the humiliation of Nicholas Scott, the minister responsible, who denied he had organised a filibuster in the third reading, and then confessed that he had. But there was no widespread public dismay at the fate of the bill – which the Government claimed would cost British industry £17 billion – and correspondingly little enthusiasm for the measures which are to be placed before Parliament in the new session. In brutal summary they call for employment discrimination against disabled people to be made illegal, for equality of access to public buildings, and for a Disability Commission to enforce the measures – in roughly the same way as the Commission for Racial Equality enforces the Race Relations Act.

Supporters of the legislation claim to be campaigning on behalf of an impressively large tranche of the population, but how many disabled people are there exactly? The "registered disabled" figures only seem to be compiled locally, and are not much help in any case, as the criteria vary so wildly from one local authority to another. In my home town of Swansea, for instance, virtually anyone with a "doctor's note" can get a disabled parking permit or "Anabl" as it is known in the land of officialese Welsh. In my family, "Anabls" are passed promiscuously from car to car as need arises: "I'm just popping down to Marks for some bridge-rolls and cocktail sausages. Now who's got the Anabl?" The result is that the currency has become devalued and orange Anabl bearers outnumber able-bodied drivers in the battle for parking spaces behind the Kardomah.

Lorna Reith of the Disability Alliance told me, "The figure we go on is 6.5 million, which is based on the OPCS 1981 census. The Policy Studies Institute put the figure a bit higher, at 6.9 million." The Alliance also estimates that there are 1 million people with "significant visual impairment" and another 7 million who are "said to have a hearing impairment". So we are up to 15 million and counting in what is clearly a country of the crippled where only multiple impairment is king. As usual it is a measure of charitable virility to get the estimate of your client base as high as possible: any lobby which can brandish 15 million votes will have a politician's attention, but with definitions so elastic as to embrace a fifth of the population there is also the risk of cheapening the vocabulary and sliding into meaninglessness.

In search of some definition of disability, which does not extend from quadriplegia at one end to tonsillitis at the other, I moved on to Hilda Bailey of the Disability Information and Advice Service. She told me that the Service roughly categorises disability as physical, sensory, or invisible. "Physical" disability means wheelchairs, crutches and so forth. "Sensory" means sight, hearing and speech. "Invisible" means things like heart conditions, sickle cell anaemia, thalassaemia etc. Obviously, she concedes, the categories blur and overlap: a person with multiple sclerosis can suffer "invisibly" for many years, with only intermittent attacks of physical and sensory disability. Someone with chronic (but not life-threatening) angina is hard to separate from someone with progressive coronary heart disease. "If a person comes to us and needs advice or information," says Hilda, "then they have got a disability." And so disability becomes self-defining, which is indeed the basis of the OPCS figures quoted above.

Perhaps the most realistic estimate would be based on the 1.5 million people who receive Invalidity Benefit from the DHSS, though this figure is still inflated by long-term sick people who will eventually return to health. To return to our original question of wheelchair ramps, the Disability Alliance claims that disabled access "is vital to more than 4.5 million people in Britain". These are presumably the same 4.5 million which the Alliance says "have difficulty in getting about", but of these only half a million actually use a wheelchair, and of *these* only 15 per cent use one all the time, so from 4.5 million we are down to some 75,000 who are "wheelchair-bound" in the literal, albeit unfashionable, sense most people would understand, and it is for these alone that we are proposing to dig up the front steps of every public building in Britain.

In a perfect world, of course, we would do just that – and indeed go further. We would take on wholesale every programme item of Rampage, the disabled access trust, and have low-floored buses to replace existing fleets, wheelchair toilets on every carriage of every train, wheelchair accessible taxis, and talking meters for the visually impaired. If it were left to me, I should want a self-steering car; a voice input wordprocessor and an express lift installed in my house as a basic minimum. It is a dreadful thing to be crippled or blinded or deafened. It could happen to any of us, and if it happened to me I would want every benefit I could wring from the wretched state and its tightfisted taxpayers.

The trouble is, of course, that it's far from a perfect world, which is why we employ hard-hearted masters of the public purse to make our cost-benefit decisions for us, so we may castigate them afterwards. It is just as well, for the disabled lobby does not have finite demands, and private generosity is unlimited when it is public money we are spending.

The disabled lobby, like so many other good people, is ultimately trying to abolish evil from the earth. They are right to be unreasonable and impossible, because their suffering is unreasonable and impossible, and we are just as right to say no at some point – or at least to appoint others to say no on our behalf.

The Spectator, 3 December 1994

Away

Border country

The teenagers with the machine guns pull us up somewhere in West Belfast. Fisher and I are just off the ferry from Scotland, arguing if we're in Lower Falls or Divis Flats or one of the other places from *News at Ten*, when the two camouflaged Army Land Rovers with the polished boots and gun barrels sticking out of the back door grumble past our bikes and pull across the road in front of us, with soldiers spilling out into firing crouches in the doorways.

So it seems like a good idea to pretend not to notice them and to teeter very slowly and casually back the way we came. Then a third Royal Ulster Constabulary Land Rover, plain grey this time, with its petrol-bomb skirts scraping on the dunes of rubble and glass, veers across the road to cut us off.

One, two, and side doors open to provide cover and narrow our escape route. Three, four, and the pink-cheeked RUC boys in their oversize caps glide to opposite pavements with automatic carbines sweeping the ground. The girl RUC officer, in dark green skirt and white blouse, frankly can't believe it. She raps out the routine questions that policemen everywhere use to establish their ascendancy. What name, where from, where to? We say we're British, and cycling around the Irish border, but she's not listening. Her straight, ginger face is just marvelling at what she sees. She's listing it in her head: two bicycles; one pair of sunglasses; one Where to Eat in Ulster guide; one tweed fisherman's hat; two pairs of bicycle clips; one silver lurex tie. Conclusion: these people do not belong here. They must go away at once.

"You'd be better off out of here," she says finally, quite kindly, and the teenagers with machine guns all clamber back in their Tonka trucks, shaking their heads, and grumble away over the dunes and wadis of broken glass.

It's difficult to do justice to West Belfast. You'd have to imagine a really bad bit of Hackney or Toxteth and square it, then cube it, then paint every surface with graffiti, and paint it over again, and again, so the buildings themselves lose their contours and blur into a mad, expressionist canvas of collective rage. You'd have to break all the windows, and fix them and break them and fix them and break them again so the glass drifted into every gutter and doorway and patch of weeds like a permanent frosting. Scatter it all with the black and orange frames of burned out cars; line the pavements with half ton boulders to stop hijackers ramming the shop fronts; cover the shop fronts anyway with massive perforated steel shutters like cheesegraters; put in some black watchtowers of armoured steel and giant windowless police stations of hastily poured concrete surrounded with 20 foot chain link fences and barbed wire and video cameras and flood lights and Judas mirrors, and you would, perhaps, begin to get the picture.

We spend the first night in a damp, catty bed and breakfast in the Antrim Road, on the fringes of the Catholic ghettos. Out of the back window is the floodlit concrete wall of Antrim Road police station and, out of the front, a street full of the sound of running feet and shouts. Further away, a burglar alarm rings endlessly, and further still there is the whoop of a police siren.

The room is a dingy pink slot about eight feet wide and 30 feet high. "It was from a room like this that Captain Nairac was kidnapped," says Fisher cheerfully. Nairac, the SAS undercover man who disappeared in 1978 was in the paper today, or at least, his skeleton was. A man walking his dog found it in the peat bog near Dundalk.

The train south to Dundalk from Belfast the next day is painted in republican livery of green and orange. It smells of disinfectant and whisky and sells the most expensive tea I have ever bought. 39p a cup. Two nuns share our compartment.

"What would ye be thinking of the Commodore 64, Sister Mary?"

"Ach, the software's not a patch on the BBC Acorn, Sister Veronica, and ye've not enough random access memory for so much as a cake recipe."

From the coast north of Dundalk, the border snakes westward for about 80 miles until it almost reaches the west coast, and then turns north for another 60 miles to meet the sea again at Londonderry, or Derry, depending on who you're talking to. It's about 150 miles by the back roads. Three or four days on a bicycle.

On minor roads between Dundalk and Crossmaglen, we cycle over the border twice according to the map; but there is no sign of it, not even a county boundary marker. The only difference between north and south has rather more of the spanking new bungalow farmhouses, set right on the road with car ports and African teak windows and a chained Alsatian on the front lawn. The old farmhouses have all reverted to barns or cowsheds.

The countryside is flat, with small fields and ragged hedgerows. More like Brittany than the manically clipped acres of the Home Counties. There are more wild flowers than England too: primrose, bluebell, comfrey, marshmallow. And regularly there is a flash of rabbit's tail, and once, a hare.

There is no sign of the army, except for a solitary helicopter that flutters briefly overhead. If the SAS really are out there somewhere, eating barbed wire and sleeping in the stomachs of dead cows, then you'd never know it.

On the way into the Ulster Catholic town of Crossmaglen, there is a Republican tricolour flying and an enormous wall painting: "You are now entering Free South Armagh – Marines Graveyard." The town centre is a very large cement square surrounded by grey terraces of small, flat-fronted houses. A black steel army watchtower in a wire cage stands on the highest side, commanding a clear field of fire. Two or three people give us stony stares, and a little boy shouts "Bang, you're dead."

In McConville's Bar, a row of bulky tweed shoulders is pointedly turned towards us and the girl at the bar spends ten minutes polishing a glass and rearranging the Mars bars before grudgingly pulling two pints of Smithwicks.

"Nice weather we're having," says Fisher.

"Rrrrhhhmphhhr," says the pair of shoulders.

"Do you know the road to Monaghan, please?"

"Left and right," says shoulders. His name is Patrick, a farmer of about 40, and he unbends fractionally after a while.

"It's hard to know which side of the border you're on around here," says Fisher, chattily.

"The border's an invisible one." He taps his head, with an air of immense significance. "You can't always see it."

"People round here aren't very fond of the British, are they?"

"You've no need to worry," says Patrick. "We only shoot the ones in uniform."

Fisher says it's the accent. People are perfectly all right until you open your mouth and then they assume you're an officer on leave. On the road out of Crossmaglen, he practises phrases like "the Brotosh Urmeh," and "Mossus Thotcher," and "legidimutt stroggle."

We stop that night in the town of Monaghan, in the Republic, and spend the evening alone in another stony bar called

McElvanneys, which is also the local estate agent and undertakers. A woman dictates down the bar telephone all evening in a dreary monotone: "Cars leave chapel of rest at 12 sharp … no floral tributes … card to read 'in loving memory' … snatched away …"

The next day it's raining steadily, so it's head down for 30 miles or so, watching the front wheel slicing through the puddles. All the wet, grey villages have names like Ballykillen and Killen and even just Kill, but probably only a paranoid Brit would notice something like that.

We cross the border into the north again at Rosslea, and this is a proper, approved crossing point, with one of the black, armoured watchtowers with a Bren muzzle poking out, and rows of savage steel spikes on expanding pantograph arms for any car that tries to jump the checkpoint. The military policeman on duty is checking the car drivers, but just waves us through.

The rain has stopped by the time we reach Enniskillen in Fermanagh, but we are cold and wet, so we sit and steam for a while in Pat's bar. There's a big international fishing tournament on in the town. Runners are setting off on the annual jogging race, and bunting is hung across the streets. It's a beautiful country town: a tumble of old streets on an island in a lake. We decide to stay.

Fisher comes from Watford, so we sit and watch his team get demolished by Everton in the FA Cup Final on the bar television. The lads in the bar are all Everton supporters, Everton being in Liverpool, and Liverpool being almost in Ireland, but they are all sympathy. Sean on the next table says this is a mixed town and a mixed bar. "Anyone starts talking politics in dis bar, they're out."

Sean, who is a Catholic postman, says he has no time for these "public bar Republicans" you get. "Dey're all country boys. A bit *tick*, you know?" he screws a forefinger to his temple. "Get the Brits out and it's a new world from nine o'clock tomorrow morning. Some of dem would kill 40 people for one soldier. I ask one, would he kill his own daughter for a soldier and he said he would, with her eight years old and standin' right over there."

Down by the lake it's a beautiful evening, with the water like a mirror and the air smelling of wet grass and midges swarming under the willows. Two fishermen have left their floats in the water, standing motionless on their own reflections beside the new wooden dock. There is nothing in the car park by the lake at all, except for a few bits of broken glass and some sawdust, stained dark brown.

The bomb went off yesterday evening when the fishermen were

loading their tackle into their cars. It killed two off-duty soldiers who were taking part in the tournament and blew both legs off a third. Ten other fishermen were injured. The local paper says it's the end of the annual competition in Enniskillen. "They all think we're fishermen," I say. "I know," says Fisher.

Our landlady, Mrs Carr, who is a Protestant, says it's a crying shame. She had a lot of fishermen staying, but only two left today. "It's nothing to do with religion at all," she says. "It's just human badness." She thinks that if Ireland had never been divided up in the first place, then there never would have been all this trouble.

Mrs Carr has two big holes in the armpits of her grey pullover, but her house is a palace, with clear plastic runners to protect the hall carpet, and turquoise crocheted covers on the toilet rolls, for modesty's sake.

Breakfast is fried bacon, fried sausage, fried egg, fried bread and fried potato bread. It's called an Ulster Grill. Breakfast yesterday was an Ulster Grill too, and dinner the night before, and breakfast before that. Neither of us has seen a fresh vegetable in four days, nor a piece of bread that wasn't white and sliced.

"Perhaps the real trouble with this country," says Fisher, moodily pronging the bacon, "is that nobody has had a crap for the last ten years. We should interview the toilet paper manufacturers to find out what their sales figures for Ulster are like."

The scenery on the last day of the ride is the best yet. Great shining lochs and inlets and wooded islands, and the odd new motor cruiser creaming along in the distance. We are passed twice by two army Land Rovers and the soldiers wave cheerfully, but Fisher is nervous, mumbling about land mines and booby traps. Eventually the squaddies stop for a chat. They are on Sunday church patrol, keeping an eye on the Protestants' cars parked outside the little border chapels. The sergeant, who is about 26, five years younger than us, calls us "lads" and looks enviously at the bikes. "You feel a right dick driving about in these things on a day like today," he says, with a wave at the Tonka trucks.

The Protestant bordertowns are all shuttered and Sunday-silent: Castlederg, Carrigans, St Johnstown. Padlocked Orange halls like barrack houses: red, white and blue painted kerbstones; Union flags painted on the road and Paisley posters on the telegraph poles: "A pound for the EEC is a pound in Dublin's pocket." The only shop we find open is very sniffy about accepting the Irish punt notes with their pretty Celtic lettering.

Londonderry is the end of the border and the end of the ride. A Disney city of spires and battlements on a crag above the river Foyle. But the centre is another burned and black and shuttered hole, patrolled by the grey Tonka trucks.

The questions I want to ask, have been wanting to ask for the last week, are stupid ones like what do you want, and is it worth it. So on the day before we take the boat back to England, we pedal down the Derry hill to the Bogside, which is west Belfast all over again, only without the charm – with knots of people staring hard at us and kids shouting and the clang of a beer can on the road behind.

The Sinn Fein headquarters is a tiny terraced house in Cable Street. We leave the bikes outside, unlocked, with bags on and everything, and they are still there two hours later. Nothing gets pinched from around here. Martin McGuinness is sitting in the small front room with a lot of shabby people standing around, and two small children, and piles of envelopes for the EEC elections on the floor. He looks to be in his late thirties. Short, fair hair, cable knit sweater, big, fashionable glasses and a practised grey stare.

He could be a young university lecturer, but was once a butcher's assistant. He is now a member of the Sinn Fein executive and a Stormont MP, though of course he doesn't attend the assembly. He was one of the young Republican leaders, along with Gerry Adams, who was flown to the secret conference with William Whitelaw in 1972. He has been accused of belonging to the Provisionals' Army Council and commanding the Derry brigade of the IRA, which he strongly denies, but he unhesitatingly supports IRA policy and tactics. "The IRA carries out the guerrilla war and we carry out the propaganda war."

Sinn Fein keeps the revolutionary socialist aims fairly low key these days, preferring to emphasise its nationalist side. McGuinness says he prefers to see the movement in the Irish socialist tradition of Patrick Connolly rather than in the Soviet or Cuban terms that the Loyalists use. The short term aim is still to use the electoral system to embarrass the British government into pressurising the Loyalists into negotiations. "If the British government said they were pulling out on July 9, 1985 then they'd start to see the Loyalists move."

It is difficult to dislike McGuinness. In a way he is the most familiar type we have met in Ulster. Perhaps he has never killed anybody, though probably he has shaken hands with the man who bombed the Enniskillen fishermen.

After a while he passes us on to Mary Nelis, a working class Bogside housewife, who is one of those passionate, articulate, self taught socialists who make you ashamed of bourgeois bet-hedging. She takes us back to her house and gives us tea and fills our arms with urgent pamphlets from a chaotic cupboard under the kitchen sink. She talks about western imperialism and the way Paisleyites play on the fear of the Protestants and try to divide the working class, and how there's no point in uniting Ireland if it's all going to be the same the day after.

What Mary wants is a proper, socialist, democratic, neutral, nuclear-free Ireland, with equality of sex and race and religion and all that, and Nato out and capitalism out and workers in. What she will get, if the malign torpor of the British government is ever stirred, and what McGuinness will probably settle for in the end, will be different coloured trains, different car licence plates, a bit more or less inflation, banknotes with Celtic letters on and the Durex back under the counter. And once again, for 2,000 deaths, or two deaths, or just two legs, is it worth it?

These are just the notes of someone passing through on a silly holiday. Talking in a few bars and eating a few meals and stopping at a few guest houses. Most of what we saw we didn't understand at all, but for what it's worth, it didn't seem worth it to us.

New Society, 14 June 1984

Ulster's diehards strike back

The bullying and shooting during Monday's strike by Ulster Protestants against the Anglo-Irish agreement is the sign that once again the Loyalist leadership has lost control of its supporters.

Unionist leaders may talk the language of impossibilism, but they have to deal with political reality, so they are regularly outflanked by their own supporters, who choose to believe what they hear. It happened to prime minister Terence O'Neill in the

1960s when he dabbled in compromise with the south, and to home affairs minister Bill Craig in the 1970s. And now it is happening to Ian Paisley himself.

Can *anyone* be more hard line than Paisley, a mainlander may wonder? The answer is yes, and his name is Peter Robinson. A 37-year-old former estate agent, the MP for East Belfast, and Paisley's own deputy in the Democratic Unionist Party, Robinson dominated the strike, from its beginning at the midnight picket at the Harland and Wolff shipyard, to an electrifying speech at Belfast City Hall the following afternoon, which was followed by a riot in the city centre.

The strike itself was largely his creation. Last week, Paisley and James Molyneux, the Official Unionist leader, met Mrs Thatcher in Downing Street to discuss their objections to last November's Hillsborough agreement between Britain and the Republic. They emerged apparently agreeing to unconditional talks. Then Robinson, and new pan-unionist groups like the Ulster Clubs and the 1986 Ulster Workers' Committee put the screws on; and Paisley and Molyneux were forced to agree to Monday's strike.

It was advertised by Paisley and Molyneux as a "dignified and peaceful protest," but there was violence from the beginning. At 6.30 on Monday morning buses were being stoned on the Protestant Shankill Road, and soon ceased running. Five or six cars were overturned and set on fire and when Royal Ulster Constabulary Land Rovers arrived, they too were stoned. At eight o'clock I took refuge in Woodvale Park at the top of the Shankill where Annie Norman, a retired English teacher, was pushing her granddaughter on the swing, while the petrol bombs whoomphed and flared down the road.

"It's the parents ye know," she told me. "Gittin drunk and letting the children roam the streets. How old are they? Eight or nine, some of them." There is a sort of Zulu ululation from the direction of the Shankill Community Centre. "Today they throw stones at the buses, and tomorrow they'll be complaining the buses aren't running on time."

By nine there are no buses in the Protestant ghettos. Most of the shops are shut and the power cuts mean that traffic lights have stopped working – but there isn't much traffic anyway. At the Harland and Wolff shipyard, men in combat jackets, with tinted glasses and scarves tied over their faces, are stopping clerical workers at the gates. Over 90 per cent of the manual workers have stayed out.

"Are they paramilitaries?" I ask one of the pickets, who has a crusty wound on his ear from a new gold earring. "Naw, they're just wee lads that have borrowed their mammys' sunglasses for the day." His friend, who is fit and bristly as a soldier, is a member of the 1986 Workers Committee, and I ask him what he thinks of Catholics. "There's about five per cent at the yard now. I could work with one if the worst came to the worst." The only trouble with them, Crusty says, is they all think they're tough, working in a Protestant yard. "That's right," says Bristly. "If one gets the sack then it's religious persecution."

A big red Granada 2.8 pulls up, full of a lot of big men, and the biggest is Ian Paisley. Well over 16 stone and six foot two, Paisley towers over the teenage pickets who mob him like a pop star. He cracks a smile for the cameras, lowering the bottom half of his face like a trapdoor to bare a set of yellow teeth that would look big on a camel. Then he makes a little speech about media smears over intimidation, so I ask him if it is intimidation for people in masks and combat jackets to copy down car registration numbers. "Writing down car numbers is not intimidation," he says firmly.

By mid morning, the road at Dundonald, outside Stormont Castle, is barricaded by a hundred or so people. But the RUC make no attempt to clear it, just stopping the traffic and turning it around. A ferrety old man in a tam-o-shanter has a whippet on a string, wearing an sort of union jack whippet-warmer. What is he doing here? "Stopping them Taigs getting in to our parliament," he says, waving across the fields to Stormont. He has his whole family with him. A podgy son with a grandson on his shoulders wearing an "Ulster Says No" sticker, and another, teenage, grandson in combat jacket with a football scarf masking his face. It's an outing for all the family: Mister Bigot, Master Bigot and Baby Bigot.

At Portadown, a country town south of Belfast, all the approach roads are blocked by fat thugs in balaclava helmets. I eventually abandon my car and walk the mile or so into town. This is the place where the RUC refused to allow Orange marchers to carry out their traditional stoning of the tiny Catholic ghetto last summer – an outrage which led to the formation of the Ulster Clubs, whose leader Alan Wright is a young electrician from Portadown.

Today the town is shrouded in smoke from brush fires the Unionists have lit around the railway station. The centre is blocked with tractors and a milling crowd of a thousand or so young people. At some invisible signal they start to run down towards the Tunnel –

the Catholic area – collecting stones as they go. The small Catholic tenements are protected from the road by steel window grilles and a high wire fence, but bricks soon start to hail over it, and children climb the fence, trying to rock it from its moorings. "Easy, easy, easy."

"Did you see me, mum? Did you see me on the fence?" says a breathless eight-year-old, "Ach, ye little divvil," says his mother, giving him an affectionate box around the ear as she stands gossiping with friends, a few feet from the stone throwers. "Portadown hasn't been as good as this in years," a young man says to me, and I grunt something noncommittal in what I hope is an Ulster accent.

English observers like me, who parachute into Ulster for the weekend to knock the Prods, are regularly accused of failing to understand Unionist politics, as if it were all too subtle and sophisticated for poor outsiders. It is all about complex, Powellite constitutional principles, about resisting American imperialism, about the sacred bond with the British crown. In fact, of course it is nothing of the kind, as illustrated by Unionist willingness to threaten UDI and to attack the state to which they proclaim their "loyalty". Unionist policy is simplicity itself. It is about keeping out the Taigs.

Take Peter Robinson's speech at Belfast City Hall this afternoon, for instance. He speaks from the wooden rostrum presented to Ian Paisley by the DUP to commemorate the "Ulster Says No" protest last year, but Paisley is far away, sulking in his Antrim constituency where there is not a camera in sight. Robinson, theatrically sombre in black tie and black cashmere overcoat for the "funeral of Ulster democracy" has all the cameras and crowds to himself. With a pile of empty coffins in front of him he talks about betrayal and treachery and the death of democracy. He compares Mrs Thatcher to President Marcos and Judas Iscariot, accepting the bribe of American silver, to push a united Ireland into NATO. This is not just a funeral, he says, but a trial for the murderer of Ulster democracy.

"People of Ulster," he roars, "You have heard the evidence. Is she guilty or not guilty?"

"Guilty!" they shout gladly.

She deserves, says Robinson, not hanging, but the electric chair. "If we did not have so many power cuts in Ulster today." Haw, haw, haw.

A few minutes later a few hundred teenagers and children break away, in response to one of those mysterious whispers that sweep

Away

big crowds. There is a Taig march coming. Some Taigs have beaten
a Protestant. They run up Howard Street and along Brunswick Street
where they start stoning The Joxer, a "Republican" pub, and
overturning tubs of conifers. A car in Franklin Street goes up with a
whoomph and a column of black smoke climbs above the rooftops
to where army helicopters are clattering overhead. Plate glass is
smashing everywhere as we run down Franklin Street, and another
car explodes, close enough to feel the heat wash. A few army Land
Rovers turn up and the crowd vanishes like mist, trotting off home
for fish fingers and beans and *Blue Peter*.

At the City Hall that crowd too has vanished like magic.
Politicians of peaceful and dignified protest have found pressing
engagements elsewhere, and I wander back towards the smoking
cars. One of the car's owners, a smart young woman in tan suit and
handbag, is circling helplessly around her vehicle, as if looking for a
single intact fragment she might salvage. To my eternal shame I ask
her how she feels, and to her eternal credit she tells me to fuck off.

Can anyone seriously say there is no connection between these
events? Can you believe there is no link between an inspired piece
of irrational invective which casts any opponent of purest Unionist
dogma as a disciple of Satan – and a foray a few minutes later into
petty terrorism? If the three-piece-suitniks of Unionist authority stand
on public platforms and denounce Mrs Thatcher as Judas, it is
hardly surprising if eleven-year-olds see it as a suspension of the
normal rules of conduct towards anyone they can identify as
political deviants. Hardly surprising either, with this sort of
authority, that a parent who ticks off a child for forgetting to brush
his teeth, will smile indulgently when he chucks a Molotov cocktail.

By nightfall there are fires and barricades all over Protestant
Belfast. In Newtownards Road, near the paramilitary UDA offices, a
group of three or four thousand is turning over lorries and setting
them alight. Empty beer barrels, thrown into the blazing wrecks
explode with a satisfying boom. If the Catholics put so much as a
milk crate in Falls Road these days, the police are out with plastic
bullets, but in Newtownards Road there are precisely two
policemen, observing benignly from behind a white ribbon.

It would take the budget of an apocalyptic pop video to do
justice to the scene. Black silhouettes of children dancing against the
flames. The rolling thunder of beer barrels on broken pavements.
The shadowy lines of barricades stretching up the hill towards
Stormont. The hot tar and diesel shining underfoot. The trim,

collected figures of the paramilitaries in camouflage jackets and berets, moving coolly through the crowds, ordering here and encouraging there. "It is the only city in Europe where the police would allow this," a French journalist says, and he is dead right.

But then, Ulster is the only place in Western Europe with a flourishing totalitarian ideology. Not the polished jackboot and brassard variety of course, but a shabby, home-grown version of Millets' combat jackets, and grubby gym shoes and Dad's balaclava. It is totalitarian, because it is incapable of modification or contradiction, because the tiniest deviation from revealed truth is the deepest treachery and because its only policy is to perpetuate its power.

Leaders like O'Neill, and Craig and Molyneux and Paisley may flatter themselves into believing that they control the apparatus of Loyalism, but once they deviate from the true faith they too become its victims. Even Peter Robinson, if he achieves political power in his own right, will feel the breath upon his collar. The only way to outface it in the end is to break it, and in Mrs Thatcher, for the first time this century, the Unionists may have encountered a prime minister prepared to do just that.

New Society, 7 March 1986

Life, death and Diet Pepsi

Incredible. There is this Turkish shop, and you know what? It has Pepsi and beer and custard creams and tuna fish and noodles and peanuts, regular and dry-roasted. *Two kinds*, and you say, so what? Listen, this shop is in the middle of a Kurdish refugee camp, halfway up the Mountain of Death or whatever the tabloid newspapers are calling it this week. Outside, there are people wading about in diarrhoea, dying of medieval diseases, digging graves for their children with penknives, and here there is a shop – a shop in a tent, OK – but still a shop, selling four kinds of cigarettes, two kinds of peanuts, and Diet Pepsi. *Diet Pepsi!*

Not only this. We are in the first shop we have found in the whole of Turkey that is both open and has something to sell. There are closed supermarkets stuffed with tempting produce and 24-hour coffee shops that sell no coffee, but the winning combination has been missing so far. I flew into Istanbul on the first day of Bayrami, which is a very big deal in Turkey, starving refugees or not. Men walk around aimlessly in very bright suits, simpering and holding hands. Everything closes down. "What are they *doing*," I ask my friend Shukruh. "They are *celebrating*," he tells me.

They simper when they tell you there is no flight, no car, no hotel room, no restaurant, no toilet. They simper, then shrug, then they say: "Impossible."

At Istanbul airport, the imported glitter of International Arrivals fades fast into the plastic-top tables and trodden chewing gum and crowded ashtrays of Internal Flights. Istanbul Airlines has cancelled its last flight east. Short-sleeved men with cupped cigarettes simper and say: "Impossible." The runways are full of old sheds and I get the last seat in the oldest, which has just been repainted with a 6in distemper brush, judging by the frayed edges and stray bristles embedded in the gloss-work.

I am flying to Kurdistan, but they recognise no such place in Turkey, so this is a pretend flight, in a pretend country where shops pretend to sell things, and hotels pretend to be places to stay, and garden sheds pretend to be airplanes, and grim, brown-rimmed holes in the ground pretend to be lavatories. And yes, I know it is the gravest cultural chauvinism to judge a country by its lavatories, but hell, if they can't run their domestic plumbing system, what can they run? So you eat Yorkie bars, chew Dio-Calms, and hold on tight for the return flight.

To get to the worst of the refugee camps, at Isikveren, you must first drive over 1,000km of bad roads, then 200km of unbelievable roads, then 5km up a mountain on a totally impossible road, with wheel-ruts of yellow clay as deep as your knee and six-axle trucks sliding sideways down the greasy slope towards you with their wheels locked. At the top is a patch of level ground with our shop, closed to refugees, and a Turkish army camp. It is the tiny stage of a vast amphitheatre of mountains, their tops still dressed in snow and their flanks covered, as far as binoculars can see, with the bright, barbaric scraps of refugee tents, thousands upon thousands of them, climbing mile upon mile over plateau and fold and escarpment until they disappear up into the skyline and the drifting smoke skeins of their camp-fires.

It is a stirring and frightening sight, and metaphors of flood and invasion are inescapable. There are 150,000, maybe 200,000, Iraqi Kurds up there, pressing down this great natural funnel towards Turkey, and the Turkish army is the stopper in the funnel.

At closer quarters the impression is less military, more pastoral – like one of the great biblical migrations of antiquity. Goats and donkeys wander among the tents; women in vivid robes of buttercup and emerald wash clothes in a stream; the steady thock, thock of an axe sounds from tree-felling nearby. "The Kurdish People," says my friend Shukruh, and the capital letters are his own.

He is a vivid hatchet-faced man, full of passion and illogic. He is a city Kurd – 40 per cent of Istanbul is Kurdish – and he is romantic about his people: their heroism, honour, hospitality. He tells me over and over of the homogeneity of a culture and a language older than Rome. "There are 30 million Kurdish people in Iran, Iraq, Turkey, and the Soviet Union," he says. "The largest people on earth with no land of their own."

He was a Marxist in his youth – he flirted with the PPK, the Kurdish People's Party, which has waged a vicious guerrilla war in eastern Turkey for 10 years; a war in which 3,000 people, mostly Kurds, have died. He laughs at Turkish bureaucracy, backwardness and inertia. He waves from the car windows as we drive at the fertile green hills and red valleys of Anatolia and Mesopotamia.

"If England or France come colonise, we have nice country. Build railways, roads, airports. The Turk he does nothing." He waves also at the little brown mosques in each village we pass. "You see. They have mosque, but no school. Mosque but no water. Foolish people, they think if they go to mosques they go to heaven and have 72 women to make love. Or if they want, 72 *Gulman* – this is a pretty boy, white like a peeled boiled egg."

Shukruh is a modern Kurd, a ship's steward, with a $1,200 Panasonic video camera on his shoulder and a knapsack of U2 and Pink Floyd tapes. He winds down the window and turns up the volume as we pass through the villages. "Consider, Mr Martyn. This is the first time maybe they hear *Ummagumma* and *Joshua Tree*."

We leave our car way below the refugee camp, because the road here is not a road any more, but a river of slime up which only tractors and four-wheel drives can slither. We hitch a ride on the towbar of a tractor hauling a trailer of bottled water. Kurdish children run alongside, begging for bottles, so we toss some down, which is a nice game.

An older child jumps on and starts heaving out armfuls of bottles, followed by a couple of men, trampling the slithering dune of plastic containers, and breaking some. A hand wrenches my shoulder; a set of big yellow teeth are very close; a boot stamps on my hand, splitting my thumb. I almost lose my balance and the spinning wheel of the tractor is very near, and there are shouting faces all around, and the tractor horn is screaming panic at the crowd and it is suddenly not a game at all.

The trailer is empty in a minute, with a trickle of broken bottles tumbling behind us. Around the corner a line of women wait patiently for the water that is not coming.

"I was quite frightened for a minute then. Were you frightened?"

"Not frightened," says Shukruh. "I was ashamed."

As we walk further up the track there is evidence of more ambushes. A muddy carpet of crushed bread; shoes and clothing trampled in the goo; burst sacks of pasta everywhere. In the centre of camp, US army engineers have bulldozed a helicopter pad the size of a football field, and all around the perimeter is a ragged hedge of refugees, three or four deep. The air fills with the whop-whop of a heavy-lift helicopter and the pad streams with purple smoke from a wind-direction flare.

As the big machine gracelessly bellies down, a shout goes up and the refugees charge forward past the helpless handful of US soldiers. One fires a shot overhead but the helicopter is engulfed in people and the pilot shoves his throttles forward. The crowd is flattened like corn in the downdraught as the aircraft lifts off again, its cargo door still closed.

In a clump of trees nearby, an army sergeant is shouting at a mild and reedy young man in rubber shoes, who leans heavily on a walking-stick.

"Now lissename, Ishmael."

"Ismail."

"That's right, Ishmael. Now lissename. Ya gotta have organisation here or no more food drops. Ya unnerstand?"

"I understand, yes," says Ismail, who has a degree in English literature from Nineveh University. "I will speak to the sheikhs but I don't know if they will listen."

The Americans believe firmly that natural democratic structures will emerge from the refugee mob, but after nearly three weeks there is still no sign of them. The Turkish army kept order in the first week by the more straightforward method of shooting food rioters dead – between 15 and 20 of them, the refugees say, but hostile press coverage has made them more cautious. "Maybe they should shoot a few more and not worry about the newspapers?" I say to Ismail.

"Then maybe the refugees will shoot some soldiers too," he says, and this is no joke. There are many deserters from the Iraqi army in the camp – I met one Christian Kurd who deserted in Kuwait – and also Kurdish guerrilla fighters from Iraq and Turkey. Many had to leave their weapons at the border – Ismail buried his own Kalashnikov "gun machine," but he did smuggle in a pistol which he shows me in his camp. "Come here Dini," and a smiling four-year-old trots up. He pulls a Soviet Makarov automatic from the child's shirt. It has a round in the chamber and the safety is off.

"You see, they do not search the children. I think, perhaps I will sell it in Turkey." And my friend Shukruh, of course, being Kurdish himself, wants to buy it, as there are only about 24 Turkish army checkpoints between us and Istanbul, and a mere 12-year sentence for carrying illegal weapons.

There are 15 people in Ismail's party, bound by inscrutable relationships made all the more confusing by the custom of referring to any female relative as "sister" and any male as "brother." "This is my brother's sister; this is my father's sister's mother; and this is my mother's father's brother's sister ..."

They sleep all together under four blankets on a narrow earth shelf, hacked from the hillside. The women fetch water, cook, wash, and mind the children. The men do press interviews. They do not join the food riots, but get help from local villagers – mostly pasta and potatoes. Water comes from melted snow, though this is rather black and oily, polluted by the fires in Kuwait, 1,000km south.

"Will you ever return to Iraq, if Saddam is dead?" I ask Ismail.

"Never, never."

He is sick of the Iraqi people, he says. They hate the Kurds. It is impossible to live there. I ask for an example.

"When I tried to join the airforce as a pilot they said, 'No, you are a Kurd'. They are afraid that I would steal a fighter plane."

"And would you steal a fighter plane?"

"Of course," says Ismail.

We visit 10 or 12 tents in our two days on the mountain and nobody seems to be starving or thirsty any more, although there is a great shortage of water for washing and of simple medicines for diarrhoea, in particular, which nearly everybody has. There are pools of liquid faeces all over the hillsides among the rotting entrails of slaughtered sheep. Women crouch, rinsing out babygrows in a stream 2in deep, which is little more than a sewer – and yet, miraculously, there are no cases of cholera or typhoid, according to the doctors of the Médecins sans Frontieres charity.

People are dying at the rate of 10 to 15 a day here at Isikveren, most of them small babies and old people, exhausted by cold and dehydration and chest infections. In the largest of three cemeteries there are 150 graves. One afternoon we watch a man dig a grave, driving furiously through the tough roots, a good 5ft down.

"He is digging very deep."

"It is for his wife."

"What did she die from?"

"She was very old."

"How old?"

"Fifty-five years old."

Her body lies under a sheet of blue plastic, pooled with rainwater, with one foot sticking out. It wears one of the rubber shoes given by the Turkish Government. They are slip-on shoes but they have laces and eye-holes moulded on to the rubber to make them look real.

Nearby, little girls are patting together clods of clay to make tiny tables and chairs, dolls-house furniture, which they put on the surface of one of the babies' graves. These are just small mounds of earth with lines of flints making an X, like a hot-cross bun.

One man in the crowd, Sadiq, has already buried his wife and daughter and son. He leans on a friend like a floppy doll.

"Why did you leave Iraq?" I ask him.

"Saddam was killing my brothers."

"Where?"

"In Dahuk."

"You saw this?"

"I hear it from my brother."

The Kurdish people make attractively Byronic images for the newspaper and TV. The women with their fine white teeth and brilliant headdresses. The men in their mountaineers' pyjamas and twisted *pushtus* on their heads. They have been persecuted by Iraqis, Iranians, Turks and Russians and yet they are famously brave, and individually kind and hospitable. We were offered drinks and cigarettes everywhere we visited – even in the most pitiable and dripping hole in the ground.

And yet, and yet, hospitality is good to receive, but the *system* of hospitality is an aspect of savagery rather than civilisation. The savage lives by personal honour and personal obligation; the civilised man by privacy, and abstract notions of the public good.

The highest form of social organisation among the Kurds is the family, or clan, which is the source of welfare, protection ... and rumour. It was panic in the clans which began the flight from Iraq, for it is not the action of a rational individual to flee 50 miles over snow-covered mountains in nightclothes, dragging tiny children to face extreme danger and privation in a hostile country – and all because of the rumour of a pogrom by Saddam Hussein. It is the clans, too, that are responsible for the chaos in the camps, for many have lost their leaders and others look out only for themselves.

The Turks, on the other hand, have received a bad press in this country – a country which refused to take a single Kurdish refugee after the 1988 exodus, and slapped visa restrictions on Kurdish tourists. The Turks have a better record towards their own Kurds than any other host nation; there are still some 30,000 refugees from 1988 in camps along the border.

But all that was then and this is now, and the Kurds remain a problem to be solved. The continuing fantasy of a Kurdish nation can be dismissed out of hand. A people who cannot organise a breadline will be unlikely to organise a nation state – particularly a state of some 20 million, landlocked between powerful and acquisitive neighbours, riven by faction and religion, with no history of state-craft.

The West will not take the Kurds in large numbers, and neither will the Turks, so they must return to Iraq under UN protection, and the sooner the better, for the babies are still dying fast at Isikveren. The last one I saw was a little girl who weighed, I would guess, about 4lb, and I took her to be new born. In fact she was two months old, the same as my son Joe, who is 12lb now and into his next size of Pampers.

"Will she be OK?" I asked a doctor, and he shook his head imperceptibly. Shukruh then sat down beside the mother and talked to her for a while in Kurdish. He had been very brave on this trip, I thought, watching his countrymen die, and be sick and humiliated, and for the first time he had tears on his cheeks.

"What's the matter?"

"Oh, it is nothing. I asked the name of the baby, and it is Beuar. It is a Kurdish name, which means without a home, without a land. That was all."

The Daily Telegraph, 21 April 1991

Kind hearts and a full kitchen

The first thing about Ludmila Prokhovenkova's kitchen in Murmansk is its absurdly tiny scale – only seven foot by eight foot, yet crammed with a fridge the size of a phone box, cooker, sink, cupboard and a table laid for five.

I am wedged in a corner against a searing hot radiator, one arm pinned by the wall and the other by Ludmila's 20-year-old son Misha, who is bigger than the fridge. His mother is a big woman too, with a suitcase-sized bosom and leg of mutton arms.

On top of the fridge is a little garden of parsley pots and a dozen onions growing in jam jars of murky water – the green shoots of which Ludmila snips into our salad "for vitamins." Every centimetre of space is used – the saucepans are stacked and interlocked so tightly in the cupboard that only Ludmila has the knack of getting them in and out.

And as there is no other cupboard all the dishes and cutlery are stored in drainer racks, one over the sink and another over the stove. The whole flat is like this, with shoe racks nailed to doors and overhead shelves stacked with shoe boxes. In the eight by 10-foot living room there are books on window ledges, suitcases under the sofa and boxes of potatoes behind the curtains.

Misha and his friend Dennis have got Depeche Mode thundering out of the stereo, with a third speaker wired into the kitchen a few inches from my ear, but Ludmila is quite serene: "What is life without children? And with two sons I have to learn to like rock and roll."

Everything on her table is homemade: bread, mayonnaise,

Russian salad, marinated mushrooms, stewed peppers, chutney, pickled cabbage. The only shop-bought things are some smoked salmon, a gift from the eldest son Sergei, in Leningrad, and a plate of Spam, which is the only meat. A generous meal but I doubt it cost more than a dollar. "Do I think there are hungry people in Russia? Only lazy people who ignore the goodness of nature."

A closet in the hallway is another complex jigsaw of jars and bottles – more than 200 kilos of preserved fruit and vegetables, all bought or collected from the wild in August, when they are plentiful. "I go to the shops only once a month for my coupon goods," Ludmila says.

We did go shopping, though, to see the markets of Murmansk, and it is easy when you do to understand the providence of the Russian woman. As the northernmost city in Russia, it has only a few hours of daylight in midwinter. Nothing grows on the tundra of the Kola peninsula but a few berries and mushrooms in the short summer. Almost everything but fish is imported: a lemon costs 25 roubles compared to 10 in Moscow; a kilo of oranges is 100R – impossible luxuries for people on 500 to 700R a month.

On the bus we chat to cheery old ladies who are scouring the city for milk – a full-time job for the grannies of the families with young children. There are rumours of a delivery in a distant suburb, so it is worth the five kopek bus ride to check it out.

Every woman carried a detailed mental map of potential supply sources. A shop three miles away is known to have shoe cream; another on the other side of town has cheese: "I forget the taste of cheese." At a rumour of sugar, or children's shoes, a queue will form immediately.

Ludmila, who is twice divorced, earns 700R from her job as an auditor, and Misha gives her 500R from his pay as a merchant seaman. These are higher wages than most of Russia, to compensate for the climate, and they get special rations of butter, eggs, fish and meat. The rent on the apartment is only 23R a month – about 12p – with heating and hot water thrown in, but even so everything goes on food, with Ludmila's six monthly trip to Leningrad to see her grandchildren as the only family luxury.

You need patience to live this shoebox existence and they are stoical, affectionate people. Misha sits close to his mother, stroking her neck as she sings a folk song. Ludmila takes my arm under her comfortable bosom as she escorts me back through the snowy streets to my hotel.

They have no interest in politics and only the most domestic interest in my outside world. Does my wife work? How many children do I have? Does the baby take after you?

In the middle of a modern industrial city they are living in a way that hardly anyone has lived in England for 100 years: with the wisdom of the peasant which lays up provisions against a siege; the wisdom which says that however bad things are they always get worse. Perhaps for now it is the greatest wisdom to possess.

The Daily Telegraph, 29 February 1992

Playing chess with Sergei

My king is a pepperpot which falls over each time the train brakes. But all the other pieces are proper ones, apart from a pawn made from a marble and a blob of chewing gum. Sergei draws black, so I open with a dull pawn to king four, which he mimics, as he does my next three moves. I think: this is going to be a pushover.

"You like this Giuoco Piano opening?" says Sergei, and then I am not so sure.

We are strangers, sharing a sleeping car on the St Petersburg-Murmansk express, which is tearing through the tundra at a good 7 mph. He's been visiting family; I'm on my way to write about the Russian submarines in Murmansk – maybe interview a submarine officer if I am lucky. We're eight hours into the journey with 20 to go, but small talk is wearing thin. "Ah, but I love getting back to the North," says Sergei, and I follow his gaze to a landscape like a sheet of cartridge paper.

"Why?"

"You should see it in the summer. Four, five different kinds of wonderful berries."

I poke a sacrificial pawn at Sergei's knight and he falls for it, giving me space for an early castle. I think: this is definitely going to be easy.

He is tall, bespectacled, with a mournful moustache. "You do cooking and washing-up in London? My wife wants me to do these things. Also she is crazy about embroidery art. Always she wants more thread, cloth, more money. I come home, there is no soup, she says, "Fix yourself, I am working'." He pushes forward a pointless bishop's pawn.

"You have been to the Russian baths?"

"I went to the Sanduny in Moscow ..."

"Tschaa. You should go to the black baths. This is steam but also with smoke from green birch log. In Sandunny baths they beat themselves like carpets, but here in the North the beating is an art." He borrows my scarf to demonstrate.

"On the chest you stroke the twigs. On the legs you scratch, so. And on the back you beat with great smartness. So!" I decide he is insane but harmless, and it's only someone to pass the time with after all. He prods another pawn vaguely into play against the gathering might of my bishop and knights. Sergei looks at his watch.

"You know in four hours' time I am free man."

"How do you mean?"

"Tomorrow I am 30 years old, which is first date I can retire."

"What is your job exactly?"

He moves the pointless pawn another square. "Communications officer on atomic submarine," he says, and I see with a sudden, sickening clarity that he has forked my bishop and knight.

In the cat and mouse game beneath the Arctic ice, Sergei is the whiskers, monitoring radar and sonar data from hostile submarines. Until a few years ago this was deadly serious stuff: "The Americans would ram us if we came close – they know it took us longer to get repaired."

When a Russian sub surfaced it would be paint-bombed by US helicopters: "From the colours they could then track each submarine on their satellites."

Ramming still takes place but generally things are more relaxed. "Sometimes we talk to the operators on the American and British submarines. We send each other messages."

"What do you say?"

"Oh you know. How's your family? What are you having for dinner? I tell you those guys eat a lot better than we do." He is impressed, and depressed too, by the superior technology he has seen on exercises and on television during the Gulf War – the speed and accuracy of US helicopters, the manoeuvrability of their boats, the sensitivity of their detection equipment. "When you have to cut your own screws from old nails like we do, I tell you it's a real eye-opener."

I don't think he should really be telling me all this, but he is demob happy and there is something of the anonymity of the confessional in this dimly lit train compartment, lurching slowly over the snowy plateau of the Kola Peninsula. I am a pawn and bishop down after 12 moves, but have only half an eye on the game now, which seems to make me play better, or Sergei play worse, for he has pushed up his queen too far and is having trouble defending it.

Senior officers on the Russian submarines are paid a supplement in US dollars these days – $7 a day, while they are at sea, which strikes me as an astonishing fact. "But it is necessary to stop them running away," Sergei explains. "Of all the people in my class at naval college I am the only one still in the service."

"But why run away?"

"Conditions are so bad in the boats now. Nothing to eat but instant mashed potato, pickles and maybe corned beef if you are lucky. No fresh vegetable, so there are problems with ulcers and skin rashes and even eyesight. And there is the paint they use which gives off really bad fumes. Sore throats, tight chest, sometimes even hallucinations. And there are rats everywhere. Really big and completely unafraid of human beings. They come sit on your neck when you are asleep. There are stories of men who go to bed drunk and the rats will take their lips or tongue."

He is a navy-brat, son of a captain in the surface fleet. "I went on a submarine trip when I was 16, and it was the greatest thing I could imagine then to serve my country in a submarine. The best job in the Soviet Union, seriously."

He was brought up on bases in Tallinn and Gremicha – a former prison camp, now an isolated naval station way down the Kola Peninsula. "Beautiful in summer, but no theatre or music, and in the cinema only films that are passed by the political commissar."

His wife Svetlana is worried about radiation from the nuclear test sites on nearby Novaya Zemlaya island and its effect on their four-year-old son. "Now they say there has been secret dumping of waste from the submarines and nuclear icebreakers. On the submarine they give us film badges to wear, but when they turn black they just give you new badges. In the reactor room and missile bays there are transparent cockroaches like glass, I'm not kidding you. They say there is no danger but how do you know? They have lied to us about everything else." And he moves his queen then, to take my rook's pawn, and to put my king in check – which is an insanely rash move, sacrificing his queen to my king.

"My wife wants me to take the early retirement, move away from Murmansk. She wants friends who are artists like herself."

"She is fed up with the naval life?"

"On the point of breaking I think, and I do not know what to do. Many people want to leave but there is no retraining, no after care for people who leave the military, and this is why there are so many of us who are frightened now and angry." And he moves his knight then, to check my king again, which is no problem, but there is another revealed check from his bishop, and only one square for me to move to. "Maybe I find work in computers."

"So leave."

"I love the North," he says again, though I understand by now that the North is only code for another deeper loss. "It is not so easy to turn your whole life inside out," says Sergei, and moves in his knight to mate my pepperpot king. "Shall we make it the best of three?"

The Daily Telegraph, 17 April 1992

The naked lunch

At the next table in the restaurant a stout German lady of 50 is taking off her knickers. She places them carefully on her plastic seat, then places herself on top of them with a small grunt of satisfaction and a tiny hiss of trapped air.

Nobody minds, because here at the Domaine de Belezy, nobody is wearing anything anyway. Waiters circle the tables in crisp shirts and dark trousers: the barman is in modest vest and baggies – but the rest of us are bare as eggs – naked as new-borns, stark and staring.

Still, there are social conventions at the Domaine. One is that when you sit on a restaurant chair you put a towel down first – though I don't know if this is to stop you leaving an impression on the chair, or the chair from leaving you with a backside like a pineapple. So in Eden everyone has a towel, worn draped over a shoulder, wound artistically around the wrist or (this is frowned upon) knotted about the waist.

Stern signs remind you "Nudity Obligatory!" and in the inverted dress code of naturism the more you wear, the more indecent you become. Wristwatches, jewellery and espadrilles are tolerated, but mildly naff. Bikini briefs attract disapproving glances. A business suit would be a cause for social outrage. Voyeur! Pervert! Exhibitionist!

The Domaine is in the hills near Avignon, and as you drive towards it regular signs remind you that this is the international capital of nudism: "Piscine Naturiste," "Camping Naturiste," "Motel de Naturisme." The French Naturist Federation lists 24 camps in this area, ranging from the enormous "nudist city" at Cap d'Agde, which takes 10,000 people, to tiny coves on the Gorge du Verdon with a dozen cabins.

First sight of Belezy is an intimidating 8ft screen-fence running for miles along either side of the road. Caroline and I left our hotel talking over-brightly about our "naked lunch" story, but the sight of the fence makes the car fall oddly silent.

The reception is normal enough, like a camp office anywhere, but for the naked couple standing beside us at the counter. Forms are filled, "passports" issued, and for 100 francs we are in, still fully dressed, though among the trees and tents naked bodies are flitting.

"Where should we take our clothes off?" I whisper.

"Perhaps we could wait until some real fatties come along," suggests Caroline.

This does not take long, for the woods are full of swag bellies and pendulous bosoms, mottled thighs and scarlet shoulders. We undress in a loo, and emerge to a scene of extraordinary *business*. There are nudists playing table tennis and volleyball; leaping boisterously into pools; playing solemnly at petanque. If they are not busy playing, they are busy striking photographic attitudes – patting hair, resting hand on hip, tossing back the head in laughter.

It is exactly like the brochure we studied before coming, or the pages of *Health and Efficiency*, furtively poured over beneath adolescent bedsheets. Deprived of costume, people reach instinctively for another set of clothes – which are the sanctioned attitudes of professional nudism – a *conscious* unselfconciousness.

At the little bureau de change I cash a cheque – just to see what it is like to go nude to the bank, and at the supermarket we buy some apples and cheese to savour the experience of a naked check-out queue. Some inarticulate impulse steers me away from sausages and bananas, baguettes and bacon slicer.

Walking up an empty aisle between ketchup and floor cleaner, I confront a girl assistant, modestly dressed in nylon overalls, and for a moment there is a terrible rent in the fabric of this surreality – like one of those nightmares of walking naked down Regent Street. But it is all right. There are naked bottoms at the cold counter and bare breasts at the till, where the check-out girl is as impassive before the queue of bodily parts as any Safeway professional.

As we drove home to Avignon, a pair of cyclists came scorching towards us on the dusty road. One was a girl in a scoop-necked top which, as she leaned forward, revealed the shapely valley beneath, and a dark, semi-circular shadow of, could it be …? I had checked out her cleavage before I knew it, in the reflexive flick of the eye every man performs a dozen times a day when I had studied, at leisure, perhaps 500 naked females.

It was reassuring, in a way, as if to say that however much nakedness one could enjoy, it would never challenge the civilised pleasures of mild salaciousness – could only ever, in fact, be skin deep.

The Daily Telegraph, 8 August 1992

Hit the road, Joe

M y youngest son Joe is a robust child – no, let us be honest – he is a little thug. One of those remorselessly energetic, tank-like toddlers, who springs from the womb wearing blinkers and hobnail boots. Who thunders around rooms crashing into the flimsiest pieces of furniture, sweeping ornaments from shelves, sticking sandwiches into video machines, pulling down curtains, and immune to any adult sanction short of major violence.

Little Joe and car journeys have never got on well – a 10-minute trip to the supermarket drives him to incandescent rage, even when heavily bribed with M'Bongo cartons and Hedgehog crisps. The two older children can usually keep him under some kind of control, but they were still at school for this holiday, and the prospect of a 1,000-mile car journey through France filled us with such dread that we spent weeks stocking up on Joe-restraints and Joe-diversions.

A new car seat (his third) from Britax offered the kind of padding, webbing and multiple tilt positions that a Foxbat pilot would envy. There was also a new Britax travel cot which would assemble itself with a flick of the wrist, to be instantly ready for the odd minute in 24 hours that Joe might condescend to sleep.

A new coolbox was stuffed with familiar brands in case his taste did not run to foreign muck. A toy bag was filled with stacking barrels (to throw about), Spot books (to tear up), crayons (to eat) and an electronic keyboard that produced assorted animal noises (to drive us mad).

Every other year we have done the mad-dash trip to the Med: an evening ferry to Calais: a shouting match at 2am when we get lost on the Boulevard Peripherique; a bleary breakfast of stale croissant near Lyons, and a crusty arrival the following evening at Cannes, where we take three days to recover.

This year we wanted the kind of adult trip which other, better-ordered families seem to manage: the cloud of white dust rising behind the rag-top Bentley; the wicker hamper in the jump-seat; the poplar-lined road; the quails' eggs and *jambon cru* at the cool little *relais routier*, where the last English customer was Elizabeth David – you know the sort of thing.

So we left Calais in the early afternoon with only 200 miles to our first stop at Epernay, near Reims. There were baguettes in the boot; the "Foxbat" seat was pitched and yawed to ergonomic perfection; The Runaway Train was on the stereo and the electronic keyboard was quacking and mooing happily in the back.

Within 10 minutes Joe was screaming his face off – but then, mysteriously, he was silent. In the quilted heat of the French afternoon he slept all the way to Epernay, then all the way from Epernay to Beaune the next day, and then all the way to Avignon on the third. Our son, we had discovered by chance, was heat sensitive. About 90 F was all it took – or about Gas Mark One in the oven back home, which is where we have now resolved to keep him.

The only worrying aspect was that he also stopped eating. At the Manoir de Montflambert, in the middle of the Champagne vineyards, we ate roast quail and sugar-browned potatoes while Joe rejected a delicate puree of *jambons et légumes* in favour of a single segment of Toblerone from the mini-bar.

Near Beaune Burgundy we stayed at the elegant Hostellerie de Vieux Moulin and ate pork *roulades* stuffed with herbs and onions.

The kindly chef-proprietor produced for our son a delicate omelette with a few *frites* arranged criss-cross on a Japanese lacquer dish, which he uncovered with a flourish at our table – and which Joe spat out over his shoe. At the hotel Meissonier near Avignon we had a wonderful *rouget tapenade* at a table beside the pool while Joe fed his *jambon* to the owner's Alsatian. Like a xenophobic Fifties tripper, our son would have no truck with foreign muck, and grew lean and large-eyed as we grew guiltily plump.

Deprived of baked beans and beefburgers he starved for four days – but at least, as we told ourselves, he was starving quietly.

The great pleasure of getting through France in this way, rather than via the brutal dislocation of a plane from Gatwick to Nice, is simply that it feels more foreign. There is time to relish the way the countryside changes, from the cornfields and coal tips of the north, through the proper, sentimental France of chalky vineyards, racing cyclists and Ricard signs in Burgundy, to the first cypresses and olive trees which signal the south.

There is time to marvel over the first footprint lavatory, which no Frenchman ever uses of course (how could they with their piles?), but which they plant in a line around their borders to repel invaders, just as we use Happy Eaters and motorway cones.

There was time to spend a morning playing football with Joe on the lawn of Manoir Montflambert, to swim and picnic at the Lac de L'Orient near Troyes, and to visit the Burgundy vineyards on the Cote d'Or, whose village names are one long list of wines you can never afford to drink at home: Gevrey Chambertin, Clos de Vougeot, Nuits St Georges and Chambolle Musigny.

The rooms we stayed in varied from the entire dilapidated wing we had at the Manoir Montflambert to a kind of space capsule of apricot melamine at the Vieux Moulin, with a view in the morning on to a vertical hillside where a herd of perfect, white Charolais bulls were stuck, surreal as fridge magnets.

They were relaxed places with very serious restaurants where, for around £20 a head on the *prix fixe* menu, you can acquire that classic French disease known as *mal de foie* – roughly translated as "eaten yourself sick".

Joe's cot fitted into the bathroom in most places – "you put your *bébé* in the *lavabo*?" one incredulous madame asked us in outrage – and we went back to the dictionary to explain.

So Joe slumbered, heat-stunned and hungry, while his parents troughed. Thus it was all made right when we reached Avignon and found the first outpost of Brit tourist occupation at the local hypermarché. They sold baked beans.

The Daily Telegraph, 14 August 1992

Brave faces

You wouldn't look twice at Pauline Moore in her Dublin hospital casualty department. Plump, pretty, bustling, she'd be swabbing cuts, setting out instruments, dimpling deferentially to the big-shot consultants. You'd never ask her name, or remember it, but here in Somalia there are thousands who know her.

"Pow-lina! Pow-lina! Pow-lina!" The children at the Wan Luen feeding centre come running out to mob her as she drives up every morning; they grab for her hand or an edge of her T-shirt, and the fortunate are favoured with a hug or a kiss.

It is a 60-mile drive here from Mogadishu and for the first few months Pauline was shot at almost every day. But she has turned back only once, when the automatic fire took out a wing-mirror and headlamp. "I was on the bleedin' floor at the time, of course – which the driver and guards thought was a great laugh." She has had a grenade explode right inside her feeding compound, feet from her office, "but, thank God, there were no children there at the time".

I don't think she really understands what I mean when I ask why she came here. She has tended diseases and injuries she would never get near in Dublin – tuberculosis, pneumonia, gunshot wounds, starvation – and saved hundreds of lives. She is managing a staff of 30-odd workers; she has designed and built a school for 700 children. In baseball cap and Raybans, Pauline's is the best-known face in town, and when her six-month tour is up in March she isn't even sure she wants to go home.

"But what do your parents think?"

"Ach, they think it's grand. Though I didn't mention yet about the shooting and the grenade."

Another morning in Baidoa, epicentre of the Somali famine: I am standing on an airstrip with Paul Enright, one-time steward with Aer Lingus, now food distribution manager for the relief agency Concern-Worldwide. "God, I love the smell of napalm in the morning," says Enright. "It smells of ... VICTORY."

Through the thorn brush, camouflaged figures are running, clutching helmets against the downblast of the heavy-lift, US marine helicopter. The take-off sends red dust 100ft high, and suddenly the chopper is a dragonfly shadow, racing over the buff plain and ragged circles of thatched huts below.

The machine-gunner crouched over his spade grips at the open door; sweating grunts cling to their webbing straps – the imagery of Vietnam and *Apocalypse Now* is inescapable, but here the payload is relief grain rather than rockets. Two hundred families are coming home to their remote village today, for the first time since the start of the civil war three years ago, and Concern-Worldwide is flying to meet them, armed with hoes and saucepans, blankets and sorghum seed.

"But how do you know if they'll be the right people?" I want to know.

"We'll mark them," says Enright.

"Shoot off one of their fingers," says Hannah Scrase, an agricultural adviser with Concern. "If they come back more than 10 times we start shooting off their toes."

"No, seriously," says Enright, "we mark their hands with gentian violet."

"And if they rub it off," says Scrase, "we shoot them dead."

Enright has earned his own pilot's licence since leaving Aer Lingus. He has paddled a canoe alone 300 miles up the Orinoco and written a book about it. He is riding a horse from Istanbul to China next year.

"But why are you doing this?" I ask him.

"Well, it beats handing out after-dinner mints to Americans," he says.

Six months or more in the madness of Somalia fosters a comic brutalism in the kindliest of aid workers – they need it to survive.

Imagine watching 50 children a day die at your feeding centre, without drugs, or beds, or even parents to grieve for them. Imagine living with armed guards, day and night, with machine-gun and mortar attacks on your compound, with weekly death threats and extortion demands. These workers in their 20s from Dublin and Birmingham and London have experienced all that, and more.

Perhaps because "aid worker" is rather a wimpish term, they call themselves "engios" after their employers, the NGOs or non-governmental organisations. There are only 350-or-so engios in Somalia, but in the past month two have been shot dead – a far higher casualty rate than in the military. Sean Devereux of Unicef was killed in Kismayu before Christmas, apparently in revenge for criticising local militia. Last week Kurst Lustenberger, a Swiss worker with the International Committee of the Red Cross (ICRC), was murdered during a robbery at his compound.

The arrival of American forces on December 9, while securing the delivery of relief supplies, has made life more dangerous for some, by disturbing Somalia's subtle balance of terror. Now the food convoys are impregnable the remnants of the bandit militias have turned their attention to softer targets such as aid workers and journalists. The American crackdown on weapons has made them more vulnerable still, since engios cannot operate without armed guards, whose Kalashnikovs are now routinely confiscated.

The guards themselves are not always a help. When Concern in Mogadishu tried to cut the gunmen's wages last year the engios were held at gunpoint in their compound, by their own "guards" for two days; around the engio dinner tables in Mogadishu and Baidoa there are endless similar war stories. An NGO director, one of whose guards had been shot, was visited by the man's family: "They wanted $50,000 compensation. All very nice with smiles and handshakes, but what they said was 'Pay up or we kill you'." When a car was hijacked from the same agency compound with a $20,000 compensation demand – and a hand grenade with the pin out. When journalists crowded Mogadishu during the American occupation, and house rents went sky-high, the Unicef agency received notice of a rent rise from $2,000 a month to $40,000, with this crisp message: "Move out or we blow you out."

Life in the NGO compounds is superficially familiar, and comfortable enough: Kellogg's cornflakes on the breakfast table; Irish whiskey on the sideboard; The Commitments on the video. There's a cook, a cleaner, a housekeeper, but other aspects of the conditions are startling to new arrivals. Rifle fire in the street outside; mortar explosions that rattle the windows and the patter of falling plaster on the dinner table – these are events too commonplace to be noted. The neighbouring NGO may be only 200 yards away, but no social call is paid without advance radio warning, and the mustering of vehicle, driver and guards.

There are more culture shocks in the teeming streets, with their roofless buildings and shell-pocked walls, their gutters running with sewage and the soil verges humped with the graves of the dead. On her first day in Baidoa, Michelle Mackin, a Belfast nurse, picked up a dying woman in the market and took her to the intensive care unit attached to the Isha feeding centre.

"I couldn't believe the place: the smell, the dirt, the people all over the floor. When someone died they were taking out the glucose drip and sticking it straight into someone else. I went back and told the people at Concern, and they said. 'Oh, Isha; that's where you're going to work' – and I just cried. Didn't think I could ever do it."

"Why *did* you do it?"

"All those pictures on the television. Everyone saying how awful it was, and not doing anything. I just felt I had to."

Mackin, who has green eyes, hennaed hair and careful makeup, is the daughter of a French mother and Irish lawyer father. She has an accountant fiancé who is putting pressure on her to come home after her six months, but she is thinking of staying on longer. "I like the responsibility – more than you'd ever get in a hospital at home – and the sense of achievement. And you do get attached to the children, though I know you shouldn't."

A lot of the children at Isha are orphans, like pretty little Fatima, who is two but could pass for one. "You should have seen her when she came in. Like a little rat. Don't know how she got here. Just found her in the corridor one day." A refugee woman, paid by Mackin, feeds Fatima, but she won't adopt her. When the baby slips her hand into mine, as the orphans do all the time, Mackin says, "You wouldn't like to have her, would you?" and it is hard to think of good reasons to say no.

Many of the children don't know their age, or even their names, so they have been christened by the Somali Concern workers: Ali Concern, Kusa Concern, Abdul Concern. "There'll be a new Concern tribe 20 years from now," says Macklin, "starting another war, more than likely."

They used to lose dozens every day at Isha, from measles, dysentery, pneumonia. Now, as the children get stronger, the morning death truck is picking up only one or two bodies; but other nightmares are taking over, as for seven-year-old Ido, a bright and affectionate little boy who has begun to bite and scratch and run away. "Some suddenly flip like that as they get stronger. They wake up screaming, 'The men are coming to burn me'." One child at Isha saw her father killed and eaten by hyenas. Another was found by an aid worker in the village of Gof Godut sitting next to the corpse of her mother, where she had waited patiently for three weeks.

The cult of comic brutalism ensures that few engios will confess to any noble motive. Denise, a legal secretary from Dublin, says it was to get away from her boring boyfriend that she volunteered for Somalia. "Ach, he paid your fare for you," says another engio.

Steve Collins, a London doctor, says he was "fed up with high-tech medicine in England. They throw huge amounts of money at chronic problems treating a huge population of elderly. Chest wards full of smokers and liver wards full of drinkers. If you spend money in one place I believe you are always, indirectly, taking it from somewhere else, and we are using up vast resources when people like these have nothing."

As the famine in Somalia begins to abate, the relief effort is turning to longer-term programmes of education and of resettlement of the land. Concern wants to put 25,000 children back in school by March, and have five villages converted to improved agricultural methods such as "row planting" and composting. It is less news-worthy stuff than feeding the starving, and harder to fund, but it is investment rather than charity: the only way to break the cycle of political instability, war and famine.

Cynicism and compassion fatigue are easily acquired as famine follows famine and crisis succeeds crisis. My own doubts were acquired, I'm ashamed to say, long before I came out here. All those millions of starving babies on the news, and the endless line of collecting boxes at the door, feeding into inscrutable acronyms of self-righteous charities. Was it really worth it?

There is an answer of a sort when our helicopter finally touches down at the village of Labaten Jirow. None of the engios is sure there will even be anyone there to receive their resettlement packs; the villagers were in Baidoa, 25 miles away, yesterday. But as the big machine kicks up its red cloud of landing dust they begin to straggle out from the trees in the distance. Fifty, 100, maybe 200 people.

They have walked here all the way, through the night, on roads still riddled with mines, to collect their modest New Year presents. Two bags of grain for each family, to last them two months; a hoe blade for cultivation; three saucepans, a frying pan and five sets of plates, bowls and spoons. It is supposed to persuade them to resettle their land: to face down looters and famine and predatory militias – and it's the kind of stuff people in England chuck away when they move house.

I try to imagine what it is like to be sick and hungry, with half my family dead, and to walk 25 miles across the African plain for a few pounds' worth of Western goodies, and of course I can't.

The abyss between my comfort and their misery is unbridgeable, unimaginable; it is a vanity even to try – but at least I don't wonder any more whether the effort to help is worthwhile.

The Daily Telegraph, 23 January 1993

Snapping at her heels

'Oh look out. Here comes Arpa. We're all right now, Cavalry's arrived." A burly man in pebble lenses and cloth cap is bearing down on the royal rat pack, camped outside the Hotel Arlberg in Lech, Austria. Arthur Edwards, *Sun* photographer and the Princess of Wales's favourite snapper, is back from his airport stakeout; the rat pack becomes visibly less agitated.

As in any pack, members are uneasy when one goes missing. If a leading blunt like the *Mirror's* James Whitaker disappears for a few hours then everyone gets panicky. Has he got an exclusive? If he checks out of his hotel, mass hysteria sets in. The rat pack ethos is an odd mixture of co-operation and cut-throat competition: "sharin'" and "squirrelin'".

"Been squirrelin', Arpa?"

"You got them jacks for me?"

"You filmin' me? Turn that soddin thing off you fourex git."

This last is aimed at a TV man with a lightweight ENG camera on his shoulder, for the pack is twitchy about stitch-up merchants from TV and blunts from the posh papers, who turn up on royal tours to make fun of their honest toil. Everyone knows that Royals sell papers, but where the tabloids do it straight, the posh papers do it by sneering at the excesses of the tabloids.

Fifty-odd monkeys and blunts have been standing two hours outside the Arlberg in heavy snow, waiting for the Princess of Wales to arrive from the airport, but it's a disappointment when she does. A coach pulls up and bundled royal kids pile out, their faces blank inside neat, 1950s haircuts. They are followed by the Princess, who is up the steps and into the hotel without a sideways glance. The only man with a decent photo is the commissionaire at the head of the steps, who has whipped a Sureshot from under his tailcoat. "Gissaneg, mate!" goes up the cry.

In monkeyspeak, the first proper "fersility" is next morning, when the Princess sets off for the ski slopes – and immediately all kinds of odd convention come into play. In the first place, since this is a private holiday, she is not officially posing at all. On the other hand, the monkeys must get the pictures they need or they will start

FROM THE DICTIONARY OF MONKEYSPEAK

All day sizzla Meal and/or restaurant favoured by monkeys

Arpa Arthur Edwards, Princess Di's favourite photographer

Belter A good picture

Bish bash bosh A rapid succession of belters

Blunt A journalist

Deffwatch Excuse to stay in exotic locations on huge expenses without producing pictures

Fersility Photo opportunity

Fill What blunts give each other when they miss a quote: "Gissafill mate?"

Free undrid A very big lens

Gissaneg, mate? What snappers say to each other when they miss a picture

Genster light Where the royals always stand

Jack Jack and Jill – bill (receipt). An appy jack is a blank bill

Monkey Photographer

Monstering Harassment

Paps Paparazzi. Unscrupulous photographers who bring the profession into disrepute by breaking the rules. Often get better pictures and make vast income

You goin' Brazil? Start of extremely boring discussion on next royal tour

hiding behind trees and generally becoming an even bigger nuisance than they are already.

Nobody actually says, "Princess Di will pose for pictures at 9.30 outside her hotel." What happens is that Geoff Crawford, her press secretary, sidles casually up to the pack, and after various pleasantries, suggests it might be a good idea if we went and stood by the ski school hut where, we infer, a certain royal person might shortly be passing.

A few minutes later the Princess appears from the ski-room door of the hotel, looking white and thin and beakier than expected. Her hair, permed in a static surf, is almost as pale as the snowflakes that are settling in it. You could find a prettier woman in every lift queue in Lech, but this is often the way with photogenic people. They set fire to film emulsion, but leave the eye unmoved.

She starts walking towards the cameras, chatting to friends and children, laughing, adjusting a ski glove, glancing at the scenery. The weird thing is that it's in slow motion, about half normal walking speed, giving the snappers plenty of time to change position, adjust focus, switch cameras.

She doesn't acknowledge the church organ of telephoto lenses, which is sometimes only a yard from her cheek, but every movement is designed for their greedy, polyocular gaze. Head to the left, so; head to the right, so; a flick of the fringe, so; an eloquent shrug; a tender pat on the head for a child. It is exactly like the supermodels of Milan and Paris, who can fire off 20 poses in the few seconds it takes them to turn at the end of a cat walk.

And the snappers themselves have their conventions: don't crowd the Princess; don't shout at her; keep out of the other snappers' shot. They get very stroppy if one of the paps (freelance paparazzi) starts shooting from the other side of the road. This is an *informal* photo, you see: Diana walking down a snowy street, chatting to her friends and kids, with no-one else at all apart from you the reader. That is the illusion, the sleight of brain which Princess and photographer are conniving at. There are no monkeys or blunts or detectives or press officers. She is appearing, unmediated, for you.

This particular fersility, the pack agree, has been "a heap of shite." "Heads down all the time; people scattered everywhere; no group of Di and the kids." Blunts are equally short of words to write, and stand around sucking on frost-clogged Biros. "I thought she looked rather miserable," says one.

"She was wearing that black ski suit last year," says another.

"It's a year this weekend her father died, isn't it?

"Must be a lot of memories for her."

In this cautiously collaborative way a story begins to take shape. "Tragic memories for downcast Di," it will be, or something along those lines. It is pitiful stuff, but in the largely fact-free world of royal journalism it is fairly typical. Most royal stories are based on the tiniest scraps of information, pumped up by conjecture, and protected from outright ridicule by careful phrasing and the fact that Royals rarely answer back. It is only when royal circles break ranks and supply a "steer" to the press – as in the Andrew Morton biography of Diana – that anything of moment emerges.

Richard Kay, a talented feature writer for the *Daily Mail*, points out that "the Morton book has made everyone forget that before it came out half the papers were saying the exact opposite – that Charles and Di were getting back together."

Rat packers are not beautiful to look upon, tending towards pallor and porkiness from expense-account living, and with a fondness for low-slung jeans and noticeable watches. Without the cameras you might take them for cab driver, bookies or publicans – one of those well-paid jobs that require few A-levels, but a lot of self-reliance, quick wits, and very thick skin. The rat packer's life is a steady drizzle of humiliation: the hours of waiting and wheedling; the contempt of their targets, the authorities and their readers; the essential triviality of what they do – and it breeds an ethos of truculent self-pity, where "everyone's out to knock us."

They are a tribe within the journalistic tribe, with their own culture and language. Necessarily perhaps, they are completely lacking in introspection. If they snatch a shot of William taking a pee, or Di falling on her nose, it's a "belter" and a "bollo," but if an eavesdropping blunt like me snatches a quote off them, then it's a "flaming liberty."

"If we don't like your article we've got your address," I was told by the barrel-chested Charlie Rae of *Today*. On the recent trip to Kathmandu, Charlie threatened to take the camera from a *Vogue* photographer who was snapping the pack at lunch and to stuff it down his neck, but with me he was only joking. At least I think he was.

Professional intruders themselves, the pack resent any intrusion into their own world, which is automatically "a stitch-up." Hypocrisy is the word for it, and like most hypocrites they talk noisily about "professional standards" which they cheefully abuse when it suits them. It is in the unwritten rules, for instance, that if Diana provides a "fersility" in the morning there is no "monstering" of her for the rest of the day, but this doesn't prevent half of the pack from piling into the ski lifts after her, and staking out the cable car stations on the mountain, and restaurants where she may have lunched.

The rules say you don't pursue her into a restaurant, but if you are there before her it's OK. You aren't allowed to take pictures, but if a pap starts to do it, and there's an ugly scene, then you might be allowed to shoot that. This was exactly what happened in the battle of the paps last Saturday, when the Princess was monstered as she went shopping in Lech in the afternoon, and her detectives started shoving paps out of her path. The British pap would not have shot her shopping (a private moment) but once the shoving started it become automatically public. See the front page of last Monday's *Daily Mirror*.

There are few tricks of the rat pack trade apart from brute persistence and spending a lot of money. "I always bring a thousand quid in cash," one tells me. "In case you've got to hire a boat or plane or whatever. You've always got to be planning one step ahead. Like chess really."

"Just like chess," says another, "only without the intellect."

In fact the Royals are highly predictable in their movements – Diana has been to Lech at the same time for three years now, and it only takes a few phone calls to hotels, ski guides and airlines to get the details. Paparazzi stars like Jean-Paul Dousset and Daniel Angeli – who took the topless photos of Fergie – maintain networks of informers in hotels and bars in the watering holes of Europe. "I can make £50,000 with the right picture of your Lady Di," one Europap told me. "How much does a hotel receptionist make?"

Angeli, according to James Whitaker, made £1.5 million with his Fergie pictures and is a millionaire several times over with a winter home in Gstaad and summer residence in St Tropez. Further up the scale is Andrew Morton, a humble blunt himself a few years ago, who has now sold more than three million copies of his book worldwide and is moving to a £650,000 house in Hampstead. A quite ordinary staff monkey will make £60,000 to £100,000 a year, while someone like the amiable and candid Whitaker, with his fruity accent, expert skiing, and plutocratic manner, is clearly set on moving into the same world he preys upon. "Wonderful restaurant in Zurs last night", he remarks as he turns up at the morning stakeout. "But expensive. Only one bottle of wine under £30."

"So he didn't have *that* one," chorus the pack.

For the most part, though, and contrary to myth, the rat pack live fairly soberly – at least two are teetotal and the monkeys are anti-smoking to a man. Another myth worth disposing of is the public perception of them as merciless predators, invaders of privacy and wreckers of royal marriages. According to Whitaker, Buckingham Palace will canvas strongly for leading reporters to accompany the Royals on an important trip like Korea or Kathmandu. "Oh yes, they'll phone up and say, 'James, we do hope you're coming'."

Diana regularly invites the press pack to private receptions, and while there is a good deal of fantasising among the blunts about which of them she is currently in love with, there is little doubt she has regarded Whitaker as something of a father figure in the past, and that she remains genuinely fond of the avuncular Arthur Edwards.

"Ten years ago," Edwards tells me, "I remember Diana walking down this high street and the press were on her like lions on a young zebra." (Arthur does tend to talk like this.) "I decided then that I'd never do it again, and I don't think you would see it now. Not from the British press."

The relationship between press and Royals is symbiotic rather than exploitative. Diana can get irritated with the pack and Charles has barely spoken to them in years, but both are more than willing to manipulate them when needs must. If there is a serious criticism of the rat pack it would be that relations sometimes verge on a cosy corruption, where the press see themselves virtually an extension of the royal household: a collection of Gold Lens Pullers-in-Waiting whose first priority is to play by the rules and preserve links with the Palace rather than rock the boat.

It was Diana's friends, or even Diana herself, who made the Morton book possible. Charles or Charles's friends have clearly used the press to retaliate in recent months. Diana, once again, is obviously cultivating the media to secure her new position as an autonomous Royal, with her own interest and overseas missions. These if anything, are the real royal stories of today; and it is a measure of the actual balance of power between press and princes that instead of writing about these things we are standing in the snow, in Lech, writing about the colour of Princess Diana's ski suit.

The Daily Telegraph, 3 April 1993

Mr Solution comes to town

'Just incredible. I mean rilly. These people lining up and walking right across hot coals. It's just rilly, rilly, incredible." Joelle has the California-girl knack of opening her eyes so wide the whites show all round, and keeping them like that all day. "These coals are like 1,000 degrees, but Tony Robbins says all you gotta do is think, 'Cool moss'. They have this wet moss to put your feet in at the end, right? So you just keep thinking 'Cool moss. Cool moss' – and don't look down."

The Virgin 747 is bumping into its final descent to Los Angeles International, like a double-decker bus rolling downstairs. Joelle works for Robbins, has been to his seminars, read all his books, and has been talking Tony for three hours but she isn't through yet. It's not enough to fly to San Diego, meet this business guru guy and write a story. Robbins gets publicity, you get an interview – this ordinary transaction is not enough. You also have to believe in Tony Robbins, for Joelle is a true believer.

"So I'm standing in line for the firewalk but I don't want to go. I rilly don't want to do this, and when it gets to be my turn to walk I just start crying. And Tony says, 'Joelle, which of your breasts is more sensitive? Left or right?' And I say, like, 'WHAAT?' and Tony says, 'GO!' and I just, like, went and did it. I did the firewalk." And her face is aglow with the memory of the epiphany.

Robbins says anyone can walk on hot coals: "There's no secret. You could do it right now. People can stand a lot more heat than they think." On his summer camps he gets businessmen to stand on top of a 50ft flagpole, with no platform. They'll be doing the firewalk in his three-day seminars at the NEC in Birmingham next month, but I'm sad to find we won't be doing it in San Diego. I suggest we do our own thing with a sack of barbecue coals and some lighter fuel but Robbins says the firewalk is part of a structured experience. "It's not about firewalking per se. It's getting people to do something they thought was impossible." The next day, at his seminar, I will do things I thought were impossible. I will shout "Yee-har" and "Whooo-hoo!" and punch the air. I will fondle the body of a large male stranger – but it's not the same as firewalking.

Tony Robbins, it says here, is the "ultimate personal development coach"; a consultant to government, leading corporations, the military and top athletes. At 33, he is a multi-millionaire, and founder of nine companies. He has written two books called *Unlimited Power* and *Awaken the Giant Within.* More than a million people have attended his seminars while 13 million have bought his tapes. He flies a jet helicopter and lives in the Castle Del Mar, an old robber baron pile up the coast from San Diego. He has a beautiful wife and four wonderful children, all free from drugs. He belongs to a breed which hardly exists in Britain: the business booster, though in Nineties fashion he also stresses his effectiveness in personal relations, spiritual growth and weight loss.

The Robbins HQ, in La Jolla just north of San Diego, is all white walls, sunlit balconies and subdued telephones, like an expensive private clinic. We meet in his vast, empty office, over-looking cool lawns. He is an enormous man – six foot seven and 17 stone, with no fat and hands like shovels. Lining his great jaw are babyish teeth, half covered by gums, and he wears his hair in a sculpted brown cowpat. The voice is big and hoarse, stumbling over clockwork pieties: "Great privilege to meet you ..." His verbal tic is to distance himself from quite ordinary remarks, thus: "The more quote-unquote successful I have become, the more quote-unquote contented." He has no idea how to do a press interview, treating it like a television encounter, where he tries to ignore questions and make boring speeches, advertising his product to a non-existent camera.

When I ask how his ideas have changed between his first and second books, he says this: "My focus then was on neurolinguistics and the focus of getting you to take action, and I'm still focused on that. But I think that the father of all action is the decision so my focus is really more on values, belief structures, rules and how they control our evaluation procedures and therefore how we think, how we feel and how we believe in life. That is my primary focus now." As he talks I doodle a preliminary glossary of Robbins-speak:

    focus = look
    belief structures = beliefs
    technologies = methods

paradigm shift = a change
analyses = thoughts
evaluation procedures = thinking

But let us press the metaphorical edit button here, and move on to Robbins's background.

He was born in Los Angeles, son of a waitress and a parking attendant who divorced when he was five. A stepfather turned up, who Tony worshipped, but when he was 11 they could not afford a Thanksgiving dinner. A stranger arrived at the house with a turkey, which Tony thought was great, but which so humiliated the stepfather that he left and never came back. When he was 18, Tony began distributing free food to poor families on Thanksgiving Day, and last year he fed 75,000 people in 400 communities, though he doesn't like to make a big deal of it in public. He gave a medical centre to Mother Teresa too, "with my good friend Marty Sheen, but we didn't have a press conference or anything".

He tells the Thanksgiving story to show that an incident is what you make of it. One person has his life destroyed; the other is set on the road to Assisi – by the same event. The notion of a person as self-defining is fundamental to Robbin's ideas, as it is to America's view of itself. "What shapes your life most is not genetics, or your family, but your decisions," – a bracing, but unforgiving theology. The story has other; more complex resonances, like the classic fairy-tales it resembles. Is Robbins showing the deserting father how it should be done? Is he repeating the episode to bring the father back again?

Thanksgiving commemorates the first New England harvest – made successful according to legend, by the generosity of the Indians. It is a festival of innocence – of prelapsarian purity, before the Indian wars, before the West was won, and industry blackened the plains, when white man and red sat down to eat. All the key American myths coalesce here – it is at the heart of the American dream, the conviction that it is always possible, like the Pilgrim Fathers, or the wagon train pioneers, to leave the past behind, to defy heredity and environment, and invent a new self. At the centre of Robbins's teaching is the notion of the mutability of the self and its beliefs. If your belief system is preventing you succeeding then change it – which you do through a system of though control we will come to later – but the basic tenet is: "It doesn't matter which belief is true. What matters is which one is most empowering."

Lacking, as he says, "any positive role models *per se*" the young

Robbins "took up with Socrates and Thoreau" and "made books my friends". He set himself a target of five books a week which he didn't make, but did read 700 in five years.

"Who are your favourite novelists?" I ask him.

"Ah, honestly, I am more involved in psychology, more involved in economics, more involved in the mind-body effect if you will."

"So which psychologists do you admire?"

"Ah, I don't much like the traditional psychologists. I look at someone like Norman Cousins as a psychologist." Cousins is not a psychologist at all, in fact, but author of a book called *Anatomy of Illness*, about how he beat cancer by watching comedy shows.

The young Robbins modelled himself on great men such as Roosevelt, Churchill, Martin Luther King, imitating their diction, habits, even posture. I was reminded of the touching scene at the end of Scott Fitzgerald's *The Great Gatsby*, when the murdered Gatsby's father finds his son's programme of self-improvement in an old cowboy book: Rise from bed – 6.00; dumb-bell exercises etc – 7.15; work – 8.30-4.30; baseball and sports – 4.30; practise elocution, poise and how to achieve it – 5.00; study needed inventions – 7.00-9.00.

Gatsby, of course, is an American archetype, the misty home background that is ruthlessly re-coloured or discarded; the shallowness of culture; the re-creation of self through physical and spiritual exercises; the ability to shed or adopt suits of moral attitudes according to circumstance; the engaging and appalling blend of innocence and cunning, idealism and brutality.

Robbins didn't go to college for some reason. There are lots of vague patches here, as in Gatsby. The life moves in and out of focus. At high school he is the kid everyone comes to for advice: "I was known as 'Mr Solution'," he tells me, and I try to imagine a 12th-grade girlfriend crisis. "I know, let's go see Mr Solution." At 23 he is a fat slob and business failure in a 40sq yard apartment, washing his dishes in the bath. At 30 he is flying his jet helicopter over the factory where he worked as a janitor ten years before. Something happened.

In the bookstore at LA airport, Tony Robbins shares a shelf with Ken Blanchard (*The One Minute Manager*); Norman Peale (*The Power of Positive Thinking*); Steven Covey (*The Seven Habits of Highly Successful People*); Mark McCormack (*What They Don't Teach You At Harvard Business School*); and Dr Barbara De Angelis (*How To Make Love All The Time*). It is a big section of the bookstore, much bigger than the area given to serious novels, and it is called *Personal Development*.

Watching a video at Robbins Corporation HQ I see some of these people again. There is Ken Blanchard, the *One Minute Manager* guy, recommending Robbins; and Barry Melrose, the LA Kings hockey coach; and Buddy Melges, the America's Cup skipper. On the backblurb of Robbins's book *Unlimited Power*, Norman Peale says it is "required reading for anyone wishing to tap his full potential", while on the back of Robbins's second opus, *Awaken The Giant Within*, Steven Covey says he is "one of the great influencers of his generation".

In Britain we do not have an endorsement culture. People such as Sir Robert Mark have advertised tyres, while Nanette Newman seldom rests from endorsing detergent, but it is fairly clearly understood that they are paid to do it. In America the exact opposite is true, in that people will endorse products without direct reward, and actually gain status by so doing. There is a kind of spiral of endorsement, where Lee Iacocca might endorse Mark McCormack, McCormack praises Ken Blanchard, Blanchard boosts Tony Robbins and Robbins endorses Iacocca. "Hey, this guy must be good," one is led to think. "All the endorsers endorse him."

Between videos the Robbins people bring fresh orange juice and wholewheat sandwiches of avocado, lettuce and grated carrot, without salt, mayonnaise or butter. I chew a mouthful for several minutes but instead of dwindling to a moist bolus in the normal way, the mouthful has the strange property of swelling bigger and bigger, and drier and drier until it is impossible to swallow or to speak.

Robbins is a non-smoking, non-drinking vegetarian who believes your body (which he calls "yorr physiology") is a decisive influence on your mind ("yorr mennul state"). Slump and sag and you will become sad. Smile and sit straight and your depression will lift. "One way to get yourself into a mennul state that supports your achieving any outcome is to act 'as if' you were already there." Act as if you just made a successful speech or sale or seduction, and you have a better chance of doing just that. Behave energetically and you are energetic.

In a sense this is just the kind of thing granny used to say: chin up; shoulders back; smile and the world smiles with you – but it's a clue to the behaviourist nature of Robbins's approach. Like Pavlov and Skinner and Eysenck, he is not interested in the unconscious of the superego or the immortal soul, or the other old-hat models for what things might be like inside people's heads. He only cares about observable behaviour and the conditions which create it – in inputs and outputs.

Classic behaviourists see the main inputs as pain and pleasure, which can be organised and applied to "condition" the subject – dog, rat or human – into new behaviour. It is an indisputably effective technique: "Of course behaviourism works," W.H. Auden said. "Give me a good behaviourist and a set of electrodes and in half an hour I will have him reciting the Athanasian Creed." In fact, when I ask Robbins if he is a behaviourist he sniffs at "all that old-fashioned stuff". What he is actually advocating is a form of self-conditioning, wrapped in a lot of flannel about "sub-modalities" and "neurolinguistic programming" but what is essentially very simple.

If you want to lose weight for instance, you create a horrible image of yourself, grossly fat and stuffing your face with food. Whenever you feel hungry you summon up this image, then insert a smaller image of yourself looking slim and healthy and gorgeous. Force this gorgeous image to swell up and replace the gross image, while saying, "Whoosh!" (No, this is serious.)

Repeat the process dozens of times until it becomes automatic, and every thought of overeating triggers the gross-to-gorgeous reaction. I tried it for a couple of days, and it seemed to work, though the waiters in San Diego's many fine restaurants did not understand why this Britisher kept murmuring "Whoosh!" when they asked for his order.

From the psychologists and sub-psychologists he has met and "modelled", Robbins has accumulated a raft of feelgood techniques and parlour enchantments: his "technologies". If you cannot spell a word, for instance, then break it up into small sections; visualise it in the top left corner of your vision field, and then – this is the clever part – spell it backwards. If your child is having an uncontrollable crying jag you can stop it by getting her to look up at the ceiling. If your wife is locked in an argument mode then break her pattern. (Which breast is more sensitive? Left or right?) I tried these suggestions at home and, depressingly, they worked – depressing because one doesn't like to think of humans as machines, available to such simple fixes.

Robbins's mass seminars, or rather rallies, attended mainly by reps and salespeople, are the test-bed of his "technologies". The rally the day after our interview, for instance, at San Diego Convention Centre lasts ten hours, 8.00am to 6.00pm with one short break, and Robbins speaks non-stop if "speaking" is the right word for bellowing, stamping, dancing, chest-beating, quiz games, comic routines and mimicry. A warm-up main called Chip Eigelberger ("GOOD MORNING SAN DIEGO!"), has the 6,000 audience in a hollering, aisle-jiving, gimme-ten frenzy before Robbins even arrives, though this is not difficult since many were visibly already in a frenzy when they ate their breakfasts, "Overweight hysterics in polyester pantsuits" would cover most of the audience. "Over-exercised narcissists" would do for the rest. There are hardly any blacks.

To a pounding Donald Fagen rock track Robbins comes jogging on stage (which is only about 8ft deep). The body language is ludicrously dynamic: pacing, punching, leaping off stage and leaping back. The gesture repertoire is elaborate: a double hand-chop for "exactly so"; finger and thumb in an "O" for an abstract question; arms in a basket for a Big Question. Strapped to his slim alligator braces is the radio mike that is his most important prop: he snaps his fingers for a pistol shot; murmurs down into it for sincerity; bangs it and stabs the air for a Big Point. BANGSTAB! and everyone's paying attention. BANGSTAB! And he's into his next energetic routine.

"Hands up who is a salesman here," he bellows, and about half put their hands up. "Hands up who has children." About three quarters obey. "How many clean their room without you telling them?" Nobody puts their hands up. "So you are ALL salesmen right?" And there is a big laugh from everybody. By continually demanding audience response and steering it where he wants, he gradually erodes its capacity to refuse him. Hands up for this, a big "yes" for that – the audience becomes his creature, willing even to get on its feet to jump about, wave their arms in the air, and give each other neck massages. Yes, even your reporter.

If all of this sounds contemptuous it is probably because I resent its effectiveness. Robbins is a great public speaker, the best I have ever heard apart from Tony Benn. And he is funny, a completely unexpected quality after yesterday's interview. He does witty deconstructions of American television ads; he performs a wonderful mime of himself as a wimpish salesman; he even turns on his own BANGSTAB! gesture, "Now this is not a good idea if you have breasts." So this is the post-modern business guru: self-conscious, self-parodying and pre-empting criticism with his own candour.

He has never performed in England and got rather shirty when I suggested he might not go down so well there: "America is not one culture. If you go to the South you get a totally different reaction from the Mid-West ..." He might be right, and play a stormer at the NEC for all I know. American attitudes are creeping in all over, from the people who shout "Yee-har" and "Whooo-hoo," in London theatres, to the baseball mitt my son wants me to bring home. I try to think of 6,000 Mondeo-driving Midlands salesmen giving each other neck massages, and walking on red-hot coals, and I suppose it's possible.

After four hours or so I have a migraine from the shouting, and walk off to the water fountain at the back of the auditorium, where I can look back on the scene. Robbins is spotlit on the stage, his shirt drenched in sweat, his cowpat glued to his forehead, and his great chest booming: BANGSTAG! BANGSTAB! The rapt crowd is a sea of waving arms, a reef of anemones, its noise a submarine roaring.

For all the thinness of its cultural soil, the strains of its ethnic mix, and the potency of its national myths, America has never come really close to having its own political demagogue – unless you count Huey Long, who in the long run was a joke. Tony Robbins is too ideologically empty ever to become such a figure. But with his battery of psychological skills and his somnambulistic sense of destiny, he might be worth watching just the same.

Telegraph Magazine, 4 September 1993

Fact and fantasy at Mission Control

Charles Conrad, Edgar Mitchell, David Scott, Charles Duke, James Irwin, Harrison Schmitt, Eugene Cernan ... Do any of these names ring a bell? They are members of the most exclusive club on Earth: the dozen human beings who have walked on another world; crewmen of the six Apollo spacecraft which, between July 1969 and

December 1972, landed men on the surface of the Moon. "The Twelve" they call them at Nasa, and they are all alive – apart from Irwin, who died of a heart attack in 1991 at the age of 62. Conrad is a vice-president with McDonnell Douglas, Mitchell is a university professor, Scott runs his own high-tech company in California, Schmitt is a senator for New Mexico ... Ticker-tape heroes once, they have merged now into the landscape of corporate America.

My son, who is nine, had heard of the first two Moon men, Neil Armstrong and Buster Aldrin. I said no, it was Buzz, and he shrugged, so what? When I told him I was going to visit Nasa in Houston, Texas, he asked what Nasa was and could I bring back a cowboy outfit? Some adults I told about the trip rolled their eyes and made remarks about Teflon saucepans and what a waste of money it all was when we had problems such as Bosnia and Aids and Rwanda. On July 20, 1969, when Neil Armstrong said: "Houston, this is Tranquility Base. The Eagle has landed," one fifth of the world's population was listening and Nasa was the most famous acronym in history, but in the spring of 1994 it was evident one was going to visit a corpse.

As it happens, a corpse is the first thing you see when you arrive at Nasa: the white dismembered body of a Saturn V rocket laid out on the lawn beside Nasa Route One – the gimcrack strip of motels and shopping malls that separates Johnson Space Center from the greasy, sluggish waters of the Gulf of Mexico. The rocket looks big from the road half a mile away, but up close it is stupendous: 36 storeys high when erect; 45 storeys on its launch pad; only a few storeys less than the building where this magazine is produced – which is the tallest in Britain.

I climb out of the rental car and the Gulf air wraps the face like a dirty washcloth. I pace it out along the springy, sub-tropical turf: a bulging white cliff of alloy and plumbing and rivets; 160 long strides from nose to tail, where there are five immense bell-shaped exhaust nozzles, each big enough to hold a family barbecue. This rocket would have taken 18 to the moon if Congress had not cancelled the last three lunar flights. There are astronauts still working at Nasa, 25 years on, who would have flown on those missions. Just imagine the mournfulness: they drive past this spacecraft every day on their way to work.

One who did go was Captain John Young, commander of Apollo 16, the only astronaut to have flown twice in each of the Gemini, Apollo and Space Shuttle programmes; the first person to fly in space six times; a former head of the Astronaut Office. One of The Twelve, and of course you have to ask the obvious question. "So what was it *like* to be on the Moon?" and Young says, "Waal, communications were so good it wasn't unlike one of the simulations down here. You felt you could turn over a Moon rock and find a microphone there with someone talking to you."

"But you must have had all sorts of emotions. Exhilaration ... fear ...'

"Waal, I don't know about fear. You are trained to cope with these situations."

"But the Moon landing must have been the most memorable experience of your life?"

"Waal, all the flights are different. I wouldn't want to trade one against the other.'

"But you were, what, only the ninth man ever to set foot there."

"Waal, you gotta remember with all the training and exercises and simulations, I'd already *been* there 'bout 60 times."

We are talking in a beige fibreboard cubicle in the Nasa public affairs office with Young across the desk from me: a dried-up gnome of a man with side-parted grey-brown hair, lined face and shrouded eyes. At 64 years old he is still on the list of the current astronauts, still working out and still flying his T-38 jet trainer twice a week. He wears a dark blue blazer, tan trousers and flowered tie knotted like a string. A lot of polyester is present. He talks in a papery monotone, drywashing his hands as he speaks, and relaxing only when he can lapse into a burst of technobabble about thrust capability and gigabytes per second.

Is it possible for Moon man to be boring? But of course. It was the constant lament of writers such as Norman Mailer who covered the first Moon-shot: these thin-lipped crewcut WASPs with their Identikit Midwest backgrounds, Mary-Lou wives, suburban bungalows and robotic mien. Men who seemed to take a positive relish in their monosyllabic replies and anonymous interchangeability, like so many back-up valves in the Saturn V plumbing. "The high society of Nasa," Mailer wrote, "was as closed to superficial penetration as a guild of Dutch burghers in the 17th century." But Mailer and the other writers were working to magazine deadlines, and it took another 10 years for Tom Wolfe's book, *The Right Stuff*, to penetrate the guild and build a more rounded profile.

Almost all the early astronauts were recruited from military test pilot schools at Pax River and Muroc (now Edwards Air Force base) and they brought to civilian Nasa the macho fighter-jock culture of drinking, driving, fornicating, flying – and frequently dying – which the grotesquely dangerous work of the test schools engendered. Not that the Nasa work was especially dangerous or demanding.

Pilots such as the legendary Chuck Yeager, who stayed on at Edwards flying X-15s at 6.7 Mach and 67 miles high, regarded themselves as the real spacemen, while the Nasa astronauts were "Spam in a can" and "monkeys on a firecracker". They were test pilots without planes to practise on. Why, the early Mercury capsules didn't have pilot controls, or an unlockable hatch, or a window to look out of. The astronaut was a biological specimen in a scientific experiment, whose only real job was to stay alive from lift-off through to splashdown. Then on May 5, 1961, Alan Shepard became America's first man in space, and everything changed.

It was a pretty puny effort: one month after Yuri Gagarin orbited the earth in Vostok 1, Shepard rode a Redstone rocket – basically an adapted ballistic missile – in his Freedom 7 Mercury capsule on a 15 minute suborbital flight. It was 300 miles against Gagarin's 24,800, and five minutes of weightlessness to Gagarin's 89. It was a glorified mortar lob, in effect, but America had a new hero of the order of Charles Lindbergh. Shepard got a Distinguished Service Medal from President Kennedy, a motorcade down Constitution Avenue and a ticker-tape parade down Broadway. Astronaut power was born, and at Nasa they graduated from Spam-in-a-can to a new branch of the services. Military? Civilian? Who cared? They got their hatches and control sticks and windows and jet trainers and anything else they asked for. Nobody outranked them now.

The Astronaut Office became a corporation within a corporation, and though the pilots (they were *pilots*!) still had to endure all the tedious and humiliating medical and psychological tests, and sit through all the press conferences with their dumbass questions (How do you *feel*? Are you *frightened*? What were your *emotions*?) they could treat them with the righteous, too-cool-for-my-trousers way they deserved, and in that laid-back, cracker drawl handed down from Chuck Yeager himself. So though Buzz Aldrin might have a PhD from MIT, and Neil Armstrong an MSc from the University of Southern California, and though John Young was born in San Francisco, and has a BSc from Georgia Tech – they too are inheritors of those clipped banalities, the stubborn resistance to introspection and the calculated defiance of glamour which is the *essence* of glamour and charisma to those who truly have the Right Stuff.

Outside the public affairs building the landscape of the Nasa campus seems similarly contrived to deny the romance of its purpose. Until recently the grounds were scattered with interesting bits of spacecraft for visitors to gawp at, but these have been moved across the road to Space Center Houston, a commercial theme park designed with the help of the Disney organisation. The land that both stand on was donated by Rice University in 1962, with the proviso that it would be restored to the university if Nasa left – so it resembles a modern college campus, albeit a particularly dull one. Forty or 50 putty-coloured concrete boxes, many of them windowless, are dotted around a glassy plain, and identified only by numbers, allocated by some inscrutable logic. "Why is Building 1 next to Building 45?" I ask a young contract worker one day, and he says, "Just to annoy everybody. This place was built by nerds. Plastic pocket protector people." And it is true that you can still spot the old-time Nasa employees by their pocket protectors – a wallet fitted in the breast pocket of the white, short-sleeve drip-dry shirt, to insulate it from the inevitable battery of Biros.

Of the 10,000 people working at JSC only about 3,000 are the federal civil servants employed directly by Nasa – known variously as the Plastic Pocket Protectors, the P3s, or simply "the Feds". These are concentrated in administration and the core functions of mission control, project planning and astronaut training. The rest are contractors, doing everything from supplying computers to running the library to maintaining the T-38 jet trainers out at Allington Field.

Another split, running vertically through the organisation, is between engineers and scientists, as Wendell Mendell, a scientist in the Planetary Projects Office, explains. "Scientists are culturally very different from engineers. Engineers are hierarchical, compartmentalised, tasks are broken down into segments. Scientists are arrogant, intelligent, individualistic – they insult each other a lot and they are fractious and freewheeling. Nasa is an engineering culture. It is concerned that things operate correctly – much less concerned that the right type of knowledge is obtained. Nasa claims to be about science but what it is actually about is building spacecraft."

Nasa has its origins in Naca, the National Advisory Committee for Aeronautics, a civilian, research-based body founded in the Twenties. When the Soviets launched Sputnik 1 in 1958, to widespread public alarm in America, Naca was merged with a number of more practically-oriented bodies: the Army Ballistic Missile Agency led by former German rocketeer Wernher von Braun in Huntsville (or "Hunsville"), Alabama; the Naval Research Laboratory; the Jet Propulsion Laboratory run by CalTech in Pasadena. Crudely speaking, Nasa was a shotgun marriage between brains and brawn: disinterested research on the one hand; bombs and rockets on the other – and as the space race intensified in the early Sixties it was brawn that won out.

In 1962, on any rational assessment, America's future in space lay with the steady, incremental development of re-usable craft that could take off and land at regular airstrips – the direction already indicated by the X-15, X-20, Dyno-Soar and M2-F1 projects. You do not, as Mendell says, "run a railroad by throwing away the locomotive after every trip," but that is what Project Apollo amounted to. President Kennedy had the botched invasion of Cuba at the Bay of Pigs to live down, and the likelihood that the Soviets would be first into lunar orbit. His New Frontier economists saw space as a useful boost to an economy becalmed by peace, while Vice-President Johnson saw a river of federal dollars flowing into his home state of Texas.

Project Apollo, as Mailer observed, "was born on the landscape of political machination, economic cynicism and the manoeuvres of Lyndon Johnson's gravyboat navy." Kennedy's promise to land a man on the Moon by the end of the Sixties was a poker player's exponential raising of the space stakes, which demanded what Nasa itself describes as "a quick and dirty engineering answer to the political situation of the time". Apollo lacked clear scientific objectives and long-term developmental logic, but the engineers were placed in the driving seat, and they are there to this day.

Steve Bales, for instance, was the 26-year-old aeronautics engineer who ran the flight computer on Apollo 11, the flight that landed man on the Moon. He is now in charge of building the new Mission Control Center at JSC – a chubby, greying man in bifocals, pinstripes and migraine-patterned necktie. "When I graduated from college I'd had three hours' instruction in computing – I came to Nasa thinking they'd want me to design them a tailfin – and they put me in charge of computing and software."

We are talking in the Nasa holy-of-holies, the mission control room from which all the Apollo flights were run: a dim-lit cavern with raked ranks of olive drab desks facing three giant back-projection screens, which are presently simulating the flight path of the Space Shuttle on its equatorial orbit. It is familiar now from a hundred television transmissions, though as Bales says, before Nasa built it nobody had any idea of what a mission control room should look like. Early designs were based on Second World War fighter ops rooms, with a central table surrounded by terminals.

On July 20, 1969, Bales was in the front row – the trench – with the decision on whether to land on the Moon in his hands. The lunar module, codenamed Eagle, had undocked from the command module, Columbia, with a slight positive air pressure in the connecting tunnel. This had created a "popgun effect", wrecking the descent calculations, "so we didn't know exactly where we were, or where we would land, and we were travelling 14mph too fast, which was scary because if it was 20mph we had to abort." Communications to Earth broke down repeatedly on Eagle's "powered descent", and then in the final stages its computer began to put out an overload message, "Error 1201", which nobody understood. "The flight computer had 60 error conditions, many innocuous and a few disastrous, with a middle group of 1 or so that we called 'You Gotta Use Your Judgment'."

The rule of thumb the computer people had developed was that if the messages were more than 10 seconds apart they would ignore them. By this point the Eagle was 50ft above the lunar surface with Neil Armstrong still unable to recognise his landing site, flying it by the seat of his pants, and with fuel down to 17 seconds. Steve Bales, 26 years old, was faced with the prospect of going down in history as the man who aborted Apollo 11 when it was 30ft from the Moon. But his timing of the gaps between the computer errors was around 12 seconds, and Bales said "Go!" His voice is squeaky on the tape recording they keep at the Nasa archive, but the Eagle had landed.

"And were you taking a risk," I ask him now, "because you knew the whole world was watching?"

"No. I think I can honestly say I cared more about what the people in the room around me thought."

Bales's boss that day – the man who did as much to land the Eagle as Armstrong – was Gene Krantz, flight director of Apollo 11. He retired last year and lives in Dickinson, 10 miles from JSC, where I drive to meet him on a foray into suburban Nasa. Since JSC was set down in the cow pastures 20 miles south of Houston it has acquired its own metropolis of some 200,000 people, known as Clear Lake after the muddy sea inlet which it borders. It has no

centre – just the gaudy highways of Nasa Route One and Camino
Reale, with their Taco Bells and Denny's Diners and Nasa Cafes.

Turn off the highway, though, and with the guillotine
abruptness of American zoning laws you are into suburbia: placid
gridirons of middle-class streets with big shade trees and wide
lawns; kids' bikes with whitewall tyres safely abandoned on the
grass, and the Stars and Stripes flying half-mast for President Nixon
– or maybe Eisenhower. There is a Chevrolet Suburban in the
driveway, a basketball hoop in the yard, and a punchbag in the
garage, with dad out back throwing a football with Junior. It is the
landscape of *ET, Back to the Future* – or *Nightmare on Elm Street*,
according to taste.

Krantz is in his garage, working on the kit bi-plane which is his
retirement project: "Had to get it from Canada. You can't buy a light
aircraft in the US, with the liability laws here now. All the firms such
as Piper have been driven out of business." He leads the way to his
den, which is stuffed with TV, video and hi-fi, and decorated with
pictures of Second World War fighters. Krantz belongs to a vintage
aircraft club and flies a Boeing Superfortress for weekend recreation.
He is a former Korean War pilot himself, but never wanted to apply
for astronaut training: "No, not even when I was young and bullet-
proof. Those guys only get to go on a couple of missions, where I
have been on 60."

He is a tough-looking, green-eyed man with a half-inch crewcut,
and he makes coffee with a wary, experimental air. Martha, his wife,
is out with the third grandchild and all four children are grown and
gone: "So really, we got it made now." He joined Nasa in 1962 on a
salary of $3,000 a year and retired on $120,000, which is pretty
meagre by American corporate standards: a planned trip to Europe
this summer is only the second foreign vacation of his life.

"How has Nasa changed over the years?"

"Well, in the Sixties you had a very young enthusiastic president
with clear goals and a 'do it now' attitude. You also had a media
and a Congress which were fresh from the Second World War and
Korea. They understood *risk* and they understood *technology*. Not
stupid risk, but the kind of risk that makes sense, to achieve great
things. The difference today is the experience of Vietnam has made
people averse to risk and to technology. People want guarantees of
risk and reward and there are still no guarantees in this business.
Not when you are sitting on top of five million pounds of explosive
material."

What Krantz is referring to, of course, is the near-total paralysis of Nasa which followed the Challenger disaster of 1986 in which seven astronauts died. I call it a "disaster" here because everyone else does, though as John Young points out, the shuttle designers anticipated they would lose a spacecraft once every 60-odd missions, which is just what they did. Of the 24 astronauts who have died to date, only six died with their boots off, and two in off-duty accidents, giving an occupational death rate of 66 per cent – though apart from Challenger all of these happened off-camera. The high risk of violent death is part of the job and the astronauts know it, but the fact did not prevent almost indecent paroxysms of grief and recrimination from engulfing the agency, with an 18-month suspension of flights and a damning report from the Rogers Commission. Bereaved relatives of Challenger astronauts, such as Ellison Onizuka, have an almost regal status at Nasa, and there are Challenger shrines and memorials wherever you turn. At the souvenir store in the Space Center Houston theme park, there is a constantly running video of the Challenger explosion, which always attracts a crowd, and is one of the best selling items in the shop (after the simulated Moon soil at $5.99 a bag). The subject seems shrouded in a spirit of morbid sentimentality that is specifically American – akin to the violent mawkishness of Country & Western music – and which is hard for outsiders to understand.

Aside from its shop, the theme park is a curiously downbeat place, and seldom crowded. "There's no queues for *anything*," one father complains. Plans by Lunox Corp for a lunar buggy which tourists can drive about the surface of the Moon by remote control from Houston are still in the dream stage, but there are some interesting things to see: the nose section of the shuttle Adventure, sticking out of the wall as if it has just crash landed; a real piece of Moon rock to touch (slightly sticky from infant fingers); a simulated Moonscape, surreally populated by Moms and Pops in slacks and bowling shirts; a demonstration by Harriet of what it will be like to live in the Space Station, should it ever get built – "Now these are the living quarters, which we call the Habitation Module ..." Harriet, who is 55 and full-figured, wears a blue astronaut's flight suit, as do all the staff at the Space Center, right down to lavatory attendant and carpet sweeper.

What is strange about the place is that there is less conviction, less sense of celebration in the real and momentous events it commemorates than you find in the fantasy landscapes of a proper

Disney park. "What was it all for?" and "Where do we go now?" are the questions it mutely asks and they are not the questions demanded by Mickey Mouse. On a wall in the museum there is a quote from Thomas Paine, former Administrator of Nasa, which tried to give an answer: "The fundamental significance of Apollo was that for the first time mankind had been given a vision of the thin blue biosphere that surrounds our beautiful planet Earth, which as far as we know is the fragile home of all the life that has so far been detected in the solar system." So it was an *ecological* mission! We went to the Moon to save the whale! You find the same feeble appeal to the fashionable pieties of conservation in every piece of current Nasa propaganda. Even John Young, that rough old technocrat, was spouting stuff to me about how a Moon base would teach us to conserve water and energy. But surely the whole point of Apollo – the essence of its insane boldness – was to assert the opposite argument: that we are not ultimately dependent on our fragile environment but can manipulate and transcend it. You don't say these things in Nineties Nasa, or at least you don't say them sober and in daylight.

The one place you hear them now is down the Outpost Tavern on Route One, where the faithful still gather to drawl in their cups about Moon bases and Mars missions. The Outpost is spiritual inheritor to Pancho's Bar at Muroc, where the first astronauts gathered in the Fifties to practise their drinking and driving and flying and fornicating. The Outpost is a dive, carved out of an old barrack hut they dragged here from Allington Field: a sagging, blistered shack with rockwool insulation bursting from the plasterboard walls. The pool tables are scorched with cigarette burns, the mats are stuck to the bartop with beer glop, half the fairy lights are burned out and the jukebox is jammed on *Surfin' Safari*. But everyone has spent time at the Outpost: Krantz and Young, Kris Kraft and George Abbey, Armstrong and Aldrin. They have all been in, and all their pictures are up on the wall, beer-spotted, fly-blown and scribbled on. A dummy astronaut hangs from the ceiling, dressed in an old Mercury flight overall that looks as if someone painted the lounge in it, with a pair of Christmas tree balls dangling from the fly zip.

Gene Ross, the old soldier who owns the place, once ran a topless bar too, and the Outpost used to be full of astronaut groupies, hoping for a cosmic grope. "Still get the odd one, asking what an astronaut looks like, and I say, 'It's the feller over there with the propeller on his head'.." Ross has been a heller in his time with five wives and 10 children, who "musta drunk a railroad car of Canadian Club whiskey." But he is sadly diminished these days: wasted with alcoholic diabetes and both legs amputated above the knee. "Funny thing is since I had the amputations the diabetes is cured, so I'm just waiting for the legs to grow back too."

Up against the bar and into his fifth beer is Kent Joosten, in baggy shorts, Hawaiian shirt and ragged moustache. He is lead designer for lunar missions with Planetary Projects, tiny rump of what was once the New Initiatives Office. It was here they planned all the big bold missions to the stars, but budget cuts have turned it into a toyshop for dreamers. Kent, for instance, is working on a nuclear-powered robot mining base on the Moon which could extract enough oxygen and hydrogen to fuel a spaceship back to earth. The technology is practical: Kent has a moon buggy in Death Valley, Arizona, that he can drive from his desk here at Nasa. He has tested the extraction equipment in a flight on the C-135 plane that Nasa uses to simulate zero gravity conditions – the so-called "Vomit Comet". And it would only cost about $10 billion – one quarter the sum Nasa was demanding from President Bush for its Moon and Mars bases 10 years ago.

"So you think it might happen?" I ask him, and Kent stares moodily into his beer.

"There is *no* commitment on anybody's part at Nasa to human lunar exploration."

All that Nasa is committed to these days is the long-delayed and heavily trimmed space station project with the Russians – which everyone expects to be cancelled any day – and the continuing of Space Shuttle flights, though it is increasingly hard to say what exactly they are for. Research into weightlessness; fabrication of new alloys in low gravity: the same vague noises that Nasa has been making since the Sixties. The Shuttle has performed fairly well but it was always a kludge – a term defined by the *Devil's Dictionary* as "a wheel made out of bricks". And the cost of the thing. It takes a billion dollars and 20,000 people to put one Shuttle into orbit around the Earth, while up at the army's old Star Wars place in Arlington it takes 10 teenagers with a couple of million dollars to put the Clementine satellite in orbit around the Moon. "I can't believe sometimes," says Kent, "that we are pouring $14 billion a year into the top of this organisation, and I have so little coming out of the bottom."

Burgeoning bureaucracy is the usual bogeyman that is blamed for the ills of Nasa, though one has to remember here that in America it is regarded as a test of patriotism that one should hate the government. Still, there is no denying that since 1960 central staff at Nasa has grown by a factor of 10 in an organisation that grew by a factor of three. Professional administrators at JSC have grown from five per cent to 20 per cent of the organisation and are twice as likely to receive promotion as engineers and scientists. "I don't believe that Nasa has a long-term future," Wendell Mendell says. "There is an enormous amount of inertia and it just has to be destroyed."

The flight of Apollo 11 was an enormous achievement, with spin-offs ranging from the micro-circuitry of the computer on which I wrote this article, to the satellite navigation systems that flew me home to London; from flameproof car seats to sports bras; from foetal monitors to long-life pacemakers; and from self-righting life-rafts to solar batteries – and never mind the old saw about Teflon, which was invented long before Apollo.

It cost $24 billion, which was less than America spent on Vietnam every eight months, and it paid back seven dollars for every two dollars invested: priming the economic pump of the Sixties boom, giving work to hundreds of thousands, creating towns and counties and serving as handmaiden to a hundred new corporations. And yet, as Mailer saw at the time, "it had failed to become a vision of technology which would put light in the eyes of every poor man ... In the hour they landed on the Moon America was applauding Armstrong and Aldrin and the world would cheer America for a day but something was lacking. Some joy, some outrageous sense of adventure. Strong men did not weep on the street nor ladies copulate with strangers. Any armistice to a petty war had occasioned greater celebrations."

The Moon shot was an inherently irrational, romantic enterprise, but in the dogged determination to achieve its end Nasa lost all register of the true complexity of the event: scaling down the scientific programme; suppressing the elements of personal adventure and courage, until all that remained was an image of impersonal efficiency and robotic men-machines who related their adventures in the language of the automatic drink dispenser, and finally bored the world into indifference. The Nasa team hit a home run with Apollo, but they lost the ball somewhere before the end of the innings and they are looking for it still.

The Gilruth Building, at the edge of the JSC campus, is a sports and recreation centre where the young bloods of Nasa come out to play: in chilli cook-offs, and beer chucking races, and grapefruit passing contests. All through the week I spend at Nasa, though, there are retirement parties running. Kegs of beer are set out in bins of ice, and big bowls of nachos and potato chips and avocado dip. And the gods of the old Nasa return to the Elysian field to say farewell to their comrades – grizzled men in Sears shirts and pegged tan trousers with belts hitched under their bellies. Gene Krantz and "PJ" Weitz and Joe Kerwin and Eugene Cernan. They are off to retirement condos in Arizona and long-delayed trips to Europe and plane kits in back garages. "Pete, you ol' sonofagun!" "Joe, you worthless sawbones!"

None of them smokes, so I have to leave the party for a cigar after a while, where I find John Young, searching for a set of car keys he has dropped in the parking lot. When I have helped him to find them he shows me a picture of his baby granddaughter welded into the plastic keyfob. "You see that. She's the reason we should be exploring space. The generation of the future. You tell that to the folks in England." And John Young – who has orbited the earth 253 times; who is one of The Twelve who have flown to the moon and back – pockets his keys and shuffles off across the carpark, into the retirement party.

Telegraph Magazine, 25 June 1994

God bless the Queen

'So then the toilet, like, exploded ..." "And then my thermostat just fell off the wall ..." "And these *fumes* started coming off the carpet ..." "And they told me to use the toilet down the *hall* ..." "And the purser's office just said: 'Well, what do you *expect* on Four Deck?'"

All over the QE2 you still hear these war stories whispered in the corners of bars but there isn't much evidence of the chaos of a month ago, when the £45 million refit left hundreds of cabins unfinished and hundreds of holidays cancelled at a few days' notice.

This week lawyers in the US filed a $50 million suit against Cunard in the New York Supreme Court, including claims for compensation of $100,000 each for 120 passengers. Cunard has said the company will defend itself "vigorously" and that its compensation package, which includes a refund, a free cruise and spending money, was "generous" by European standards.

But not all the American passengers are litigious "whingers," as the Cunard public relations office rashly dubbed them. My friend Dottie, from Akron, Ohio, for instance, has war stories to rival any of them: a shower that alternated between freezing and scalding; a non-flushing toilet; a basin tap that ran dark brown; carpet glue fumes fit to make your eyes water; broken-down air conditioning ...

But Dottie is the philosophical type, and she didn't want to write off a $40,000 holiday. "So I just asked the purser's office for another cabin and they said they couldn't do it because the cruise was fully booked – but real *snotty*, you know, like I was about 12 years old. But I couldn't face a fight. I am on my vacation, right? So I just paid them $8,000 for an upgrade."

I can vouch for Dottie's story in the matter of the purser's office at least, which can display a spectacularly jobsworth attitude. Just before writing this article, for instance, I went to ask them for some A4 paper (which they do not sell on board) and was told crisply: "We can't go handing out sheaves of paper to just *anyone* you know." So I said: "OK, you can charge it to my cabin." "But they didn't have the *facilities* to do that and it took a minor temper tantrum before I was grudgingly issued with 12 sheets of paper – and this to write something which they hoped would *improve* the image of Cunard.

At the bottom of these frictions there is a clash of cultures, I think. On the one hand you have those who virtually worship the QE2 as a unique British institution: last of the great Atlantic liners; the biggest, strongest, fastest passenger ship afloat, etc, etc. Supporters of this view include the majority of British passengers, the QE2 officer caste, and the innumerable QE2 enthusiasts who travel on the ship year after year – a fraternity of ocean-going anoraks – who can recite every statistic from its top speed (32.5 knots) to its caviar consumption (2.5 tonnes a year) to the amount of clingfilm they use annually in the kitchen (enough to wrap the ship 731 times).

On the other hand there are those (mostly American but with a few Europeans) who see the ship as a floating hotel – and a damned expensive one – which should be able to make its showers work properly and should not patronise its customers.

I am in the floating-hotel group myself but I don't write off the romantics. You sense the density of the QE2's history the moment you step aboard, and the many eccentricities which go with it. Just a few weeks ago, for instance, a mystery passenger was spotted at a captain's reception – a striking-looking woman in spike heels and sequinned ballgown. She turned out to be a transvestite steward who had taken to relieving the monotony of the galleys by popping into the occasional passenger party between shifts.

Or there is the "soft-toy lady," a Mrs Jerry Kay, who goes everywhere with a stuffed animal under her arm and books a stateroom for every world cruise, with a separate room for her collection of toys (and this for a minimum of £12,495 a room). Or there is the woman from Tallahassee, Florida, a sombre society matron at home who comes on every cruise simply to get falling-down drunk for three months (when she falls down, she can fall back on her walking stick which is filled with gin).

Or what about Ike from Utah, who spends all day every day working on the 3,000-piece jigsaw in the Chart Room bar? I spent an hour with him one day, did not get a single piece in place, and was virtually in tears from the boredom and frustration. "Don't you think it's just a bit dull ?" I asked him.

Ike replied: "Oh no. You got these wavy pieces and these other pieces with little bumps on the side ... there's lots of variety." The puzzle we were working on showed a scene of fiord and forest, remarkably like the one sliding by outside the window as we cruised down the New Zealand coast. But Ike never looks out of the window.

I joined the ship in New Zealand for a five-day cruise to Sydney and spent the night before embarkation in Auckland. When I went to bed, my hotel window had a view of Auckland Harbour, which is pretty big. When I opened the curtains in the morning, all I could see was the QE2. There was a ship-shaped shadow over downtown Auckland. People had stopped their cars and got out, and were standing around, scratching their heads. They were saying things like "Phew, she is *big*?" and "Man, that is a *big* ship".

I was lost within minutes of getting on board, among cavernous theatres and lounges and stairwells and quarter-mile corridors. The signs and the stewards talked about aft and forward, port and starboard, quarterdeck and boat-deck, but what did they mean? And these sea-going types are so slippery with their jargon, for as soon as you pluck up courage to ask for the bow, they say: "Sharp end? It's back the other way, sir."

My cabin is on One Deck, so called because it is fourth from the top of the ship, or fifth from the bottom – I can't remember now but someone explained it to me. It is a good-sized room, about 15ft by 12ft with a walk-in wardrobe and bathroom, which has just been done out in that swanky corporate style – all grey granite tops and marble tiles. There is a pool of water on the floor but I *swab* it up – with the complimentary face flannel – and it does not return.

The cabin has a new raspberry-coloured carpet and easy chairs but the overall effect is still rather dingy. The QE2 was built in the 1960s, and the style is still apparent in the yellow teak of the ceiling, the grubby hessian panelling on the walls and the brown sticky-backed vinyl covering all the horizontal surfaces – and coming unstuck in several places. The strip light around the mirror does not work. There is no mini-bar, just an empty fridge crudely fitted into an old life-jacket chest. None of the phone buttons – for room service, purser's office, etc – produces a response.

These may just be the gripes of a spoiled journalist who has stayed in too many five-star hotels at no personal expense but if I *was* paying the $1,800 a day which this room costs I would not be happy.

As it isn't costing me a penny, I am deliriously happy and go skipping upstairs (sorry, aloft) to the ship's rail to survey, with patrician indulgence, the huddled masses of Auckland who have gathered to see us off – roughly 5,000 of them. A brass band on the quayside is playing *My Way* and *Seventy-Six Trombones*; cameras flash and people call to us: "Bon voyage! Safe journey! Have a lovely time!" A cruise on the QE2 is still a thing most people wish for when asked what would be their dream holiday and so I suppose we represent a kind of secular heaven to those below us on the quay. They wish us well, these people who do not know us, because it keeps alive their own dream of bliss.

If you are British, of course, then heaven must have a class system and the QE2's is quite elaborate, though, just like the shore-based system, it's existence is officially denied. At the top end a full world cruise in a penthouse cabin can cost £175,000. Many passengers book two cabins, one for themselves and one for their clothes. On this trip there is a pharmaceuticals tycoon who has booked eight suites for three months at a cost of £1.2 million.

At the bottom end, which is a cabin with bunks on Five Deck, you can get 11 nights on the final leg of the world cruise, which is Istanbul to Southampton, for £1,595 which is not at all bad when you remember it includes all you can eat.

The way we tell each other apart is where we eat: the Queen's Grill for the plutocrats; the Princess and Britannia Grills for the bourgeoisie; the Caronia and Mauretania Restaurants for the sansculottes (though the captain, very democratically, keeps his table in the last two restaurants). The food does not vary much from one another (it is wonderful).

Obviously, nobody who goes cruising on the QE2 is going to be poor but there are plenty of ordinary people, like Alan and Pauline who run a pub in Southport, Lancashire, and have been cruising on the QE2 for six years now; or there is Madge, a former Blackpool landlady, on her third world cruise. Women out-number men by about five to three, and inevitably there are many divorced and widowed women travelling alone. Dorothy from Akron, Ohio, is cheerfully spending the alimony she extracted from her doctor husband when he left her six years ago: "He pays, I play."

In the Queen's Ballroom every night there are 12 "Gentlemen Hosts" employed by Cunard to act as dancing partners for the single: silver-haired retired American men for the most part, who receive bed and board but no salary for their efforts. "And do you ever sleep with your dancing partners?" I ask one of them. "All I can do to keep them awake on the floor," he tells me.

Although Cunard makes an effort to promote a more useful image – the staid Yacht Club bar is shamelessly described as "a glittering fashionable discotheque" – the style of the ship is late middle-aged and lower middlebrow. Glancing through the daily-events guide I find, at random, a "non-surgical facelift demonstration," an "informal gathering of the Masonic Brethren," "Teatime with the Lester Lanin Orchestra" and "Golden Oldies Aerobics".

But most passengers decide not to do anything at all – even to go ashore – and devote their time to eating enormous meals and sleeping them off. To wander around the QE2 in mid-afternoon is to find the pools empty, the lecture theatres almost deserted, the games equipment abandoned, and the only sound the giant susurration of engines and sea. Hush! The entire ship is snoring.

In a world where the well-off become more timid by the day,

the cruise ship is a perfect cocoon, a floating condominium. "You are in a hotel that moves," Captain Burton-Hall says.

"You pack and unpack once, there are things to do all day and you get a doctor in 30 minutes. You can visit somewhere like Rio and encounter real poverty but be back on the ship for a bath and dinner."

I think of his words when we pull into the harbour at Lyttelton on New Zealand's South Island, and I somehow miss the day excursion because I'm having this big breakfast.

And then I think about getting a taxi into Christchurch but there is this book I am quite enjoying. And then, when I've had a little sleep after lunch, I think about a bit of a walk on the quayside.

But it is so comfortable here – with the purr of the waves and the snore of the engine, and the smell of dinner rising from the gallery – that it hardly seems worth the effort.

The Daily Telegraph, 11 February 1995

Novels

Do It Again

"He is *amazing*, isn't he?"

When people asked other people over dinner what Malcolm was doing these days, they liked to recite these facts about him. "Oh, he *hasn't*. You're *kidding*," they used to say. "He is *amazing*, isn't he?" Malcolm's friends, the ones who had succumbed to jobs and children and mortgages, liked to be amazed by Malcolm, but Malcolm was entirely unamazed by himself. He was the least sentimental of all the people he knew. He had the same awareness of past and future as a pussy cat, which is to say, none at all, and like a cat, Malcolm was always warm, comfortable and well fed.

At five to one the computer beeped softly and he padded across the room in his socks to switch on a row of radio cassette recorders. Each radio was tuned to a different local station and after lunch Malcolm would listen to the recorded news broadcasts in turn, picking out stories that could be sold to the diary columns of national newspapers.

The newspapers liked local colour in their diary columns. It gave them an air of solidity and breadth; provided ballast to their shrill campaigns and misinformed opinions. If there were no sufficiently interesting titbits in the radio news, then Malcolm would make some up. The newspapers never minded so long as the stories were sufficiently amusing, malicious and legally fireproof.

"Anything else you want ..."

Melanie had taken all her clothes off and was sitting facing Alec, with her knees crossed and her chin propped in her hands. Two brown nipples peeped from behind her forearms. They were always called Melanie wherever you went: strip club, massage parlour, peep show, escort agency. A whole world of Melanies.

"Shall I tell you what I will do for you?" she asked.

"Yes, please," said a croaky voice, very far away. Quite like Alec's.

"I will masturbate myself and you can masturbate yourself at the same time. That will cost you £20."

"Oh," said the Alec voice, feebly.

"What's the matter? Too much money?"

Melanie explained some of the other options. For £5, she said, she would spread her legs and show Alec her cunt. For another £5 she would stick her fingers up her cunt. And so forth. She did not actually say "cunt". She said "myself", as if acknowledging the bleak economic fact that herself and her cunt were, to all intents and purposes, the same thing. The plastic bench she was sitting on gave a little fart every time she shifted her buttocks. For £25, she told Alec, she would put a dildo up herself. She took the dildo from a Safeway's carrier bag on the floor beside her to show him. It was chrome-coloured and ribbed like a giant lipstick. He noticed a shrink-wrapped packet of butcher's mince in the carrier bag.

Everything seemed to have a price, except for actually touching each other, because there was a half-inch sheet of plate glass between them. The sign outside in the street had read "Nude Encounter Parlour" and Alec had imagined a dimly lit, sybaritic salon of divans and tasselled drapes, with candlelight gilding naked bodies. But the parlour had turned out to be only a plasterboard cubicle in the cellar, a little larger than a lavatory, with a door at each end, and two of the farting benches, each completely sealed off from the other by the six-foot sheet of smeary glass.

He had come in through a narrow passageway off Greek Street. A pink-cheeked girl with the cheerful smile of a Woolwich advert explained the protocol to him. It was £10 for ten minutes, £15 for twenty minutes and so on. "The girl will strip off completely and talk to you for ten minutes," said Woolwich, in a level, matter-of-fact voice. "Anything else you want" – her voice lingered briefly – "is arranged between you." Someone's fingers, nimble as bananas, found the money in his wallet. Someone's feet tramped solidly, resignedly downstairs, carrying his body with them, to the basement cubicle where Melanie was waiting.

"Sir would like some sash lifts ..."

In times of trouble, some people buy doughnuts and others new clothes. Alec Smith found solace in hardware, and Meakins in Wykeham was his favourite hardware shop in the world. It was 112 years old and staffed by ancient, withered men in brown cotton shop-coats who treated their customers with weary contempt, who weighed everything in tiny brass scales and wrapped each purchase laboriously and individually in brown paper and string.

Meakins was lined from floor to ceiling with tiny, polished mahogany drawers filled with rare and curious items that were smelted and cast and turned to order in backstreet workshops in the Midlands: tiny screws; enormous bolts; hinges for doll's houses; lion's head door knockers with tongues that went in and out; and flushed brass handles for eighteenth-century sea chests.

Alec had bought many of the fittings for Uplands here, and for the house in Islington, and he came equipped with careful lists and sets of sketches. The Meakins countermen had served their apprenticeships in the age of the professional builder and decorator: monosyllabic and authoritative men, with folding rules and square carpenter's pencils tucked behind orange-peel ears. But the customers now were the DIY Blackandeckermen, strong on their dignity as consumers but weak on terminology, and the Meakins men despised them.

In the front of Alec's queue was a man in a leather blouson jacket and trainers, drawing wild diagrams in the air. "I want some of those, erm, some of those little nails for, fixing the leather to chair seats, sort of like drawing pins, only bigger ..."

"You mean some *chair nails*, sir," said the counterman smugly.

Further along the counter another Blackandeckerman was miming the opening of an invisible sash window. "Some of those little curved brass things you fix on the bottom of sliding windows, for, erm, sliding them with ..."

"Sir would like some *sash lifts*," said a second counterman.

The trick, Alec had learned over the years, was the *obviousness* of the names of these obscure pieces of hardware. A brass corner piece for protecting the corner of a military chest, for instance, was known as a *military chest corner*. A sliding bolt for a lavatory door, which indicated whether there was anybody in the lavatory or not, was a *lavatory indicator bolt*. The cast-iron ends of old-fashioned wooden ceiling airers were called *airer ends*. And just in case a regular like Alec ever got cocky, the countermen could throw in a name as unguessable as Rumpelstiltskin. Alec had once asked firmly for a "Brass swivel match" for a kitchen cupboard, only to be told, loftily, that what he required was *a button-on-a-plate*.

His father, Harry, hated this sort of place, of course. Harry had made his money in the wholesale clothing business. He disliked retail establishments on principle, but hated DIY and tools and hardware even more. He could have hated Meakins just for its olde worlde name, or for the dusty pyramid of Polyfilla packets that was its hopeless window display, or its complete lack of commercial acuity. He would have loathed its queues and its sluggish, condescending service; raged at its cruel little courtesies and its finnicky nomenclature; despised its total lack of interest in selling merchandise and making money in preference to irritating and baffling its customers.

Alec Smith was an ordinary man who had begun to feel his life sliding inexorably towards oddness. He had grown up in Watford, had supported Arsenal, collected Robertson's gollies and constructed Airfix models of British fighter planes. He had eight 'O' levels, three 'A' levels and a 2:1 in Political Science from an ordinary university. The book jacket of *The Republican Reader* stated that "Alec Smith is married with two children, and lives in north London" – and what could be more ordinary than that?

He was ordinary, but Susan, Rachel and now Melanie had, successively, made Alec begin to feel very odd indeed. He had begun to fear that he was on the verge of making some impatient, dramatic, self-revealing gesture that might ruin everything for ever. Some terrible and shameful act which would change him in an instant from wealthy, successful, affable, family-man Alec to a freak-outcast-pervert Alec, fit only to be stoned in the cathedral precincts by brown-coated shop assistants, Scots Presbyterian Education Secretaries and students with Sebastian Flyte haircuts.

So he came to Meakins in search of the finely graded inefficiency and fractionally modulated rudeness which are the indices of ordinary English life. He came for the stoicism, the flinty reserve and the fanatical attention to meaningless detail which, for Alec, were quintessentially English, and to which he quite naturally responded, and which reassured him, therefore, of his essential Watfordian, Battle of Britain, Robertson-gollyish dullness. And he needed to buy some hardware.

"This is a serious exercise …"

Alec was making mayonnaise in the Uplands kitchen, trickling a thread of thick green olive oil into a white china pudding basin while his other hand worked the egg yolks into golden ointment. The gentle piddle of oil into the bowl, the suck and click of the wooden spoon in the thickening goo, was soporific in the hot, sunlit kitchen where William sat, dozing over the Sunday papers on a table white with plaster dust.

"It's an argument for the existence of God, you know."

"What?"

"Mayonnaise." said Alec. "It's one of those things that couldn't have been discovered by accident. Nobody could ever have guessed that simple eggs and oil would do this when you mixed them together. Even when you know how to make it, you can often get it wrong if you rush, or if you're feeling bad-tempered. My mother used to say a menstruating woman should never try to make mayonnaise."

"If you feel your period coming on," said William, "there's some salad cream in the fridge."

"Toothpaste," said Alec dismissively. "Dried eggs, chip-shop vinegar, anti-oxidants and E numbers."

William took a jar of Safeway's mayonnaise from the refrigerator, set it down next to the pudding basin and scooped up a dollop of each on to his grimy forefingers.

"Right," he said, "close your eyes." Alec did as he was told, and took two ginger licks.

"Okay," he said. "Number one was Polyfilla and number two was sand and cement."

"This is a serious exercise," said William. "If you can't do this, you can never bullshit me again about wine smelling of pencil shavings and blackberries."

"All right, seriously. Number one is Safeway's toothpaste and number two is my own mayonnaise."

"Lucky," said William.

"Luck has nothing to do with it," said Alec smugly. "The Safeway's is a good 10 degrees colder."

"Funny thing is," said William, just to keep his end up, "they were both Safeway"s."

"Like most friendships ..."

In university holidays they had run their own housepainting business in London. Working for the sharp-toothed minnows of the speculative building boom, William had met the businesslike, omnicompetent Alec and been depressed by him. Alec with the cleanest overalls and the grit-free glosswork. Alec who chased around with pursed lips and a critical squint, straightening the edges of William's painting, picking up his stray bristles and paint dribbles.

It wasn't the university Alec of the six-joint sessions over the latest Dylan album, and he liked him not nearly so much. "They're only speculators' hutches, squire," he told him touchily. "Woodchip paper and magnolia emulsion is what they want, not fucking David Hicks."

But Alec seemed incapable of the genial slovenliness which William felt was all their gold-braceleted employers deserved, and which, in any case, came naturally to him. They were only making a few quid in the holidays, after all. Taking a ride on the property spiral. But as they tarted up plasterboard bedsits in Finchley, Alec was dreaming of Highgate restaurants and Hampstead mansion blocks. He talked of fleets of white Mini vans, power spray guns, industrial wallpaper strippers, illustrated catalogues and a special line in decorative finishes. He took to saying "Islington Interiors" when he answered the telephone to their clients, while William enraged him with a cheerful "Quickslosh Decorators".

William knew that like most friendships – like most of the marriages he knew – theirs was based on the past. It had been founded on common undergraduate appetites for dope and Dylan records and mildly subversive behaviour. It had been cemented by shared houses and minor ordeals: rebuilding the old MG, hitching across Turkey, hustling a living together in the building trade. Over the last fifteen years, and through long separations, it had been kept adequately topped up with pints in pubs and do-you-remember conversations.

But he had often thought, in the years since university, that if they had met now, for the first time, their worlds, their boundaries, would have barely intersected. They would have tapped and diverged like billiard balls. Alec with his houses and children and board meetings. William with his string of unsuitable girls and addresses scribbled on cigar packs. He was not displeased with his life, and he was not especially jealous of the solid accumulation of property and achievement which was Alec's. But as he watched this sudden wobble develop in his best friend's steady trajectory, it was not without a trace of satisfaction.

"The democracy of decline ..."

Alec drove Rachel south through Bedgebury Forest in his Audi Quattro and worried about his stomach. He had been fat once, nearly sixteen stone, and had made himself thin again by swimming and starvation and by drinking gin instead of beer. But the paunch had remained. It was a compact little apron of suet, which had never spread to his hips or breasts but had also proved immune to sit-ups or to Susan's Trim-wheel. He had got up to 200 sit-ups a day at one time, but the paunch had just changed from being flabby and prominent to rubbery and prominent.

Fashionably baggy trousers in the 1980s had made it less of a problem and on Greek beaches it could be camouflaged with a sun tan. But after nine months in London the paunch was codfish white and swimming trunks, however generously cut, were unforgiving. With Susan it didn't matter so much. In the democracy of decline, his gut and her bum cancelled each other out. But without ever having seen Rachel in anything more revealing than a decorator's overall he already knew she was going to make him feel about sixty.

"You look lovely."

"I think I'm going to keep this dry for the way home," said Rachel, and peeled down the shoulders of her swimsuit. Alec tried the usual techniques for looking casual: staring up at the leaves above his head; tracing patterns on the ground with his fingers; whistling noiseless tunes between his teeth. Then he gave up and looked instead at Rachel who was naked now and picked her way gingerly through the litter of broken twigs and beech mast to the water's edge.

The perfect hemispheres of her rump, with their brief triangle of white skin, were painful to Alec. The buried pipeline of her spine sliding smoothly beneath her skin was agony. The hint of spun sugar pubic hair that flickered in the blue V of sky between her thighs was quite intolerable. He pulled off his T-shirt and bathing trunks, and marched resolutely to the water's edge.

"Stop sucking your stomach in," called Rachel, bobbing and shuddering in the cold water. "You look lovely."

They swam side by side out to the ski ramp. The windsurfers had disappeared from the far shore, and the sheet of water was dark and flat as engine oil in the still afternoon. The only sounds were the tiny splashes of their arms breaking the water now and then, and the susurration of their own breathing.

He enjoyed the strange sensation of the cold water coursing between his buttocks as they clenched and unclenched with the steady stroke. Even in a hundred yards you could begin to feel the heat starting to retreat from the skin, inwards to the body core as the coldness pressed in. Half and hour, he knew, and muscles would begin to knot with cramp. An hour in this sort of water and you would be unconscious.

Alec imagined himself down on the dark floor of the gravel pit, 200 feet below, looking up at the insect scurrying of their own bodies on the calm surface of the water. Way down there among the rusted cars and supermarket trolleys and the jumbled bones of birds and badgers and the odd, unlucky swimmer.

He could see from there that he and Rachel, splashing happily across the surface of a sunny pond, were feeble little heat engines, leaking energy into the millions of tons of freezing water beneath them, seeping inexorably towards equilibrium with the chill indifference around. Down there at the bottom of the gravel pit Alec Smith stopped worrying about his wife, Susan, and his children, Dora and Jonathan, and about the indignities of age and paunch. His testicles were shrunk to the size of lentils and his penis was a bluish acorn, but he knew with great certainty that he wanted to fuck Rachel.

The Mother-in-Law Joke

"It's what London is ..."

At university in Cardiff my friend Reg, London lad and worldly wise, had schooled me in the subtle snobberies of the metropolitan postcodes. "South of the river, forget about it. Nobody lives there but blacks and bank clerks. E3 to E8 is all sawn-off shooters, soccer yobs and Paki sweatshops. Stamford Hill, Golders Green, Hendon is Jews and Jags. W3 to W8 is big mick boozers, small-time TV people and Sikh sweatshops –"

"Hang on, hang on," I stopped him, bewildered. "Does everyone walk about *knowing* these things?" The Welsh town I came from had an ordinary bit and a posh bit. There were tidy people and people who were common. I'd learned the English categories of working, middle and upper class by now, but these new complexities seemed overwhelming.

"It's what London *is*," Reg told me patiently. "SW3 is better: Sloanes and Kensington crocodiles. NW5 and NW1 are trying hard: Alan Bennett, Jonathan Miller, Hunter Davies, A.J.P. Taylor. But the real colour supp. country is N6 and NW3. That's where you want to be."

And that was where I was, stamping up East Heath Road against the wind, fingertips digging for warmth in the fluff and grit of pocket seams. I turned right, across a cinder car park that was piled high with black plastic bin bags. There were rats in the streets of London that winter the tabloids said, but only photographers seemed able to find them. I crossed a dam between two ponds, where narrow gardens filled with wet furniture and mossy statues ran down to the water. Behind a picture window a man was working at a typewriter. Novel, poem, play? He glanced up, and from behind his desk I watched myself, a dark figure in denim and shoddy moving across the shining water, rubbernecking the swans and gentry gardens. He looked down again at his typescript and I was switched off.

I started up a dim tunnel between dusty evergreens, sensing space and light beyond. Over the hill ahead I could see coloured kites flying; scraps of simple geometry on Fuzzy-Felt blue. I climbed a steep asphalt path towards them, keeping my eyes left to the big red-brick houses which fringed the Heath, saving the view which I knew would be there until I reached the top.

It was one of those winter days when the sky lifts its lid on London and floods the city with a hard, splintering light which shrinks distances and pulls into focus the blue ranges of downland which define its limits. In the shallow bowl of the Thames Valley the lava flow of the city had halted. Brown and massy, it was still smoking lightly, hardening here and there into the cubes of office blocks, firing light off their new-formed edges, and the crystal spikes of churches, stabbing through the brown slurry of terrace and traffic.

The noise of the city was a vast and muffled grinding, like the shifting of tectonic plates, which I heard through the feet rather than the ears, as I stood there feeling the new geography form around me. The river ran from right to left, which meant I must be looking south. The pale slabs marching leftwards were the East End. An airliner sinking towards the gleam of the river on the right signified Heathrow Airport. Beside the path was an etched steel panorama, scribbled cockandballs with felt tip. Leaning over it I located the Telecom Tower, St Paul's, St Pancras, St Bride's, St Clement Danes.

"No music and machines"

Reg was leaning over the bar when I found him, reading the *Guardian* crossword puzzle upside down. On the public side an old soak with a roghan josh complexion and a blue Barbour jacket was wheezily sub-vocalizing the clues beneath a trembling purple forefinger.

"A torque twisted into a fancied circle. Seven letters."

"Try 'equator'," said Reg, raising a hand to me in greeting. Muttering ungratefully the soak filled in the clue with a frayed Bic, its point rucking the damp newsprint. Reg was wearing vast black magician's trousers with silk braid seams, and a breezy Dan Tempest shirt which blazed in the treacly twilight of the pub. For the sake of effect he jabbed at a few optics, crashed a wire tray of pint pots into the dishwasher and whisked an invisible droplet from the bar with a spotless towel.

"Right then. What will you have?"

"Gin and Tonic, please."

"Large Gin and It for the young man with the cheekbones, Eugene," he sang out to his non-existent assistant.

"You like our little *estaminet, Philippe?*"

At eleven thirty in the morning the saloon bar of The Jar was almost empty, apart from a few shaky livers-on-legs, drinking their hangover cures two-fisted out of Duralex tumblers. The colour scheme was phlegm and nicotine, smoked haddock and used teabag. Golden plumes of cigar smoke spiralled through the rays of winter sun that filtered through the frosted glass. The smell of frying sausages floated from the kitchen. No music and no machines. I approved.

"Just like pornography"

"Have you noticed how much the old hacks talk about death?" I said to him. "The audience they murdered in Birmingham. The crowd they killed in Crewe. They're always socking them with punchlines and slaying them with putdowns. Knocking them stiff, laying them out and stopping the show."

"Just like pornography," said Reg.

He was lying on his bed in the attic bedroom, his hands behind his head, gazing complacently at his newly painted ceiling. Reg moved in to Aberdare House a month after me, but he fitted in a lot faster. He had charmed my mother-in-law, made Hon laugh and Saul hoot. My clothes had never quite made it out of the suitcase a second time, but Reg had painted his room white all over – ceiling, walls, floor and furniture – so it had lost its shadows and perspectives, like the inside of a ping-pong ball. All around the walls his breezy shirts were hung on the picture rail, freshly ironed and stirring in the draughts like spinnakers.

"Why pornography?" I asked him.

"Because, *Philippe*, comedy is the only form of communication apart from the stroke-mag that has an actual physical effect on the audience. This cheery chappie up on stage is effecting a physical change on the people out there. You're taking charge of their bodies. It's intellectual assault, verbal rape."

"And the audience are just victims?"

"Not at all," said Reg, "because if you're not a very efficient rapist, then they're going to kick you in the balls."

"I'm a father already ..."

Another meeting, the same day. I am sitting in, on, around a sag bag, on the floor of a Highgate sitting room. Evening sunshine, filtered through the leaves of a giant fir tree, sprawls over the polished parquet floor. In the centre of the room, her tasty brown legs arranged in an effortless lotus position, is Serena Arum, the leader of our natural childbirth class. Around the walls in attitudes that range from discomfort to rapt enthusiasm are another dozen people, all in couples. We have all taken our shoes off and they are lined up beside the door: Reeboks, Timberlands, desert boots, Korean canvas sandals, Natural Shoe Store clonkies, and a still-archaic pair of Kickers (no longer, thank God, Diana's). Not a polished toecap to be seen.

We are going through the process of introducing ourselves, an inevitable ritual now of every large meeting, from corporate boardroom to Kilburn squat. Officially it is to set everyone at their ease, to draw them into the circle. Unofficially, I suspect, it has the same purpose as calling the register at school – a disciplinary routine which establishes the ascendancy of the leader, and stops everyone nattering.

Robert is a healer, Jasmine runs a stall at Camden Lock, Damien is a gardener, Chloe makes jewellery, Edward runs a schools' theatre project, Amanda is a community liaison officer, Joe is looking for himself, and helping out meanwhile at an after-school play centre ... They're joke jobs, all of them ("What's *your* job then?" – Diana), but they must make money at them somehow or other, because it's fifty guineas a head for just three of Serena's feelgood sessions. I contemplate being a South American mercenary, a pork butcher, a whale processor, a tester of shampoos on bunny rabbits. But when the turn comes around to introduce myself, I decide on a more modestly vicious career.

"I'm a management accountant for Price Waterhouse."

"*Phil!*" This is a fierce whisper from Diana, at my side, and a ripple of gentle bafflement spreads around the room. "I thought you said he was Phil Thingummy ... Could have sworn he was the one that used to be on TV ..." But Serena handles it deftly. "Of course, we all know Philip better as one half of First and Last. Welcome to prospective fatherhood, Phil."

"I'm a father already."

"Then we'll all be able to benefit from your experience," says Serena smoothly.

She is dressed in a purple leotard with a broad black sash. Long, black, glossy hair, a handsome hooked nose, and a brown bendy body that holds my attention a lot more closely than anything she says. For this is all to do with recapturing childbirth from the male hegemony of doctors, and throwing off the tyranny of drugs and anaesthesia, and learning to understand the rhythms of your body, and all that crap.

Diana is more and more into all this stuff: homeopathy and reflexology and aromatherapy and astrology and acupuncture and meditation and yoga and Rolfing and Alexander Technique and shamanism. And that's the most stupid thing about it – that you can be into *all* of them, at the same time.

"It's like Chesterton said," I tell her. "When people stop believing in God they don't start believing in nothing, they believe in *everything*."

"But you don't believe in God," says Diana, "and you don't believe in everything." So she's not stupid you see, or if she is stupid, it's in quite a clever sort of way.

"That's not the point."

"And you always used to say Chesterton was a reactionary old fart."

"Old *fuck*. And that's not the point either. The point is how can you go around believing in all these contradictory things? How can you believe one day that sticking needles in yourself makes you better and the next day that you have to swallow squashed buttercups in brandy?"

"Bach flower remedies."

"Whatever they're called. They're mutually exclusive systems."

"They're not. They're complementary."

"Only because all these profiteering quacks who peddle them are unwilling to push their theories to any logical or coherent conclusions. They won't even *test* them properly."

"It's because double-blind testing isn't appropriate," she says. "It's a hostile, technocratic approach which upsets the fragile, symbiotic environment in which alternative medicine can work."

"Well I call it moving the fucking goalposts," I tell her, "and the day I'll believe in it all is the day I see someone crawling out of a car crash with his leg hanging off and asking for a Bach flower remedy. There's no atheists in foxholes, and I bet there's not many homeopaths in labour wards when a baby's coming out back to front and sideways."

"Telephoning the Pope ..."

Funerals begin to accumulate in middle age. There was a time when I was eight or nine that my father seemed to be getting out his black coat every Saturday afternoon, and coming back after tea with red-cold ears and whisky breath. "Where've you been, Dad?" I used to ask. "Telephoning the Pope," he would say, and I imagined him in his black coat at a phone box on a windy heath somewhere, trying to get through to Rome. I never made the connection with the bottle of Vat 69 in the kitchen cupboard, and it was years later, mindlessly screwing the optic on to a bottle at The Jar that I laughed, finally understanding his small joke.

His own father died when I was seven, an enormous man with white, muscular breasts and a black soupstrainer moustache. Sepia-coloured uncles with sock-suspenders died as well, and beer mates of his from the Labour club, with gurgling, catarrhal laughs and receding gums. They died of strokes and heart attacks and cancers and bronchitis and emphysema. Bred on beer, fags and chips they never lived long enough to develop sophisticated ailments, but their wives lived for ever. Spry, leathery old ladies who were still hopping over garden walls at eighty.

Women never went to funerals, since it was a South Wales tradition that burials were too terrible for womenfolk. They stayed at home preparing an enormous tea, it being another custom that the thing had not been done properly unless you were buried with ham. And I took that literally as well when I was small, imagining the wet pink ham with its crust of yellow crumbs and blanket of white fat and the paper ruff around its shank, being tucked tenderly into the coffin beside the corpse.

"Survival means five years"

The doctors should just pull out the plugs on my little boy and let him die. Is that what you want?"

And I just stood there and didn't say anything, because it was what I wanted. I didn't want my son to wake up from his sleep to face chemotherapy and radiotherapy, and pain and fear and humiliation. The bleeding gums and nailbeds and wigs and lies and then death in the end anyway, because all the figures for cancer are fiddled, and everyone knows that survival means five years, which is not a life for a little boy of seven. So yes, I did think the doctors should pull the plugs and let him die, but I didn't even have the courage to say it, much less do it, so I stood there and didn't say anything.

I just got on with the numbing routines of hospital life instead: sitting every other night beside Dewi's bed and watching spikes march steadily across the grey phosphor screens. The time passed terribly slowly, even with a book to read, even with the routines of drip changes and catheter emptying and blood-pressure checking. His skin was always cold and waxy, and in the blue electronic light the fine down on his cheek became a rime of frost. When nobody was around I used to comb his lank hair, and trim his fingernails, and push down his cuticles, and moisten his dry grey lips with glycerine. I didn't ask myself at the time why I did it, but I suppose I'd have said it made him look more alive.

When I could not sit beside him any longer I patrolled the empty corridors and waiting rooms and concourses. I got to know the withered old volunteer ladies on the tea stall, and the night cleaners. I began to grasp the hierarchies of staff and sister; houseman, registrar and consultant. I fell asleep on sticky plastic banquettes and grew flatulent on canteen food and dispenser drinks. An oily film descended between me and the world and I would wash my face in empty lavatories, four or five times a night, scrubbing at the film with hard water and stinging hospital soap.

On the Sick

Martyn Harris with his son Joe photographed at home on 21 May 1996 by his wife Caroline.

"As the gossamer stuff of ambition and money and possessions fades away, as it always does in times of crisis, I have seen more clearly how the real structure of my life is my wife and children, family and friends."

Something understood
The Daily Telegraph, 25 May 1996

This is not the time to die

The scene is by Woody Allen – from *Annie Hall*, I think. The professional hypochondriac is sitting in the doctor's surgery, hands and knees knotted, waiting for the results of "the Tests". The doctor enters, snaps his X-ray photographs on to his light box, fiddles with his spectacles, shuffles some paper and says. "Well, these are preliminary results, of course, but I am very sorry to have to tell you ..."

And then you wake up. Or at least Woody Allen wakes up and the doctor is saying, "Well, these are preliminary results, of course, but I'm pleased to be able to tell you everything appears absolutely normal ..."

I keep waiting for this to happen. For myself to wake up in damp and knotted sheets with a shudder of relief and a "God, that was *so* real ..." But somehow I am still sitting in the doctor's surgery in Harley Street, and he is tapping more nails into the rapidly rising architecture of my terror. Through the buzzing in my ears I can hear disconnected phrases: "I have made an appointment for you this evening to see a cytologist ... Very good chap who works at Barts ... He will probably send you off for a CAT scan and some more blood tests ..."

"So I *have* got cancer?"

"Well, as I said, the results are only preliminary, but it does seem to be a tumour ..." And I start crying, which curiously enough is the last time I do cry in the next six months, even though some pretty horrible things are to happen to me. And the doctor says awkwardly, "There, there," and, "I know, I know," and, "It's never easy. It's never easy ..."

I am the last person who should have got cancer – not because I am 42 and reasonably healthy, and a fine chap all round, though these are all good reasons, but because I have imagined myself getting cancer at least once every day of my life. I am a compulsive brooder over minor spots and lumps, and an obsessive consulter of medical dictionaries. It is people like that who are supposed never to get cancer, but to drop dead of unheralded heart attacks at the age of 89.

I am also indecently terrified of death – a fear which has sat gibbering on my shoulder like a mad monkey since I was seven or eight years old. I can remember now the first realisation that one day I simply would not "be" any more. That I would have no more consciousness. That the world would go on without me while I was just a void, a nothing, and that there was nothing I or my supposedly omnipotent parents could do to avert that conclusion. Everyone died, so I would die, and the only comfort was the tissue-thin promise of an after-life held out by my family's Methodism, which I was already beginning to doubt. I sobbed for hours until even my kind and patient mother got fed up with it: "Well, yes, you will die one day, and there's nothing anyone can do."

So that was that. The only way to deal with the intolerable truth was to shut it out, to force the mind into other channels as soon as the black dog came scratching at the door, to induce a kind of white noise in the mind which would obliterate the pathway down into spiralling panic.

Every now and again, of course, the mind control would fail, and the fear would come flooding back, sometimes for months at a time. Looking back at my life, this seems to have happened at roughly ten-year intervals, and to have coincided with emotional upheavals: the onset of puberty; leaving home to go to university; the break-up of my first marriage in my early thirties. This is not a universal pattern, though, as I discovered when I occasionally mentioned the subject to friends, who were either politely baffled or cheerily dismissive. "Why worry about something you won't know anything about?" was the typical response. This has sometimes seemed the wisest thing anyone can say about death, and sometimes no more than an idiot tautology. It is precisely the fact that I won't know anything about it which I find so scary.

Martin Amis, whose latest novel, *The Information*, is largely about middle-aged mortality panics, told me that he had never felt the same searchlight illumination as a child: "At six I had some inkling, and at ten I could entertain the idea that it would happen to me, but there is this strong mechanism which exceptionalises you – it will never happen to me – I'll be the one who gets away. And that's how it is until you are about forty, when suddenly it is a full-time job looking the other way."

Amis also told me that he thought he was getting over the fear now, turning up the white noise, as everyone does, and I said, but what about Philip Larkin, his father's best friend, who just seemed to have got stuck in that state of terror all his life? There are Larkin poems such as *Aubade* and *Next, Please* which I find so frightening that I have been unable to read them for years at a time, however much I admire them.

"Oh, but he got that in his twenties. And my father, I think. They were both gibbering in the face of death as undergraduates. At least I got the full forty-year holiday before that came. But I think the Larkin condition is not so uncommon, particularly among writerly types." My own journalism and my two out-of-print novels would never earn me the title of "artist" but I know that even minor literary efforts demand a drive and a vanity which are simply not available to most people, and which probably do have their roots in a heightened, even neurotic fear of extinction.

The surprising thing about being told I had cancer was that I did not succumb to all these terrors. During the weeks of ominous symptoms and endless tests which led up to my diagnosis, I was terrified, twitchy, tearful, garrulous – swinging between optimism and despair and driving my wife demented with discussion of every possible symptom. "I think I'm just going to *explode*," I told her one night, and I really believed it, but when I finally knew the truth I became calm.

I had a form of cancer called lymphoma which was fatal if untreated, but for which there was a good chance of complete cure. In my own case, it was better than 80 per cent, which was frightening enough (who would ever cross the road if there was a 20 per cent chance of never coming back?) but it was not paralysingly frightening. The exceptionalising mechanism came into play, and rapidly I was thinking in terms not of extinction, but of getting to the other end of the treatment, as through a particularly gruelling set of exams. It would be six to eight "pulses" of chemotherapy, one every three weeks, with each "pulse" consisting of four big injections of cytotoxic drugs. There would be a few days of tiredness and nausea after each pulse, but the anti-sickness drugs were very good nowadays, and there was no reason I should not continue with light work. It would be five hard months, but once more I would be the one that got away, who fluked his way through maths and brilliantly bluffed the final history question.

One decision I made early on was to ignore all the "positive attitude" merchants who suddenly started targeting me by letter and telephone. "You must think positive," they told me, as if it was some great secret only they were privy to – as if without their important insight I would be smearing myself with ashes and rolling in the dunghill. For most of them, I suspected, it was just a convenient way to wash their hands of you and your problems. Have a "positive attitude" and you can defeat anything. Drop dead, and it's obviously your own fault for not being positive enough.

For similar reasons I decided to have nothing to do with alternative medicine. As soon as word got out, I started getting letters on gritty recycled paper from old friends in Glastonbury who wanted to introduce me to healers and homeopaths and herbalists, and I turned them all down. There is not a scrap of evidence for alternative or complementary medicine doing any good at all apart from cheering you up, and I had my own ways of doing that. I also resent the implication which lies beneath complementary approaches that a disease is always your own fault. You ate the wrong food, lived the wrong lifestyle or thought the wrong kind of thoughts. Lymphoma, as it happens, does not appear to have any links to smoking, drinking, diet, or environment, but whatever the disease it seems wrong for a "healer" who can't prove his own healing techniques to hand over responsibility for the cure he is peddling to the sufferer himself. Contrariwise, I also resolved that if big medicine did not do the trick and my tumours did not disperse, then I would try anything going, up to and including Bach flower remedies, Rolfing, a deathbed conversion to Roman Catholicism and cryogenic preservation in a Californian deep freeze.

Two weeks after the first chemotherapy all my hair fell out, which was the first real test of friends and relations. Up until then, the cancer had just been a horrible new fact, but now I was visibly the cancer victim, with his stigmata of raw pink scalp, albino eyelashes and ruthlessly plucked pubic hair. I made a point of telling people on the phone to prepare themselves before they came to see me, but most of them – men in particular – did not handle it well. They avoided looking at me; made jokes about Duncan Goodhew; said it would soon grow back. Women on the other hand seemed to make an effort to imagine themselves into my position before meeting me, and I seldom saw shock on their faces.

One of the luxuries of having cancer – and there aren't many – is the increased ruthlessness it allows you in dealing with people. If a bore or a sponger invites himself around to see you, you say no.

If an invitation to a dull dinner party arrives, you turn it down. Conversely, if you need to see a real friend, then you ask for their company or invite yourself to their house, because there is no room for shyness anymore. The sharpness of vision a fatal disease brings to your life casts other people in clear, sometimes cruel focus. Why have you bothered to all these years with the old friend who seems to have nothing to say to you now about your disease, who is unable to remember the name of it, or what treatment you are having? Why, on the other hand, have you not valued properly the brother-in-law who now writes to you twice a week for six months – with funny, newsy, perfectly pitched letters which give you a lift every time you open one? I had always rather despised the middle-class habit of constantly sending notes and cards, but the many dozens I have received have been a comfort, and it is one of my many good resolutions, post-cancer, to become a better correspondent myself. (I have also promised myself to move out of London, change my job, stop being cruel to people in articles, eat better, exercise more, spend more time with my youngest son and to become a regular churchgoer.)

In the meantime, however, I was beginning to wonder if there would be a "post-cancer" and if the exemption mechanism was still operating. I had two tumours – one in my neck which had disappeared rapidly and another in my abdomen, which after three "pulses" had failed to respond at all. The doctor decided to shift me to a more intense regime of chemotherapy and everything suddenly became very nasty indeed. Up until then, the effects of the treatment had been similar to a combination of flu and a bad hangover: nausea, headache, tiredness, aches and pains – mostly over in four or five days. The new treatment three times heavier than the old, took five days in hospital just to administer, and knocked me senseless for weeks on end. I had, in addition, to be fitted with a permanent intravenous line in my chest, which promptly became infected and spread septicaemia into my blood, where there were virtually no white cells to fight it. I was on intravenous antibiotics for a week; I didn't eat for three weeks; I was running a temperature of 104 for a lot of the time, and delirious for the first time since childhood. Somehow or other, in a mood of gruesome objectivity, I managed to compile a list of my symptoms at this point which reads as follows: "Blinding lumbar headache; continuous nausea; shortness of breath; very weak and tired; cannot lift arm from bed; strange taste to all foods; persistent unpleasant smell from own body; no appetite; skin going very soft and papery; spots all over back; diarrhoea; thickness in ears; numbness and tingling in fingertips; watery eyes causing blurred vision. Could be worse?"

Racked out on my hospital bed, unable to talk or read or even listen to the radio, I contemplated the eight more treatments which lay ahead of me, and began seriously to plan how to kill myself. A hosepipe from the exhaust put in through the car window was the traditional coward's way out, but mightn't that invalidate all my insurance? A high-speed crash into a bridge-support on a quiet motorway was braver, but it might not work, and I'd end up as a quadraplegic cancer patient with third-degree burns all over his body. One night when I was in hospital on a heroin drip, I asked the doctor (casually I thought) if it would kill me to press the plunger all the way. "Nah. Too dilute," he told me kindly. "We think of everything."

And then something happened, though I find it hard to explain, committed rationalist as I am. The best I can do is to say that up until this point there had been something rather passive in my attitude to the disease. I had never gone so far as to entertain the idea that I deserved cancer, but I had been saying things to myself such as, "Well, you've had a pretty good life. You have fulfilled your ambitions in journalism. You have written a couple of fairly decent novels. You have fathered three lovely children. You may have mucked up your first marriage, but you have been wonderfully happy in your second. There are more things you would like to do, of course – to see your children grow up and so on – but after the age of 40 life is mostly repetition. There are lots of people who have had a lot worse luck …"

Somewhere in the fever and delirium of this long stay in hospital I found this attitude had evaporated. I couldn't contemplate suicide any longer. I badly wanted to live. I was very angry that I had cancer. It wasn't a conscious, rational decision, or even an emotional conversion – more as if the cells in my body had undergone some mysterious shift at a fundamental, bio-chemical level, and arranged themselves for a fight. And almost at once I began to get better. The infection cleared up; I had a CAT scan; and then a biopsy and then a laparotomy which finally confirmed – to a set of incredulous doctors – that the lump in my abdomen was not malignant at all. Miraculously, I had a complete remission, and only three more of the "mild" treatments before I was free of chemotherapy – which is approximately where I find myself as I write this.

I don't like the implication of the above, because, as I said before, the whole idea of "positive attitude" seems deeply suspect to me, and yet here I am describing some kind of attitude shift in myself, and attributing to it a semi-magical outcome. I got angry and I began to get better – or am I simply finding a writerly metaphor for healing processes in my body which were as ultimately explicable as the onset of the disease itself? All I really know is that I have discovered I *need* to think about the disease in this way, as something I have the power to make choices about.

In a way, it is parallel to the choice not to commit suicide, or the more modest decisions most of us make every day to be good rather than bad people. In the long run they make no difference. In a universe without a God or even an after-life, which is what most of us are reluctantly obliged to accept, the only imperative to behave well is the knowledge that it is more dignified than to behave badly. It is better to resist entropy than not. It is better to live than not to live, and in deciding to live we make ethical creatures of ourselves. It is just about the only tiny moral truth that the 20th century has been able to extract from the wasteland left by scientific materialism. At bottom, whether I now live a long or a short life is outside my control, but I know clearly now that I want to live, which is all that really matters.

The Spectator, 19 August 1995

Something understood

E ight months ago I wrote an article about having cancer, which ended on quite an optimistic note. After a long course of chemotherapy I seemed to be getting better and I had found out things about myself which I felt gave me some new reasons for living. Since then I have had two relapses, two courses of radiotherapy, and two stem cell transplants. The words I wrote last September seem rather smug in retrospect, but in certain ways I feel calmer and more optimistic than I did then.

I was, as I wrote then, the last person who should have got cancer – not just because I was only 42, with three children, and reasonably healthy, and a fine chap all round – but because I had imagined myself getting cancer at least once every day of my life. I was a compulsive brooder over minor spots and lumps, and also indecently terrified of death. Since the age of seven or so I had found the idea of ceasing-to-be quite paralysing – so much so that my only way of dealing with it had become to induce a kind of mental white noise, to blot out the pathway down into spiralling panic which opened at the prospect of my own non-existence. There were certain poems about death, such as Philip Larkin's *Aubade* and *Next, Please*, which I found so true and so frightening that for years I could not even read them, however much I admired them. Larkin's bleak vision of "the total emptiness for ever/The sure extinction that we travel to/And shall be lost in always" seemed as unanswerable as it was intolerable.

Perhaps it is paradoxical, then, that one of the things I kept asking myself when I was very ill in hospital last summer was "Why not kill yourself?" My treatment did not seem to be working. I had no hair, my skin was tissue thin, I had continuous nausea, diarrhoea, blinding headaches, blurred vision – so in some ways it would have been a physical relief. There was also the illogical idea that I could cheat the hangman, evade the furnace glare of the fear of death by pre-empting the whole process, with an overdose of pills or by gassing myself in the car. That would teach Death to scare me.

The best reason I could come up with for not killing myself was that it was always better to keep on keeping on, even when life was pointless. The decision to live is, in a way, parallel to the decision most of us make every day to try to be good rather than bad people. In a universe without God or an after-life, which is what I felt reluctantly obliged to accept, the only imperative to behave well is the knowledge that it is more dignified than to behave badly. It is better to resist entropy than not. It is better to live than not to live, and in deciding to live we make ethical creatures of ourselves. It is just about the only tiny nugget of moral truth that the 20th century has been able to extract from the wasteland left by scientific materialism.

As I say, that was where I stood eight months ago. A philosopher would call it the "existential" position, and I still think it is good solid ground for a moral atheist. But my own ground, I find, has shifted beneath my feet. The most important influence is the great kindness which other people have shown me while I have been ill. I have always had a kind of stupid optimism about people and the world, which no amount of misery and suffering seems to dent, and being seriously ill has only helped to reinforce it. As the gossamer stuff of ambition and money and possessions fades away, as it always does in times of crisis, I have seen more clearly how the real structure of my life is my wife and children, family and friends: their love for me and mine for them. People I hardly knew have been immensely kind, beyond any call of social duty, with visits and gifts and phone calls. Complete strangers have sent letters which went so immediately to my heart that they made me cry. And the crying did not come from pain but from the poignancy of the way people can speak so directly to each other when they try. The feeling that there really is a kind of co-inherence to humanity.

In spite of my sturdy existentialist stance there were still too many times when I became intensely frightened and depressed – by the prospect of dying, or by yet another round of hospital treatment. The only thing I found that really helped me then was to try to get outside myself: to write a letter to a friend; to ring up someone else who was sick; or just to make myself play with my children. The little devil of scepticism which lives on every journalist's shoulder might sneer and say it was mere self-interest – I was just taking my mind off myself to cheer myself up – but the devil could not deny the fact that here was a benevolent magic which really worked. Writing my original article about cancer was the same kind of experience, and I was repaid a hundred times.

I begin to sound a bit soggy and platitudinous now, I know, like an earnest young curate on Radio 4. All ye must do is love one another! People drum their fingers impatiently at this kind of stuff, and wish they would get on with the traffic updates and weather forecasts. I was brought up in the Methodist Church but stopped going when I was 14 or so, and refused to be confirmed. As an arrogant, would-be intellectual adolescent, I wanted to hear arguments about things that mattered such as the existence of God, the truth of the Resurrection and the problem of evil. I liked the pretty Welsh village chapel, founded by my ancestors, whose names were commemorated on tablets around the walls. I was fond of the plain services with their pattern of two readings, six hymns, a sermon and home for lunch. But there wasn't much intellectual meat to be had in chapel; the ministers never seemed to deal with the basics of belief, instead making laboured attempts to draw up-to-date parallels with the Gospel stories. It was as if science and the modern world had terrorised religion out of tackling its own central mysteries.

I couldn't help noticing either that most of the congregation seemed to consist of old widowed ladies, and that such young people as there were always seemed to be the least attractive and most badly dressed types that one avoided at school. I concluded, with the cruel certainty of youth, that religion was for old people frightened of dying, and for young people who couldn't pull.

I was never quite an atheist though. The triumphalism of science (any minute now and we'll show you the face of God) seemed quite as silly to me as the foam-flecked enthusiasm of fundamentalist religion. I was set on a literary career and it seemed impossible to imagine a literature which thrived within the closed systems implied by a science that promised Ultimate Answers to Everything. Literature – or any other art for that matter – seems to insist on open-ended multiplicity: "a universe based upon metaphor rather than measure" as Norman Mailer put it.

There were also, as I was growing up, certain areas of experience that I was very reluctant to hand over to mechanistic explanation. There was the intense pleasure of the landscape of the Gower coast for instance. There was the similar shiver of pleasure or shock of recognition I sometimes felt when I encountered a really good work of art. It might not be religion or even evidence of a God, as Wordsworth tried to argue, but it seemed in some way parallel to religious experience. The frisson you get from a fine line of poetry comes chiefly, I think, from the sheer pleasure that someone has recorded something you thought only you had felt before. More than that, it comes from the realisation that many others have shared and will share this moment you had thought was unique and inexpressible. The loneliness of the individual life is dissolved briefly in the flicker of that same sensation, of co-inherence.

The core of Christianity as I'd always understood it was love. Not just love your neighbour, but love your enemy. Turn your other cheek. Suffer the insult not seven times but 70 times seven. As an impatient and short-tempered person I'd been bad at practising it but at least I could see that it was a tremendously potent political insight.

From a hamlet in Palestine it conquered the Roman Empire in three centuries and without a battle. In our own age, in the form of peaceful resistance, it has displaced the British from India; won the fight for civil rights in the southern USA; overturned apartheid in South Africa; even brought down Communism. For although you could argue that it was economic forces and political manoeuvre and even sporadic violence which helped defeat those regimes, it was ultimately those great pacific crowds of common people, from Delhi to Mississippi to Warsaw to Berlin, that were decisive.

One of the most privileged adventures of my life as a journalist was to be sent to spend a few months in Soviet Russia as it was falling apart, and to be one of the first reporters to travel freely across it, without official guide or approved schedule. Brought up on the black prophecies of George Orwell and Arthur Koestler, I expected to meet a semi-brain-washed population, mouthing Marxist dogma, ignorant and suspicious of the West. As it turned out I found people barely different from those I had left in England; in many cases better educated and informed and, spiritually, virtually unscathed by 75 years of indoctrination.

Among the young Russians Christianity was all the rage. This was partly a fad, like Levi jeans, but it was also a deliberate gesture of dissociation from the most serious attempt ever to build a materialist kingdom of heaven on earth. Some time in the 1930s a commissar warned Stalin of the depth of religious resistance to his "reforms". His response, possibly apocryphal, has gone down in the history of the 20th century as a kind of motto for the crushing of spiritual values by technology, materialism, military might. "How many divisions does the Pope have?" Stalin asked contemptuously. The answer, it suddenly seemed to me, as I wandered in the ruins of Stalin's empire was, "All of them."

So it was strong stuff, this love, but what did "love" mean exactly? Obviously things like compassion and tolerance, but there was some central kernel of meaning more important than these things, which I could sense, but only express approximately with phrases such as "self-surrender". I had to reach for parallels from ordinary life to explain it to myself. I knew, for instance, that when I had been in difficulty in my life the answer often lay in handing myself over to the logic of events, or to the truth of my feelings. I knew from one failed marriage and one successful one that love between people did not work properly without self-surrender to the other. Hold yourself back, preserve your pride, hang on to your habits or dignity or shame, and you will never really love.

On a more banal level I had similar intuitions about my work. Every journalist knows the moment when you walk into a strange pub or violent demonstration, or whatever, and embarrassment or fear paralyses you. Invariably the way forward is to do the bold and honest thing – introduce yourself to the biggest thug; declare who you are; ask the dumbest question, and a mysterious momentum often begins to unfold in your favour. I don't often have the courage to do it, but I have complete faith in it as a form of magic. And writing itself seems to obey similar laws, as a sustained act of self-exposure – and I do not mean the narcissism of "me journalism", or "emotional features" like the one you are reading. All decent writing, from reportage to poetry, is about a struggle to strip away clichéd expressions, hackneyed ideas, and general obfuscation; about taking off your character armour and exposing your thoughts and feelings to the scalpel of language.

What these different examples seem to have in common is a kind of confession of inadequacy; an admission that I am not entire and self-sufficient, and that I must throw myself open again and again throughout my life to other people, to my ignorance and weakness. And beneath that again, and deeper still, there seems to lie a recognition of connectedness and mutuality. I cannot function properly in society as an atom of pride and self interest: I cannot survive in the universe as a chunk of matter randomly generated by impersonal physical laws. I have to hand myself over to the idea that I am reciprocally connected to other people and to the universe in ways I cannot understand but have humbly to accept. And that, in far too many words, is what I think I mean by love.

I have been talking so far as if all this pondering took place in a vacuum, but in fact I was reading a good deal at the same time: Pascal, C.S. Lewis, Richard Holloway, Gerard Hughes, Alan Jones – but especially the New Testament. Although I went to Sunday School until I was about 14, I am ashamed to say I had never read a single Gospel all the way through, though they are such slender things which you can get through in an hour or two.

Still more grotesquely, I found I was embarrassed to be seen reading them, and would shuffle the Bible under some other book if anyone came into the room. Christians, after all, were people who knew nothing about Bob Dylan or Jarvis Cocker, who had fish signs on the back of their cars, and terrible taste in shoes. What would my friends think? Poor old Martyn; the cancer has made him go over to the God Squad. I was terrified that I might be running to religion out of fear, but there was a quote from Martin Luther which helped: "God uses lust to impel men to marry, ambition to office, avarice to earning and fear to faith. God led me like an old blind goat."

And in any case, I found I enjoyed the Gospels: the poetic compression of language; the suggestive and paradoxical thought patterns of the teaching; above all the force and authority of Jesus's personality which comes scorching through all the small faults of repetition and translation and human recollection. No fair-minded person could read these stories without acknowledging that here at the very least was a phenomenon in history, whose mere acquaintance drove ordinary men to sacrifice their homes and families and ultimately their lives to spread the story across the known world in a single generation. These were not the vaguely remembered children's stories of gentle Jesus meek 'n' mild but an account of spiritual transformation and revolution.

And once again at the centre of it all was this love, repeated over and over. "Those who love me will be loved by my Father and I will love them and reveal myself to them"; "Those who love me will keep my word, and my Father will love them"; "Love one another as I have loved you". The repetitiveness might quickly become a meaningless chiming were it not for the way in which the life and the story pick up and exemplify the theme of self-surrender. The disciples are asked to give up everything to follow Jesus; the rich man is invited to abandon his wealth and the Pharisees their self-righteousness and rigidity. The common people, driven by toil and care, are told to live as the lilies of the field and even Mary must set aside her motherly love for her son. In the end Jesus has to give up his own life to cast himself upon the ocean of the unknown.

In the crucifixion, the mystery of the transaction becomes overwhelming. God is telling man that only in the self-loss of love and faith can he find redemption, and Jesus enacts the sacrifice – but it is not play-acting. Jesus is God, but he is also a man, and he really does not know the outcome of the drama. God asks men to trust him and deliver themselves to him, but in token of his earnestness he binds his own hands and delivers himself up to man. Any single summary is too crude but here was a story, it seemed to me, which was saying that the creation is not ultimately accessible to or controllable by human reason, that it is the root cause of our human misery to demand that it must be, and that God was willing

Considered# On the Sick

to die to show us the way out.

Considered merely as literature – and that was just how I read it first – the New Testament was extraordinary. Add to that the powerful congruence between the shape of the story and my growing intuition about the necessity of self-surrender and it promised to become much more than literature or myth. I could go on for quite a long time from here: about my surprise at the intellectual coherence of Christianity; at the feebleness of much of the materialist position which I had assumed to be so impregnable. But one of the things I have learned while writing this article, which has taken me longer and cost me more drafts than almost anything else I have written, is that ultimately you cannot simply argue yourself or anyone else into a faith. There is a quote from Cardinal Newman: "It is as absurd to argue men into faith as to torture them," and another from Dean Inge, "Faith begins as an experience and ends as an experience." I have had to spike about 6,000 words of really quite impressive argument to find myself giving reluctant assent.

Faith is crucially and essentially nonsensical. It is confirmed, if at all, by the most elusive kind of personal experience of order and comfort and belonging for which the frissons provided by art or nature or human love are only clumsy metaphors. I believe the experience is there for anyone if you are desperate enough, as I have been, or open enough, or perhaps simple enough, but even the best poets have been able only to sketch around the edges of it. T.S. Eliot in *Four Quartets* talks of "the unattended/Moment, the moment in and out of time". George Herbert writes of "Church bels heard beyond the starres, the soul's bloude/The land of spices. Something understood".

The sense of a reality outside and beyond time, unifying and making sense of experience, is a matter of "hints and guesses", sometimes there, more often not. Sometimes I have been filled with well-being and serenity. Sometimes I am convinced it is nothing but self-delusion brought on by a terror of my own mortality; that the whole of religion is just what Philip Larkin suggested: a "vast moth-eaten musical brocade/Created to pretend we never die." The pendulum still swings between the extremes, but I think the swings are becoming shorter. I can read Larkin's *Aubade* now, without that sick terror of total identification I once felt. I look more steadily at my own death without the spiralling panic it once evoked. My wife even says I am not quite as bad tempered as I used to be.

On the Sick

Nobody really knows what is "out there" beyond our death, beyond the stars, not Stephen Hawking or Richard Dawkins or Philip Larkin or the Rev Billy Graham. All the ways we have of approaching our existence, from science to religion, are ultimately no more than models or paradigms, and you have the power to choose your own paradigm. Larkin was a brave man in his way, but he chose a model which left him drunk, suicidal, self-obsessed and paralysed by misery. The scientific atheist who, like Richard Dawkins, sees life as the chance outcome of a cosmic singularity chooses a model which leaves him in an attitude of existential bravado, shouting his discoveries at the edge of a cooling and indifferent universe. As I sit here in my room, looking at my fingers on the keyboard, smelling the Wisteria flowering outside, listening to the sounds of my family in the house below, I think I know which model I choose. Put the gun to your head Harris, and say it: Yes. I think so. I don't know. No. I hope so. Yes.

The Daily Telegraph, 25 May 1996

Introducing ...
Chief Whitecoat

"What do you think of white coats?" my consultant demands as I totter in for my post-holiday assessment. He is of the old school – wry and spry, with bow tie, pocket watch and backswept wings of grey hair. Senior registrars leap to his command and brilliant students lose all power of speech. He takes his dog on rounds and sends us patients to the pub between doses of chemotherapy. The man is a god.

In a democratic age, captains of industry must attend brainstorming sessions with their salesmen; army officers must "toss ideas about" with their sergeants, but the consultant is still an outpost of autocracy. In his power to spend money, take mad decisions and terrorise his underlings, he has no secular rival save perhaps the newspaper editor – which is perhaps why I feel so at home.

307

Like all the grandest doctors at this London teaching hospital, my consultant goes to work in a three-piece suit, but today is wearing a white coat, so I must be cautious. "I think they can be, um, reassuring ..." His face darkens. "But also intimidating ..."

"The *patients* have voted that the doctors should wear more casual clothes. Which is why I am wearing a white coat for the first time in 20 years." It is the same one he discarded 20 years ago to judge by the strain on the buttons. Actually, I do find it more reassuring than the trainers and T-shirts of the housemen, and in any case my consultant needs a name if he is to feature regularly in this narrative without suing me, and so, by his own hand, he becomes Chief Whitecoat.

His Canadian registrar, by association, is christened Tonto, and the sister who is always so ready with a joke and a urine bottle, she shall be Laughing Water. After 18 months with cancer, you develop an argot for communicating with other patients and comparing the rival hospitals. The Cromwell in west London, for instance, does excellent egg-and-cress sandwiches and offers VIP suites of magnificent sleaziness. But its foyer resembles an airport hotel and there are always Arab men sitting cross-legged on the banquettes, picking their toenails.

The London Clinic on Marylebone Road has a faded Thirties' grandeur, panelled lifts and a whiff of history: the Queen comes here, and so did Harold Macmillan for his post-Profumo prostate. The Whittington in Highgate is a Kafkaesque nightmare of cockroaches, cancelled appointments and lost X-rays, but the views from the wards are good. The local pubs are also excellent for those special Hamlet moments that you want to spend with yourself and six gin and tonics after the doctor tells you that you have had another relapse.

On the whole though, I would still recommend NHS if you want to be seriously ill. You see a lot more of your consultant in a private hospital, but it is always possible to wake up in the middle of the night with a major haemorrhage and find there is nobody on duty but a junior house officer of 55 with shaky hands who speaks only Greek. The NHS is slower but has a democratic chirpiness and coverage in depth, which means there is always a surgeon on duty, even if he does lose your X-rays afterwards.

Two years ago, I was interviewing Marti Caine about her cancer which, she told me, was the best kind to get. It was curable and relatively painless. The only major symptoms were lumps in the lymph glands caused by uncontrolled growth of white blood cells known as lymphocytes. She had had three courses of chemotherapy, but had been clear for a year: if you could stay clear for two years, you were generally reckoned to be cured. The disease was called lymphoma, she said, the fifth commonest cancer around. I said I had never heard of it. Six months later I had it; six months after that, Marti Caine was dead.

I decided then that it was a bad idea to identify yourself too strongly with a particular cancer patient, though I did the same thing with little Jaymee Bowen who was treated at the London Clinic with me. Remember the statistics, not the individuals. I have had two big courses of chemotherapy, and am about to begin a third, with a bone marrow transplant from my sister. It is rather like entering a tunnel where you know your senses will be dulled, your terrors exaggerated, your brain slowed.

I want to try and write about it as it happens, to make myself feel better, perhaps some others, too; but if you are ill or frightened of illness, do not believe in "me" too much. Remember Evelyn Waugh's epigraph to *Brideshead Revisited*, which applies with equal force to Chief Whitecoat, Laughing Water and the Greek doctor with the trembling hands: "I am not I: thou art not he or she: they are not they."

The Daily Telegraph, 30 August 1996

Why my hair's falling out for the third time

Chief Whitecoat, the consultant, has gone to Renfrewshire to knock a little white ball about and Laughing Water is "on a course" together with half the rest of the nursing staff. Some tic in the hospital budget dictates no nurses can be hired over the Bank Holiday, so the whole cancer ward has been evacuated downstairs complete with drip stands and catheters.

The kettle in the new kitchen doesn't work because someone

has pinched the flex to use in the cell separator unit. The wheels have disappeared from my bedside table, along with all the saucers from the tea trolley. Most patients are sent home and the hospital assumes an abandoned air in the dog day afternoons: empty white wards with blowing curtains; the only sound the squeak of trolleys and the cry of seagulls in the square outside.

Tonto and the surviving nurses are kind and cheerful. Blitz spirit rules, but it took about two days to get us all down there and another two to get back. This has cost more money in staff hours and postponed treatment time than could conceivably have been spent on hiring a few agency nurses in the first place. Everyone understands this apart from the bean counters in management who, in some future full-colour report, will describe the process as "cutting out waste in the NHS".

The lumps on my head and neck are smaller, which means the chemotherapy still works, thank God. My "tumour burden" (horrible Whitecoat phrase) must be half the original size before they will consider a bone marrow transplant. The trouble is the more times you have chemo the more "refractory" the cancer cells become. I have had three courses of chemo, three of radiotherapy, and five operations. The patient may be getting refractory but at least my cancer cells are still well behaved.

I get so used to this gruesome stuff I forget how little I knew about cancer two years ago and how little most of the people near me still understand. A bright journalist said to me the other day: "Sorry, but how does chemotherapy differ from radiotherapy?"

Basically it is just drugs which stop cells dividing. Some are drugs with other primary uses, such as antibiotics and steroids. Some are descended from poison gas used in the First World War. Cancer cells generally divide faster than other cells so the theory of chemo is to cripple as many tumour cells as possible with each dose without knocking out too many normal ones. You do destroy normal cells of course, especially other fast dividing cells in the skin, gut and blood. This leads to the most notorious side effects: baldness and nausea – though both are temporary and there are good anti-sickness drugs (though none as good as marijuana).

You won't meet a Whitecoat who is enthusiastic about chemo. It is too mad and crude, like using a machine gun to switch off the kitchen gas, but it can work. For systemic cancers such as my lymphoma it's also pretty much all they have. With all the progress in genetically engineered antigens there will probably be a pill in 20 years' time which will get rid of lymphoma as septrin gets rid of spots. It's a nuisance that all I can do now is soak up First World War poison and watch my hair fall out for the third time, but when the magic bullet arrives I would like to be around to take it.

After six nights I am out, and off to the old mill in Yarmouth on the Isle of Wight, much to the disapproval of Laughing Water. "You're neutropenic, Mr Harris," she tells me, which means I have no white blood cells and no resistance to infection. You can catch runaway septicaemia from your own skin bugs, and the only thing which will pull you around are massive intravenous antibiotics within 12 hours.

Just as well Laughing Water can't see the old mill which is a place of truly imperial squalor, with about 30 bedrooms, several occupied by pigeons and others by young descendants of A.J.P. Taylor, the historian, whose summer place it was. There are leaky boats and a snooker table covered in sand dunes and, I would swear, the same piece of bacon bait on the hall floor as three years ago. Yet from the bedroom window is one of the most beautiful views I know, across the herons and mirrored water and piling clouds of the Yarmouth estuary. The children fish for crabs all day; the grown-ups walk and drink gin and cook dinner and watch the sun set.

We have not been totally daft. We could tear back to London in three hours, but in any case a different kind of calculation takes over when you have a potentially fatal illness. I want to be around in 20 years, but I have also got used to the idea I may not be around next week, which means learning to live one day at a time – that most profound of clichés. Every moment is here in this moment.

One more sunset across the estuary really might be worth as much as the next 20 years – or at least that is the illusion I have almost come to believe.

The Daily Telegraph, 6 September 1996

Lie back and think of ... peace and quiet

As a bookish teenager I used to imagine it might be rather nice to be sent to jail or hospital for several months with a picturesque, but not painful disease such as consumption. Just think of the reading you could get done without all those irritating interruptions from parents and teachers. I might even be able to get down to writing that grandiose epic poem or magnificent novel sequence over which I constantly brooded but of which there existed not a single concrete idea, nor one completed line.

The fantasy was destroyed by my first stay in Chelmsford hospital for a mastoid operation in my twenties. The roaring TV set on the communal ward; the insane but cast-iron hospital schedule which turfed you out of bed at six, gave you lunch at 11am, dinner at 4pm and woke you in the middle of the night for a sleeping tablet, not to mention the constant harassment of tests and "obs" of functions fantastically remote from my ailment – "But nurse, I've got an ear infection. Why do you need a stool sample?" "Just fill the container *please* Mr Harris."

Writing, reading, or even consecutive thought were impossible and for the first time in my life I began to understand the consolations of *Emmerdale Farm* and the *Sun* crossword. Things are better nowadays (everyone may hire their own TV set) but hospital life is still all about discontinuity, boredom, being mucked about. Pulse, temperature, blood pressure; drugs round; Tonto's round; bed changing; room cleaning; lunch trolley ... It has taken me all morning to write this paragraph and Laughing Water has just popped her head around the door. "Now you mustn't work too hard Mr Harris. Hospital is for *relaxing*."

When the battling TV sets become intolerable I retire to the linen cupboard landing on the fire escape, which has a pleasant view over the roofs of Smithfield and Little Britain, and where I can smoke a cigar. One tiny consolation of being diagnosed with lymphatic cancer was being told there was no link to smoking.

I started pinching my parents' cigarettes at nine and kicked a 50-a-day habit only at university. Where did we find time to eat, drink and make love? Old family photos and cine films show people playing tennis, swimming and pulling sweaters over their heads with fags in their mouths. There is one of me brushing my teeth with a cigarette smouldering on the soap dish. People smoked *seriously* then. From 20 to 40 I was giving up smoking. It became mostly a habit for cigars that I didn't inhale (much) and which stopped for lengthy periods. When doctors asked if I smoked I could say "no" with only a slight twinge of guilt. Smoking on the linen cupboard landing is not official but the nurses don't mind because half of them smoke anyway. Sitting there the other day I started reading the labels on the shelves.

Sheets, towels, dressing gowns, shrouds, theatre gowns ... Did that say shrouds? It did and there they were, neatly stacked and laced at crown and foot: a garment I had used in metaphor 100 times but never seen. Shrouds. Funny how cigars have lost their savour these past few days.

Back to the TV then, and a programme on Sir John Crofton who pioneered the use of combination antibiotics against TB in the 1950s. Crofton's cure rates were so impressive and his techniques so simple and cheap that many colleagues accused him of fiddling. TB had been the biggest killer of people between 14 and 44 for 500 years. Remedies had ranged from purging with cod-liver oil to infusing sufferers with gold.

Even by 1950 the main treatment was based on "fresh air" regimes in immense sanatoria where patients lived lives of semi-isolation in unheated chalets and snow was allowed to drift across the counterpanes.

Crofton's advances were to save enough money to pay for *all* medical research in the NHS for the next 10 years.

The terrifying disease led to the growth of a whole folk mythology and cult of personal guilt about its causes. D.H. Lawrence blamed his consumption on his inability to stand up to his mother's smothering.

Much the same is true of cancer, which has a whole industry of counselling and alternative therapy battening upon it, suggesting that the causes lie in failure to control stress, or poor eating habits or buried guilt. I have wondered if I would have got it if my first marriage had survived, if I had devoted myself to writing novels instead of journalism.

I have decided it is corrosive nonsense, and that the clinching argument is this. If a cure for cancer emerged as suddenly as for TB then the whole culture of guilt and self-reproach and quack remedy would be gone as completely as the snow that once drifted across the beds in those long demolished sanatoria.

The Daily Telegraph, 13 September 1996

This marrow can also prolong active life

Two visitors have already asked me which bone is taken out of me to extract the marrow when my bone marrow transplant is done. I think it's the fault of that old dog food advert about prolonged active life, in which they used to shovel this yucky jelly out of a cow bone with a spoon. Real bone marrow doesn't look like that. It looks like thick blood and it is simply sucked out through a needle.

I say "simply" because it doesn't happen to me but to the donor, my poor sister, who is in the operating theatre as I write this, having needles pushed into her pelvis and a litre of marrow hoovered out. Quite apart from the risks of the general anaesthetic, you wake up feeling like you have been kicked in the backside by a brewer's dray and it can take weeks to get all your strength back. Thank you Judy Reynolds and donors everywhere.

The main point of a transplant is it allows the Whitecoats to give you a much higher dose of chemotherapy – so high in fact that it completely wipes out your own marrow, the factory for most blood cells. As one Whitecoat said to me: "Basically we *have* a cure for cancer. Chemotherapy will kill anything. It's just a matter of how high we can turn up the wick." The second point of a marrow transplant, once it has "rescued" the patient from the chemo, is hopefully to kick-start an immune reaction which will see off any residual cancer cells.

So all I have to do in about a week from now, when they have finished giving me the chemotherapy, is to lie back and have the marrow fed back into a vein. The stuff then finds its own way back through my body and engrafts itself in the bones. Isn't that amazing? No sawing bones up, no yucky jelly, no teaspoons and hopefully a lot of prolonged active life.

Watching the television news from my hospital bed the other night I was twitched from a mild chemo-coma by *that* phrase: "fixed NHS resources and continually expanding patient demand". The newscaster (the oleaginous Alastair Stewart) had welded the words together and delivered them in that maddeningly irrefutable air which is the hallmark of propaganda humbug. The idea that people have infinite demands on the health service and that the NHS is a mysteriously finite thing is a glib advertising slogan which appeared in Saatchi-land sometime in the Eighties. It is designed to give an air of common sense inevitability to an ideological claim. It is not true.

In two years of travels through the health system, I have yet to meet a patient with "infinite" or unreasonable expectations. There is nobody out there who thinks there is a right to immortality, a personal CAT scanner and a mercy flight to America for every tragic tumour tot in the tabloids. People just expect prompt appointments, beds for acute cases, clean wards, functioning equipment, doctors and nurses who are not exhausted, harassed and underpaid, and a general level of treatment comparable to the other well-off countries. Anyone who has spent time in an NHS hospital recently knows we are not getting all those things ...

Naturally, people have rising expectations of health and longer life. We have the same rising expectations in all sorts of areas: higher wages, nicer houses, safer cars, a continually expanding economy. It may be an illusion but it is the same illusion of the possibility of general betterment peddled by every government at every election since 1945.

Why should health be different? It is because the NHS is still the most popular and successful monument to post-war welfarism – it is also one of the cheapest and most effective, and it sticks in the craw of the free market fanatics.

Thanks to the magic of modern newspaper technology this column should continue to appear for the next fortnight or so even though its author may be out of radio contact, somewhere on the dark side of the moon. The only weight on my conscience is several hundred letters from readers, for which thank you and apologies for not always answering. I have had to adopt a kind of triage approach of sending postcards to my fellow sick, postponing the kindly well-wishers and questioners (the vast majority) and ignoring the insane of whom there are only a few. One of these told me it was my own fault I had lymphoma because of the six gin and tonics I drank after the doctor told me I had relapsed. Another asked who did I think I was, moaning about my illness in the paper and spouting my cracker barrel opinions, when other people just have to put up with things.

I don't have an answer to that except to say I know how much luckier I am than the old woman down my corridor with no friends or family to visit her, no platform to pontificate from and no thousands of strangers wishing her well. I have enough letters to worry about for now, so send one to the old lady down your own corridor and look out for radio contact to resume.

The Daily Telegraph, 20 September 1996

A slow dance to Buffalo Soldier

I received my sister's bone marrow transplant on my wedding anniversary, which seemed a good omen. I also got given a remote control CD player, so I can languidly switch records from my bedside. Tonto the faithful registrar was so taken with this that we played Bob Marley all through the procedure – he holding up the bag of liquid bone marrow as it dripped into my vein, and shimmying gently to *Buffalo Soldier*.

I now have to wait about three weeks for it to engraft in my own bones and then another three weeks or so to make sure I don't have any disastrous reaction. The odds on the process killing me through infection or rejection are roughly the same as curing me – about 25 per cent. The other 50 per cent of us, I suppose, end up back where we started, but I'm already massaging these statistics. The mortality figure is bound to include a lot of old and young and feeble, and I'm still in pretty good shape. Assuming I get through to the other end, we are talking 25 per cent of 75 per cent which is a one third chance of a cure. A good bet at any bookie, and so we beat on boats against the current.

Does anyone know, while we are on the subject, who wrote: "Absurd longevity, more, more it cries / More life, more wealth, more trash of every kind"?

Just outside the gates of St Bartholomew's Hospital, a few hundred feet from where I am lying, is the place where Sir William Wallace was disembowelled in 1305. There are fresh flowers there now, laid by the Scottish Nationalists, or more likely by fans of Mr Mel Gibson. It was on the same spot that the Peasants' Revolt was crushed in 1381. Wat Tyler was actually treated here in Bart's by the monks. Many of the Marian Martyrs were burned in Smithfield outside.

In the pub across the road you can still see the benches where the resurrection men brought their corpses for inspection by Bart's surgeons. From my window I can see Little Britain, where Hogarth grew up (his pictures decorate the Great Hall of Bart's) and where Dickens placed Jaggers' offices in *Great Expectations*.

There is something satisfying to me in these random facts: a feeling of reassurance in continuity which I never expected to need when I was younger, and when the very word "institution" seemed oppressive. I had never encountered then the Burkean idea of the institution as the organic expression of human needs and wisdom. I had not then visited the collapsing Soviet Union and witnessed how frightening it is to live as a citizen with nothing – no church or union or club – between you and the wintry power of the state.

Places like Bart's take a long time to grow – nearly 1,000 years – and now a Conservative government has chosen to dismantle it like a Portakabin. Shove it into a trust, merge it with the London Hospital in Whitechapel, perhaps close it altogether. It is just being squeezed and bled to death at the moment with one department closing after another and all in the name of a dogma which says there are too many hospitals per head in London.

You might as well say there are too many art galleries per head as well, and too many theatres, universities and football teams. To close Bart's because there aren't enough patients living nearby makes as much sense as to close Smithfield market because there aren't enough cows in Clerkenwell. London is all about these complex, stirring institutions it has generated over centuries, and they are more important than ever now that enlightened forces are trying to reverse the hollowing out of cities by office development and private cars. It all makes you wonder exactly what one means with labels like "conservative" nowadays.

Visitors keep saying things like "Oh, you're so brave", which I think often translates as "for God's sake keep on being brave for my sake." In fact, you don't really have much choice in the one-way street of cancer. It is either curl up and die, or carry on as best you can.

Once a week or so, I do curl up and have a good cry – from rage or self-pity or frustration – and feel better for it. A year or so ago, after my first relapse, was the only time I thought I might really crack up. I wasn't sleeping, and I was having mild panic attacks. I was also having radiotherapy to my neck which involved having my head clamped down in a sort of plastic mask. Quite without warning one day, I got an overwhelming attack of claustrophobia and had to tear myself free of the table. It took three more goes and 30ml of Valium before I could get back in the mask – together with a kindly suggestion that I might benefit from some counselling.

I took it and it has helped a lot with the panic and sleeping and claustrophobia, and with some of the more general terrors of serious illness. I used to think strong drink and stubborn silence was the answer to most emotional problems, and I have made too many snide remarks about the counselling industry in my columns over the years – but as I say, I'm only really brave for the visitors.

The Daily Telegraph, 27 September 1996